THE CATHOLIC UNIVERSITY OF AMERICA
CANON LAW STUDIES
No. 316

DISPENSATION FROM THE INTERPELLATIONS

AN HISTORICAL SYNOPSIS AND A COMMENTARY

by

ARTHUR ANTHONY SEGO, B.A., J.C.L.

Priest of the Diocese of Lafayette in Indiana

A DISSERTATION

Submitted to the Faculty of the School of Canon Law of the Catholic University of America in Partial Fulfillment of the Requirements for the Degree of Doctor of Canon Law

THE CATHOLIC UNIVERSITY OF AMERICA PRESS
WASHINGTON, D. C.
1951

Nihil Obstat:

LUDOVICUS MOTRY, S.T.D., J.C.D.,
Censor Deputatus.

Washington, die 13 februarii 1951

Imprimatur:

✠ JOANNES GEORGIUS BENNETT, D.D., LL.D.,
Episcopus Lafayettensis in Indiana.

Lafayette, die 16 februarii 1951.

Printed by
THE ABBEY PRESS
ST. MEINRAD, INDIANA

RESPECTFULLY DEDICATED

TO

MARY IMMACULATE

PATRONESS OF THE

DIOCESE OF LAFAYETTE IN INDIANA

TABLE OF CONTENTS

PART II

PART III

FOREWORD

THE Catholic Church has always shown itself zealous for the welfare of its children, and has repeatedly throughout its long history evidenced this concern in its official legislation. Conscious of an obligation imposed immediately by Christ to extend His Kingdom to the boundaries of all known lands and to all people the Church has, even from its infancy, manifested a sincere and ardent desire to welcome all within its fold. Early developments of a purely canonical or juridical nature give adequate testimony of this desire.

Christianity introduced an altogether new concept of conjugal love and relationship in giving to it the sacredness that derives from a sacramental character. And yet it is precisely in regard to this institution that the Church has most effectively proved its maternal solicitude for those who have but recently embraced the Faith.

Pursuant to the warning of Christ the Church met with early and constant opposition. St. Paul, who only shortly before had assisted at the first martyrdom, saw an even more pernicious evil facing converts who had pagan consorts. He knew that these latter could be a constant source of trouble to the new Christians even to the extent of occasioning spiritual or temporal harm. He knew further that many would refuse peaceful cohabitation out of hatred toward the convert's newly won Faith, thus depriving the Christian of his just conjugal rights.

It was for the benefit of such as these that St. Paul used his Apostolic power to grant converts the privilege which now bears his name, for he considered it improper that a Christian be under bondage to a pagan who would make the convert's Faith a burden.[1]

That St. Paul legislated well is evident; for almost fifteen centuries there was adequately provided a power to be in-

[1] I Cor., VII: 12-16—*The New Testament,* Confraternity of Christian Doctrine Edition (Paterson, New Jersey: St. Anthony Guild Press, 1941).

voked in favor of the Faith. In the years preceding the Council of Trent canonical thought and practical usage clearly determined the fundamental conditions for the use of the Pauline privilege, particularly the necessary requirements of interpellating the infidel. Already at that time, however, it had been pointed out that the interpellations were only a means, and not an end in themselves, and that therefore, when their purpose had been fulfilled by other means, they became entirely unnecessary.[2]

It later became clear that not all problems concerning the marriages of converts could be solved by means of the provisions of the Pauline privilege. Once more the Church proved its concern, and then reaffirmed by way of practical use the supreme authority given to it by Christ.

Indicative of this are the sixteenth century Papal Constitutions of Popes Paul III, St. Pius V, and Gregory XIII, in which the supreme authority of the Church mitigated the rigor of its matrimonial legislation to prepare the way for the conversion of many who, in their sincerity, were desirous of embracing the Faith, if some of the strictures which were attached to the current matrimonial legislation would be effectively neutralized. Without departing from its invincible attitude on the indissolubility of the marriage bond, the Church employed to the full its power over the bond of non-sacramental marriages for the good of souls and for the spread of the Faith.

Since the basis of the power to dispense from the interpellations, in virtue of the common law, is found principally in the Constitutions mentioned in canon 1125, one is bound by

[2] Gandulphus Bononiensis, *Sententiarum Libri Quattuor* (ed. Joannes Walter, Vindobonae et Vratislaviae: Amelius Haim et Soc., Bibliopolae Academici, 1924), Liber. IV, n. 279: " ... aut non est verum, quod contumelia Creatoris solvit ius matrimonii circa eum, qui relinquitur. Ad haec dici potest quod si fidelis cognoverit pertinacem eius infidelis voluntatem, *non eum debet admonere* vel retinere. Voluntas ergo non quaelibet, sed pertinax et ipsa discessio circa eum, qui relinquitur, solvit ius matrimonii, vel pertinax infidelitas scilicet quae horret nomen Christianorum."

the general principles of canon law to interpret that canon according to the norms of the pre-Code law of which the Constitutions were a part. In fact, the origin, the precise nature, and the extent of the power must be determined ultimately from the interpretations accepted by the approved authors of the pre-Code law as well as from the official interpretation of the Holy See in its pre-Code faculties and responses.

Conscious of the obligation deriving from this fundamental principle of interpretation, the writer has sought to consider thoroughly and necessarily at length the historical antecedents of the Church's power to dispense from the interpellations. It is solely in this manner that one can find a safe juridical guide for the further study and interpretation of canon 1125, in the light of which are revealed the conditions under which a dispensation from the interpellations becomes applicable in the Church's present law.

In Part Two of the dissertation the writer considers the interpretation and application of these constitutions in the United States today. Due emphasis is attached to the extensive interpretation accorded to these Constitutions and their privileges by recent commentators.

Part Three considers the Constitutions in the light of the Code of Canon Law. It offers a canonical commentary and analysis of the dispensation from the interpellations.

The writer wishes here to acknowledge his filial respect and gratitude to His Excellency, the Most Reverend John G. Bennett, D.D., LL.D., Bishop of Lafayette in Indiana, for the confidence he has bestowed, for the opportunity of advanced study in Canon Law he has granted, and for the topic he suggested as the matter to be treated in this dissertation. At the same time he expresses his thanks to the members of the Faculty of the School of Canon Law of the Catholic University of America for their attention and invaluable direction. He feels obligated also to his fellow priests of the diocese of Lafayette in Indiana, to his classmates at the University, and to his many friends for their constant encouragement and often generous assistance.

PART I

POST-TRIDENTINE LEGISLATION AND HISTORICAL DEVELOPMENT UP TO THE CODE OF CANON LAW

CHAPTER I

REACTIVATED INTEREST IN MATRIMONIAL LEGISLATION

WITHIN the first fifteen centuries of the Church's existence there was a minimum of legislation relative to the sacrament of matrimony, and what there was of such laws was intended to strengthen the matrimonial bond. Surely the Church never doubted the doctrine regarding the privilege promulgated by St. Paul, but there may well have been circumstances in history that did not warrant its application.[1] That seems to be the inevitable conclusion as it may be drawn from the silence of the past centuries.

One can only speculate about the reason for this, for indeed there must have been some reason. It seems an altogether logical explanation that during the early years of its existence the Church struggled to maintain and preserve the Christian notion of the indissolubility of marriage against

[1] From the beginning the writer wishes to acknowledge three earlier dissertations relative to the matter under consideration in this thesis and recommends them to the attention of the reader: Donald J. Gregory, *The Pauline Privilege,* The Catholic University of America Canon Law Studies, n. 68 (Washington, D.C.: The Catholic University of America, 1931); Francis James Burton, *A Commentary on Canon 1125,* The Catholic University of America Canon Law Studies, n. 121 (Washington, D. C.: The Catholic University of America Press, 1940); Edward M. Woeber, *The Interpellations,* The Catholic University of America Canon Law Studies, n. 172 (Washington, D. C.: The Catholic University of America Press, 1942).

the Jewish[2] and pagan[3] philosophies of divorce and marital repudiation. This struggle of the Church to preserve unvanquished its ideal of indissolubility forced it to adopt an exceptionally rigoristic attitude toward any practice, no matter how legitimate, that might tend or even could seem to lessen its traditional stand on this essential mark.[4]

But then came the opening of the 16th century, a turning point indeed in canonical matrimonial legislation. Territorial discoveries and expansion encouraged popular migration and missionary activity. The missionaries, often encouraged by civil authorities, brought to pagan countries their first contact with the Christian moral and disciplinary laws so fundamentally at variance with their own pagan rituals and tribal mores. The theoretic formulas and rules in their consideration abstracted from the polygamous marriages and wholesale divorces among the natives, many of whom could not even remember their former spouses, and the existing ecclesiastical matrimonial legislation did not make provision for the negro slaves who had been forcibly

[2] Deuteronomy, XXIV: 1-4; Matt., XIX: 7-8; Mk., X: 3-4; E. Neufeld, *Ancient Hebrew Marriage Laws* (New York: Longmans Green and Co., 1944), ch. XIII, *Divorce*, pp. 176-188.

[3] *Corpus Iuris Civilis*, Vol. I, Digesta Iustiniani Augusti (ed. stereotypa 15, recognovit Theodorus Mommsen; retractavit Paulus Krueger, Berolini: apud Weidmannos, 1929), (24, 2) 9; Vol. II, *Codex Iustinianus* ed. stereotypa 10, recognovit et retractavit Paulus Krueger, Berolini: apud Weidmannos, 1929), (5, 17) 8; *Codices Gregorianus Hermogenianus, Theodosianus* (ed. Gustavus Haenel, Lipsiae: Prostat Bonnae apud Adolphum Marcum, 1837), III, 16, 1 and 2; Emmanuel Gonzalez-Tellez, *Commentaria Perpetua in Singulas Textus Librorum Decretalium* (Lugduni: Sumptibus Laurentii Arnavdi et Petri Barde, 1673), Lib. IV, tit. XIX, *de divortiis*, cap. 1. This latter work offers an excellent commentary on the history of divorce among the Hebrews and the Romans, its meaning, kinds, causes, solemnities involved and penalties inflicted for unjust separation.

[4] George Hayward Joyce (*Christian Marriage: An Historical and Doctrinal Study*, [2nd Ed., London and New York: Sheed and Ward, 1948.] [p. 475]) asserted "that it is possible that the Church even refused to recognize the exception permitted by the Apostle." (Hereafter this work will be cited *Christian Marriage*.)

separated from their native countries and abducted into distant lands without any hope of reunion with their legitimate spouses.

In truth, the existing legislation was woefully inadequate in the face of these unique but nevertheless urgent circumstances. The missionaries soon found that this fact proved an obstacle to the conversion of many, for to join the Church under these conditions meant either that the new convert would have to live with a pagan partner who might or might not be his valid spouse, or it meant giving up all conjugal relationship. The first could not be allowed; the second would be imposing an almost insupportable burden on the new convert. It was evident that the cause of Christianity would be partially stifled in the new world unless something was done to relieve the dilemma of those natives who otherwise were ready to embrace the Faith.

Though Pope Paul III (1534-1549) had in 1537 granted an extension of the power of the Pauline privilege in favor of polygamous converts, and though within a few years after the close of the Council of Trent two other Pontiffs were to grant even greater and almost unbelievable concessions relative to the dissolution of the marriages of converts, one does not find any similar frame of mind in the Tridentine legislators. The canons and decrees of that Council evidence the extreme rigorism of the early Church toward the unassailable bond of every valid marriage. Not only in the canons but also in all of the preliminary discussions one finds indications of this reaffirmation of the Church's doctrinal stand on this essential note of the matrimonial contract.[5]

There was a valid reason for this, of course; coincidental with the celebration of the Tridentine Council the century old tradition of the Church was flagrantly violated in the

[5] *Concilium Tridentinum, Diaria,* Tomus I, Herculis Severoli Commentarius, Angeli Massarelli Diaria (Collegit, edidit, illustravit Sebastianus Merkle, Friburgi Brisgoviae, St. Ludovici, Americae: Sumptibus Herder, 1901), pp. 709, n. 23; 716, n. 7; 728, n. 30.

protesting dogmas of the great religious revolt. Expressly directing its stand against the new heresy,[6] the Council firmly reiterated the Church's doctrine on the indissolubility of Christian marriages in precisely worded canons.[7] It moreover anathematized those who contested the Church's defined teaching in this matter.[8]

[6] Conc. Trident., sess. XXIV, *Doctrina de Sacramento Matrimonii*: "And since with regard to this teaching ungodly men of this age, raving madly, have not only formed false ideas concerning this venerable sacrament, but, introducing in conformity with their habit under the pretext of the Gospel a carnal liberty, have by word and writing asserted ... many things that are foreign to the teaching of the Catholic Church ..., this holy and general council ... has thought it proper ... that the principal heresies and errors of the aforesaid schismatics be destroyed ..."—H. J. Schroeder, *Canons and Decrees of the Council of Trent* (St. Louis: B. Herder Book Co., 1941) pp. 180-181.

[7] Conc. Trident., sess. XXIV, can. 5-6.

[8] *Canones et Decreta Concilii Tridentini ex Editione Romana 1834* (Neapoli, 1859), sessio. XXIV, cann. 11-12; Schroeder, *op. cit.*, p. 182.

CHAPTER II

PAPAL SOURCES OF NEW MATRIMONIAL LEGISLATION

IN the face of seemingly insoluble dilemmas the missionaries in the new World looked to Rome for an answer and for direction in solving the matrimonial problems prompted by the conversion of polygamists, and fortunately they found in Rome a zeal to match their own. Three Popes—Paul III (1534-1549), St. Pius V (1566-1572) and Gregory XIII (1572-1585)—enacted legislation relative to the perplexing problems of natives who knew not for certain who, if any, among their many wives was the legitimate one. This legislation also benefited many converts who had become separated voluntarily or forcibly from their spouses without any hope of reunion.[1] Actually these Constitutions not only offered a solution to the difficulties at hand, but they also served to clarify the practical use of the privilege in that they introduced an altogether new interpretation of the power of the Holy See over the marriages of the unbaptized, for it thus became clearly evident that the *privilegium fidei* was far wider in its application than was the *privilegium Paulinum.* This fundamental distinction must be kept constantly in mind in any discussion of these privileges. A failure to do so will lead only to confusion and inevitably to an unwarranted restriction of the privileges herein contained.[2]

[1] In the consideration of these Constitutions the writer does not intend a minute critique of the texts and their destination. That seems unnecessary in the light of the subject matter of this work. These questions are thoroughly and capably considered by other authors: cf. Burton, *A Commentary on Canon 1125;* Francis J. Winslow, *The Pauline Privilege and the Constitutions of Canon 1125* (New York: The Field Afar Press, 1948) (hereafter cited, *The Pauline Privilege*); Francis F. Woods, *The Constitutions of Canon 1125* (Milwaukee: The Bruce Publishing Company, 1935).

[2] Franciscus Wernz et Petrus Vidal, *Ius Canonicum ad Codicis Normam Exactum,* (7 vols. in 8, Vol. V, *Ius Matrimoniale,* 3. ed., a P.

Article I: The Constitution *Altitudo* of Paul III[3]

This papal Constitution was issued on June 1, 1537;[4] directed to the bishops of West and South India, it covered a great number of topics concerning the administration of the Church in these missionary countries. In treating of marriages it granted the first in a series of privileges to native converts. In this regard specifically it was directed toward those natives who before their conversion had had many wives, and, *de facto,* could not remember which one of these they had married first, and who was, therefore, the legitimate spouse. Paul III decreed that upon their conversion the natives were to be allowed to choose whichever one of their many wives they wished, and with this one they were to contract marriage according to the required formalities of ecclesiastical law. If, however, the convert remembered who was the first wife, then he was to remain with her and to dismiss all the others.[5]

In all of these constitutions the privileges granted to the men polygamists were extended, by the equity of law, to native women converts who had lived in polyandry.[6] The

Aguirre, Romae: Apud Aedes Universitatis Gregorianae in Piazza della Pilotta, 1946) (hereafter cited, *Ius Matrimoniale*), n. 636; Woods, *op. cit.*, p. 17.

[3] Cf. Appendix A, *infra* p. 243.

[4] *Collectanea Sacrae Congregationis de Propaganda Fide,* (2 vols., Romae: Ex Typographia Polyglotta S.C. de Propaganda Fide, 1907), Vol. I, n. 114 (hereafter cited as *Coll. S.C.P.F.*); Petrus Gasparri, *Codicis Iuris Canonici Fontes* (9 vols., Romae: Typis Polyglottis Vaticanis, 1923-1939), n. 910 (hereafter cited *Fontes*); *Bullarium Pontificium Sacrae Congregationis de Propaganda Fide* (8 vols., Romae: Typis Collegii Urbani, 1839-1858) I, 25 (hereafter cited as *Bullarium*).

[5] G. Payen, *De Matrimonio in Missionibus ac Potissimum in Sinis: Tractatus Practicus et Casus* (altera editio, 3 vols., Zi-ka-wei: in Typographia T'ou-se-we, 1935-1936) II, n. 2405; III, n. 2405 (hereafter cited *De Matrimonio*); Petrus Gasparri, *Tractatus Canonicus de Matrimonio* (ed. nova, 2 vols. Romae: Typis Polyglottis Vaticanis, 1932), II, n. 1157 (hereafter cited *De Matrimonio*).

[6] S.C. de Prop. Fide, 14 ian. 1793—*Coll. S.C.P.F.*, n. 611; S.C.S. Off., 12 iun. 1850—*Fontes*, n. 910; S.C.S. Off., 5 sept. 1855— *Fontes*, n. 933; Payen, *op. cit.*, II, n. 2404, Part 3; II, n. 2405; Woods, *op. cit.*, p. 39; Winslow, *op. cit.*, p. 53, q. 90.

constitution demanded as an essential requirement for the use of the privilege, that the convert be not able to remember with which one of his many wives he had first contracted a true marriage, and it simply gave him the right upon his conversion to choose any one of those with whom he had lived at any time before his conversion even though he had dismissed them previously. Though it was not expressly required that the one chosen have become converted and have received baptism, nevertheless there seemed necessary on her part a tolerant attitude toward the Faith, to the extent at least that she was willing to live with the convert in full respect for his Christian faith. The significant thing was the fact that the constitution gave the convert a full right to enter a second marriage without making any attempt to learn whether the first spouse was willing to resume peaceful cohabitation, or even whether she was still living. Not only did the constitution not demand that the interpellations be made to the first and legitimate consort, which up to that time was generally accepted as essential, but actually nowhere did it make mention of the interpellations at all. When, accordingly, the essential conditions were verified, the full privilege as granted in the constitution became applicable so that the Christian could contract a second marriage. The interpellations were simply omitted, and no dispensation was deemed necessary or was in any way called for.[7] However, as a matter of precaution and to assure the unquestionable validity of the marriage the parties should be required to renew their matrimonial consent.[8]

Article II: The Constitution *Romani Pontificis* of Pope St. Pius V[9]

The Constitution of Paul III was originally directed to

[7] Winslow, *op. cit.*, p. 61; Burton, *op. cit.*, p. 45; Woods, *op. cit.*, p. 45.

[8] Francis J. Winslow, "The Application of the Pauline Privilege", *The Jurist*, Vol. X (1950), p. 321.

[9] Cf. Appendix B, *infra*, p. 244.

West and South India; the Constitution of Pope St. Pius V[10] was directed not to a determined country, but rather to a class of people who were termed *'Indi'* in the Constitution.

It seems that some missionaries among these people had been allowing their converts, who had been polygynous and polyandrous before their conversion, to retain after their baptism any one of their many wives or husbands who had likewise become converts. In time, however, this practice came to the notice of the Bishops, who, along with most of the missionaries, were disturbed by the fact that very probably encouragement was thus given for invalid marriages, since the converted spouse with whom the initial convert was cohabiting was in many cases not the first and therefore not the legitimate spouse. Since, in cases of indiscriminate polygamous unions, it was very difficult to find the first spouse or to separate a convert from the wife baptized with him, Pius was moved to grant this privilege.

Again the conditions for the use of the privilege were few and simple. The fundamental consideration derived from the very great hardship that would be inflicted upon a polygynous or polyandrous convert if there were demanded a separation from the converted partner with whom he or she was living. If the one chosen was actually not the first in the polygamous series, it was necessary that they renew their consent according to the prescribed canonical form.

The constitutions of Paul III and Gregory XIII met with generally accepted interpretations. This Constitution *Romani Pontificis* of St. Pius V, however, from its first promulgation to this very day has been the object of various and even contradictory interpretations and the subject of numerous and detailed studies.[11]

[10] *Coll. S.C.P.F.*, n. 849; *Fontes*, n. 138; *Bullarium*, I, n. 45.

[11] The writer recommends to the attention of the reader two articles that deserve particular mention for their careful analysis of this Papal Constitution: Puthota Rayanna, "De Constitutione S. Pii Papae V *Romani Pontificis* (3 augusti 1571)", *Periodica*, XXVIII (1939), 112-134, 190-209; and Francis J. Winslow, "The Application of the Pauline Privilege and the Constitutions of Canon 1125 in the United

The first of these interpretations demands as an essential condition for the use of the privilege of this constitution that the lawful spouse cannot be found. The second interpretation asserts simply that the constitution grants a dispensation only from the second interpellation, so that the convert is permitted to enter a valid marriage if the answer to the first interpellation is negative. The third interpretation maintains that the constitution grants a dispensation from both interpellations so that the convert is not required in any way to investigate the mind or intentions of his former polygamous spouses before contracting a valid union with any one of them who is willing to be baptized with him. This interpretation, however, excludes the use of the privilege in all cases where the first and legitimate spouse has voluntarily and of her own accord expressed her willingness to be baptized.[12]

The fourth opinion agrees with the third in that it holds that no interpellations are required, yet it further asserts that the convert has the right to enter the second marriage even in the case where the first and legitimate spouse has volunteered the information that she wishes to be baptized.[13]

States", *The Jurist*, X, (1950), 304-333 (hereafter cited "Application of Canon 1125 in the United States").

[12] Burton, *A Commentary on Canon 1125*, p. 160; Vromant, *De Matrimonio*, n. 344; Woods, *The Constitutions of Canon 1125*, pp. 44-45; Payen, *De Matrimonio*, II, n. 2407, "Exceptis tamen, ex dictis, esset, si habentes plures, v.g. duas, uxores, iam certe, *sine interpellatione*, scirent, ex dictis vel factis legitimae uxoris, primam velle converti et baptizari."

[13] Felix M. Cappello, *Tractatus Canonico-Moralis de Sacramentis*, Vol. V, *De Matrimonio*, (ed. 5, Romae: Domus Editorialis Marietti, 1947.) n. 787, p. 777: "Si prima uxor, quin interpellata fuerit, sponte declaret se baptizari velle, vir conversus potest nihilominus uti favore constitutionis Pianae, si durissimum sit eum separari a muliere quam nunc habet et quae cum eo baptizatur." Matthaeus Conte a Coronata, *Institutiones Iuris Canonici: De Sacramentis, Tractatus Canonicus*, Vol. III, *De Matrimonio*, (Taurini: Domus Editorialis Marietti, 1946.) n. 648, p. 906: "Si uxor prima legitima etiam non interpellata declaret se paratum esse ad conversionem aut ad cohabitandam pacifice potest nihilominus vir concessione sibi facta a S. Pio V uti, saltem si durissi-

There are several possible explanations for this wide difference of opinion, and the restrictions of the first three interpretations might be prompted by any one or several of the following causes:

1. A failure to read the Constitution in its literal and evident sense.

2. A failure to consider properly the sociological and moral background of the constitution and its proportionate influence on the mind of the legislator and as a cause for the legislation itself.

3. An erroneous and restrictive interpretation of the papal power over the bond of natural marriages.

4. And finally, a consistent but illogical attempt to interpret this constitution and its privilege within the limits of the Pauline privilege.

The fourth and final interpretation mentioned above alone is fully consistent with the text of the constitution; it alone objectively takes into consideration the elements that originally prompted the constitution, and it alone recognizes the fullness of the power of the Pope over the bond of natural marriages.

According to the text of the Constitution *Romani Pontificis* and judging from its explicit wording two conditions alone are required and are sufficient for the valid use of the

---

mum sit ei se separare a muliere quae secum baptizata est et quam sibi pro legitima elegit." Franciscus Wernz,-Petrus Vidal, *Ius Canonicum ad Codicis Normam Exactum,* 7 vols. in 8, Vol. V, *Ius Matrimoniale,* (3. ed., a P. Aguirre, Romae: Apud Aedes Universitatis Gregorianae in Piazza della Pilotta, 1946.) n. 633, p. 828. A. Vermeersch-C. Creusen, *Epitome Iuris Canonici cum Commentariis,* (Vol. I, ed. 7; Vols. II and III, 6 ed., Mechliniae, Romae: H. Dessain, I, 1949, II and III, 1940 and 1946) II, n. 436, p. 303, "Vi constitutionis Pii V non videtur interpellanda uxor legitima, etiamsi cognoscatur." William J. Doheny, *Canonical Procedure in Matrimonial Cases,* (Vol. II, *Informal Procedure,* Milwaukee: The Bruce Publishing Company, 1948), p. 553: "The privileges of this Constitution were granted to the Indians, even when the first wife was certainly known and could have been interpellated." Rayanna, "De Constitutione S. Pii Papae V, *Romani Pontificis*", *Periodica,* XXVIII (1939), 205; Winslow, *The Pauline Privilege,* p. 71.

privilege granted by Pope Pius V. In promulgating his constitution Pius V was aware of the privilege granted by his predecessor, Paul III, and the writer can scarcely believe that he wished to duplicate the privilege granted by his predecessors. He must have intended, therefore, that his constitution provide precisely for those cases not covered by the Pauline privilege or that of *Altitudo.*

The only two conditions expressly stipulated in the Constitution are:

1. That it would be difficult to separate the convert from the wife with whom he was living.

2. That the spouse would be prepared to receive baptism with her partner.

To add further conditions or to demand any other restrictions than those listed is to force the obvious meaning of the words of the constitution and to do an injustice to the mind of the legislator.

The writer recognizes that there are strong objections against this extensive interpretation of the Constitution *Romani Pontificis.* Many demand as an essential condition for the use of the privilege that it be impossible to find the first wife. These canonists find reason for this requirement in the words of the constitution, *"maxime quia difficilimum foret primam coniugem reperire."* Even accepted on its face value alone it is clear that this cause does not at all constitute an exclusive condition for the use of the privilege of Pius V,[14] but merely points out one example in which the constitution is certainly applicable. For even the strictest interpretation must recognize that "the *'maxime'* clause clearly leaves room for other reasons that would make the separation of the convert couple a severe hardship."[15]

A second objection is based on the necessity of the interpellations and demands that the convert interpellate the first of his former spouses. It is to be noted that the constitution

[14] Winslow, "Application of Canon 1125 in the United States", *The Jurist,* X (1950), 323.

[15] Burton, *A Commentary on Canon 1125,* p. 155.

does not require any interpellation of any of the former spouses. This objection can find its basis in the supposition that the only power that the Church has over the marriages of the infidels is through the use of the Pauline privilege, and for that reason this objection demands the interpellations. The answer to the objection is simple. The privilege of Pius V is in no way the use of the Pauline privilege, but quite distinctly it is an entirely different application of the wider Apostolic power over natural marriages.

"Just as the conditions for the use of the Pauline privilege are determined from the words of the Apostle, so the essential conditions for the privilege of Pius V are to be taken from the words of the Constitution *Romani Pontificis*."[16] Thus the valid use of the Pauline privilege is conditioned upon the departure, physical or moral, of the infidel, and therefore the necessity of exploring the will of that infidel by explicit questions. The faculty of Pius V is entirely different, for it does not depend on the departure of the infidel party nor upon the inability to determine who is the legitimate wife or where she is, nor upon the difficulty of finding her but simply on the hardship that would be caused the convert if he were forced to abandon his Christian wife with whom he is now living.[17]

A much more valid objection than either of these two asks whether the Pope can dispense in a case where the rights of a third party are injured. For if the convert is permitted to remain with his second wife would this not be prejudicial to the rights of the first and therefore legitimate spouse? For natural equity ordinarily demands that a person whose rights are being restricted be given the opportunity to be heard, and the general law of the Church requires that in the granting of privileges the required rights of others be respected.[18] Yet all will admit the validity of the principle that the rights of the individual are subordi-

[16] Rayanna, "De Constitutione S. Pii Papae V *Romani Pontificis*", *Periodica*, XXVIII (1939), 203.

[17] Rayanna, *op. cit.*, p. 204.

[18] Canon 50.

nate to that of the common good. Thus the Supreme Authority of the Church can deprive by law an individual's private right even regards the matrimonial right, if it be for the common good, namely for the good of the Faith. Thus, as a clear example, the law of the Code explicitly states that the Holy Father can dissolve a non-consumated marriage even if one party is unwilling.[19]

And certainly nothing more than this was done in the use of the privilege of Pius V. For this privilege was granted in the favor of converts from polygamy and gives them the right to enter a valid union with any of their former spouses who was willing to be baptized with them as long as it would be a hardship to separate them from their converted spouse. No interpellation of any of the former spouses was required, and the privilege was applicable even if the former spouse voluntarily makes known her willingness to be baptized.[20]

Article III: The Constitution *Populis* of Gregory XIII[21]

On January 25, 1585, Pope Gregory XIII issued the Constitution *Populis,* which was even more specifically exclusive in regard to dispensing from the interpellations than were the earlier two. Unlike these two, however, the Constitution *Populis* applied not only to polygynists and polyandrists but to any and all converts who had been parties to marriages contracted in infidelity. Again unlike the earlier two constitutions, this one did not provide unconditionally for the omission of the interpellations, but rather accorded to three definite groups of persons, i.e., to all local ordinaries, to all pastors, and to Jesuit confessors, the power to dispense from the making of either or both interpellations.

This constitution was granted expressly for the benefit of

[19] Canon 1119.

[20] Winslow, "Application of Canon 1125 in the United States", *The Jurist* (1950), 327; Cappello, *De Matrimonio,* n. 787, p. 777; Coronata, *De Matrimonio,* n. 648, p. 906.

[21] Cf. Appendix C, *infra,* p. 244.

[22] *Coll. S.C.P.F.,* n. 400; *Fontes,* n. 155; *Bullarium,* I, 103.

those infidels who, after having been married according to their own tribal and pagan rituals were captured and forcibly separated from their native countries and spouses in such a manner that neither of them could upon conversion to the Faith find the other in order to question them relative to their willingness to continue or resume cohabitation, as was required when the converts wished to enter a second and Christian marriage through the ordinary use of the Pauline privilege.

The essential condition for the use of this privilege was the impossibility on the part of the convert to interpellate the infidel party. The constitution expressly listed three causes as sufficing to establish this impossibility: when communication with the other spouse was impossible, even through the agency of an intermediary, because of the hostility or enmity of the country where he or she resided, or when the actual residence of the infidel consort was unknown, or finally when the length of the journey necessary to make the interpellations rendered this formal task extremely difficult.[23]

When any of these reasons was verified, then those to whom the faculty was given could, in virtue of the grant made in this Constitution and apart from any recourse to the Holy See or to any other authority, dispense the convert from making the interpellations.

According to the provision of the constitution it was necessary that the impossibility, either of making the interpellations as required by law or of furnishing an answer

[23] Woods, (*op. cit.*, p. 66) writes: "In this case, however, it is necessary that the infidel be in a distant place, the exact location of which is not known or to which access is difficult. The difficulty of interpellation must arise from the distance and the place and not from some other cause." From the wording of the Constitution it is impossible to find any basis for his combination of circumstances of distance, unknown residence, and difficulty of journey. The Constitution listed these as separate causes and nowhere demanded the simultaneous presence of all three as a condition for the use of the privilege. Burton (*op. cit.*, pp. 167-169) and Winslow (*op. cit.*, p. 76, q. 132) are in agreement with this.

within the time fixed in the interrogation, be definitely established through some form of summary and extrajudicial investigation. For it was certain that one could not in these cases act on a mere presumption of impossibility in granting the dispensation; it was, however, the more common opinion that a moral impossibility sufficed, and that for the application of the privilege there was not demanded as a condition that which likewise proved physically impossible.

Subsequent to the validly granted dispensation[24] the convert was permitted to licitly contract marriage with any Christian even of a different rite and even though his first spouse was still living. So absolute was the juridical effect of the dispensation that the second marriage was valid and indissoluble, so much so that it could not be dissolved even though it later became known that the spouse of the earlier union had been prevented from answering the interpellations. The second marriage likewise could not be dissolved if later it was proved that the spouse of the earlier union had also become a Christian before the second marriage was contracted. All of this was explicitly decreed by the Sovereign Pontiff. The constitution with sweeping finality abrogated all contrary constitutions, decrees and particular laws.[25]

This constitution shall be given thorough consideration throughout this work as the dispensation from the interpellation is considered in its various details.

[24] Matthaeus Conte a Coronata (*Institutiones Iuris Canonici*: *De Sacramentis, Tractatus Canonicus*, Vol. III, *De Matrimonio* [Taurini: Domus Editorialis Marietti, 1946], n. 649) points out: "Hic non conceditur directe dispensatio a Gregorio XIII, sed conceditur facultas dispensandi determinatis personis et in determinatis circumstantiis." (This volume is hereafter cited *De Matrimonio*).

[25] Gasparri, *De Matrimonio*, II, n. 1159; Payen, *De Matrimonio*, II, nn. 2408-9; Burton, *op. cit.*, pp. 164 ff; Winslow, *op. cit.*, p. 75; Wernz-Vidal, *Ius Matrimoniale*, n. 634.

CHAPTER III

LATER DEVELOPMENTS AND PROBLEMS ARISING FROM THESE SOURCES

Already at the beginning of the 16th century the necessity of the interpellations had been well established. This requirement has been acknowledged without exception since that time by authors of all periods,[1] and by responses of the Holy See,[2] and is now made of obligation in the Code.[3]

Therefore, the constitutions of the 16th century occasioned much argument in the following centuries. The first two Popes, Paul III and St. Pius V, allowed the complete omission of the interpellations; the third, Gregory XIII, granted the faculty of dispensing from the making of the interpellations. All three postulated definite conditions as necessary for the use of the privilege granted, and all required that there be some form of extrajudicial knowledge that these conditions had been fulfilled. Actually these pontifical declarations prompted two questions in the interpretation undertaken by later canonists and commentators.

[1] Thomas Sanchez, *De Sancto Matrimonii Sacramento Disputationum Libri Tres* (3 vols., Venetiis, 1614), lib. VII, disp. LXXIV, nn. 12 sq. (hereafter cited *De Sancto Matrimonii Sacramento*); Petrus Leurenius, *Forum Ecclesiasticum in quo Ius Canonicum Universum Librorum ac Titulorum Ordine Exploratur* (Venetiis: Apud Joannem Baptistam Recurti, sub signo Religionis, 1729), lib. IV, tit. XIX, q. CCLXXXIII; Henricus Feije, *De Impedimentis et Dispensationibus Matrimonialibus* (3. ed., Lovanii, 1885) n. 487; Franciscus Wernz, *Ius Decretalium* (6 vols., Vol. IV, *Ius Matrimoniale*, Romae: ex Typographia Polyglotta, 1904), IV, n. 703, (hereafter cited *Ius Matrimoniale*); Gasparri, *De Matrimonio*, II, n. 1143.

[2] S.C.S. Off., instr. (ad Archiep. Quebecen.) 16 sept. 1824—*Fontes*, n. 866; *Coll. S.C.P.F.*, n. 784; S.C.S. Off., *Florentina*, 17 ian. 1722—*Fontes*, n. 687.

[3] *Codex Iuris Canonici Pii X Pontificis Maximi Iussu Digestus, Benedicti Papae XV Auctoritate Promulgatus* (Romae: Typis Vaticanis, 1917, reimpressio, Wesminster, Md.: The Newman Bookshop, 1942), can. 1121, § 2.

The first of these questions related precisely to the nature of the privileges granted in the constitutions, and the second concerned the exact nature of the dispensation for the granting of which provision was made in the faculty granted by Gregory XIII.

Article I: Practical Application of the Privileges

Section 1: Omission of the Interpellations

The problem seemed immediately to pave the way for the expression of two different opinions as represented by Sanchez (1550-1610)[4] and Pontius (1569-1629).[5]

Sanchez held that under given circumstances the interpellations could be omitted even apart from any granted dispensation, while Pontius demanded a dispensation in every case of their omission. Though Sanchez clearly insisted on the absolute necessity of the interpellations, he saw that there were times when the making of the interpellations would be useless or impossible. He acknowledged a principle that was to become fully defined only later, namely that the interpellations were not an end in themselves but simply served as a means for determining the good or evil will of the infidel consort. Accordingly, when this will was known through other means the purpose of the interpellations had already been served, and they were, therefore, of no further need.[6]

He gave as his authority the wording of the Constitution of Pius V, and in reliance on an earlier writer, Gabriel Vasquez (1549-1604)[7] he coined the statement: "*Non est*

[4] *Op. cit.*, Lib. VII, disp. LXXIV.

[5] Basilius Pontius, *De Sacramento Matrimonii Tractatus cum Appendice de Matrimonio Catholici cum Haeretico* (2. ed., Bruxellis, 1627) lib. IX, cap. 2 (hereafter cited *De Sacramento Matrimonii*).

[6] "Quod ea monitio solum petatur, ut de infidelis pertinacia constet. Non ergo ea opus est, quoties aliunde habetur certitudo moralis." *Op. cit.*, lib., VII, disp. LXXIV, n. 13.

[7] *Commentaria ac Disputationes in Primum Secundae D. Sancti Thomae* (2 vols., Lugduni, 1630), Tom. I, q. XIX, art. VI, disp. LXVI, cap. V, nn. 25-26 (hereafter cited *Comentaria in I, II*).

necessaria monitio, ubi moraliter est certa obstinatio." Thus there was clearly indicated that what was required was a moral certitude of the ill will or of the obstinacy towards the converted spouse on the part of the consort who remained in infidelity. Taking a cue from the papal constitutions of Pius V and Gregory XIII, Sanchez felt that moral certitude on this score was sufficiently in evidence when the infidel's place of habitat was unknown, or when he lived at too great a distance for normally possible communication; he likewise felt that the interpellations were no longer necessary, if the infidel had given expression to his ill will through the external facts of his life.

Thus Sanchez not only considered the absence of the spouse as sufficient evidence that there was no desire for the resumption of cohabitation or for a conversion to the faith, but he moreover declared that such unwillingness was all the more indicated if the unbaptized spouse had entered a second marriage.[8] At the same time Sanchez insisted that the convert could omit the interpellations only when he was certain, morally at least, that his partner, who till then had remained obstinate in his infidelity, did not wish to be converted, or was determined not to resume the required conjugal life. If there remained any doubt regarding this obstinacy, the convert was fully required to use some means for determining more definitely the state of the will on the side of the infidel party.

Sanchez explicitly listed three earlier authorities in support of his theory. The first of these, Vazquez (1549-1604) stated that these constitutions set up a presumption of law that the spouses of these converts did not wish to be converted and had no desire to resume marital life with the christian. Since this obstinacy was acknowledged in law, there was no longer any need for the interpellations and therefore they were to be omitted.[9] The second, Navarrus

[8] *Op. cit.*, lib. VII, disp. LXXIV, nn. 13, 14, 15.

[9] *Commentaria in I, II*, q. XIX, art. VI, disp. LXVI, cap. V, nn. 25-26.

(1493-1586), acknowledged the necessity of the interpellations by way of general rule, unless some other means sufficed for the securing of proof regarding the intention of the infidel.[10] Finally, Henriquez (1538-1608) suggested in particular that the interpellations could be omitted altogether as long as moral certitude of the infidel's obstinacy could be gained in any other way whatever.[11]

A contemporary of Sanchez, but left unmentioned by him, was Fernandus Rebellus (1547-1608). This author held that the interpellations could be omitted when communication with the infidel was forbidden by ecclesiastical precept, particularly because of the danger of perversion.[12] As long as such danger was certain it was sufficient to determine the will and mind of the infidel by some general means. But this danger would have arisen only if the convert made the interpellations personally, and hence the doctrine of Rebellus seemed applicable solely when the interpellations were to be made privately.

Caponi, writing in the latter half of the 17th century, referred to the teaching of Sanchez and in agreement with him held that the interpellations were to be omitted when the unbaptized partner lived at a great distance.[13]

Section 2: Dispensation Required

In his consideration of the application of the Pauline privilege, Pontius[14] took exception to those who held that

[10] *Consilio et Responsa* (Lugduni, 1594) lib. III, tit. *de conversione infidelium*, concil. I, n. 4; cf. Sanchez, *op. cit.*, lib., VII, disp. LXXVII.

[11] *Summa Theologiae Moralis*, (Venetiis, 1660), lib. II, *de matrimonio*, can. 8, n. 5, in comment. lit. S, quoted in Sanchez, *loc. cit.*

[12] *Opus de Obligationibus Iustitiae, Religionis, Charitatis* (Lugduni: Sumptibus Horatii Cardon, 1608), Pars. II, lib. III, *de matrimonii impedimentis*, q. 10, sect. 2, concl. 5.

[13] Iulius Caponi, *Institutiones Canonicae* (ed. nova denui revisa, emendata, atque aucta, Coloniae Allobrogum: Sumptibus Marci Michaelis Bousquet, 1734) lib. II, tit. 12, *qui matrimonium impedire possunt*, q. 5: " ... si inveniri commode nequeat, non est opus monitione, quia moraliter certum est, quod nolit sponsus converti ... "

[14] *De Sacramento Matrimonii*, lib. IX, cap. 2.

at times it was not necessary to make the interpellations. He quite emphatically stated that they had no grounds upon which to base their teaching, and cited as his authority the Constitution *Populis* of Gregory XIII. Pontius summarized the cases in which the making of the interpellations could be regarded as outside the pale of possibility. Only in the cases wherein the infidel could not be questioned because of the certain danger of death did he deem it allowable and feasible to determine the intent of the infidel in some general way. But, if he could not be interrogated simply because of such factors as the difficulty of travel or the distance of the journey, or because the Christian did not know where his consort lived, then the convert was not to be allowed to enter a second marriage until he had first obtained a dispensation from the Roman Pontiff, which dispensation was to take the place of the interrogation normally required for the use of the Pauline privilege. Such a dispensation, according to Pontius, was implied in the act of Pius V when he honored as valid the marriage contracted by the Indians of the new Spain who, not knowing where their first spouses lived, had entered other marriages. Pope Gregory, so Pontius averred, had granted a similar dispensation. If such dispensations were not necessary, as Sanchez contended, why had the Roman Pontiff issued them?[15]

Laymann (1574-1635) writing in the early 17th century, urged the seeking of a dispensation in practice as the safest solution to any doubt in the matter.[16] Later in the century Caponi referred to Laymann as an authority for the opposition, since he himself agreed with Sanchez.[17] Rebellus, cited

[15] *Op. cit.*, lib. VII, cap. 48, nn. 21-22.

[16] Paulus Laymann, *Theologia Moralis in Quinque Libros Distributa* (ed. nova, ab auctore recognita, Venetiis: Typis Georgii Valentini, 1630) lib. V, tract. 10, part 2, cap. 3, *de matrimonio infidelium*, n. 4: "Quamquam ab auctoritate in contrariae sententiae, longe tutius erit in hoc casu Summum Pontificem consulere atque dispensationem petere; idque etiam in praxi observari, testatur Veracrux (hereafter cited *Theologia Moralis*).

[17] *Institutiones Canonicae*, lib. II, tit. 12, q. 5, resp. ad 3.

by Pontius, had held that the interpellations could be omitted if the convert was absolutely certain that he would be subjected to a proximate danger of the perversion of his faith in consequence of any attempted communication with the infidel spouse, but demanded that in every case of doubt the Holy See should be consulted and a dispensation obtained.[18] In a later conclusion he considered the argument specifically, and in adverting to the doctrine of Navarrus and Sanchez disagreed emphatically with their opinion that the interpellations could be omitted when, because of the distance or in view of the difficulty of travel, the making of the interpellations became at least morally impossible. He again adverted to the exception mentioned above by allowing the omission only when the interpellations could not be made because of a certain and proved danger of spiritual perversion. He challenged Sanchez' interpretation of the Constitution of St. Pius V, and then pointed to the Constitution of Gregory XIII in warrant of the fact that no difficulty was of itself sufficient to justify the omission of the interpellations, and that accordingly a dispensation had to be obtained from the Holy See.[19]

In addition to the two official documents which Pope Benedict XIV (1740-1758)[20] issued and in which he considered questions similar to these insofar as they were evidently based on the Constitution of Pope Gregory XIII, he published the *De Synodo Dioecesana,* in which at considerable length he set forth his personal and private opinion on this question. Though he definitely followed Pontius, he considered the problem thoroughly in vindication of his own stand in the dispute. Pointing to the necessity of the interpellations[21] he cited the famous Decretal Letter, *Quanto te*

[18] *Opus de Obligationibus Iustitiae, Religionis, Charitatis,* Pars. II, lib. III, q. 10, sect. 2, conclusio 5.

[19] *Ibid.,* conclusio ultima.

[20] Ep. *In Suprema,* 16 ian. 1745; Const. *Apostolici ministerii,* 16 sept. 1747—*Fontes,* nn. 353; 381.

[21] *De Synodo Dioecesana* (2 vols., Romae: Ex Typographia Joannis Baptistae Connetti, 1783) lib. VI, cap. IV, n. 3.

magis, of Innocent III[22] and a response of the Sacred Congregation of the Council under the date of January 23, 1603.[23] When he expressly referred to the opposite opinion he summarized Sanchez' teaching that the convert could enter a second marriage without making the interpellations if the infidel had gone to distant countries or if he could not be located,[24] but lated answered precisely that "neither distance, nor difficulty, nor presumption suffice to excuse from the obligation."[25]

Benedict XIV, a strong defender of the papal authority, asserted that it belonged to the Holy See exclusively to declare in what circumstances the divine precept to interpellate the unbaptized party no longer was of obligation.[26] He based his interpretation on the Constitution of Gregory XIII,[27] and on this point he cited Pontius with full approval.[28] But as the Supreme Pontiff he likewise insisted that the Holy See should willingly grant the dispensation to those who seek it as long as there was an urgent cause in a case wherein it was morally impossible to make the interpellations.[29]

[22] 1 maii 1199—*Regesta Pontificum Romanorum* inde ab anno post Christum natum 1198 ad annum 1304 ed. Augustus Potthast (2 vols., Berolini, 1874-1875), n. 684; c. 7, X, *de divortiis,* IV, 19.

[23] Pallottini, S., *Collectio omnium conclusionum et resolutionum quae in causis propositis apud Sacram Congregationem Cardinalium S. Concilii Tridentini Interpretum prodierunt ab eius institutione anno MDLXIV ad MDCCCLX, distinctis titulis alphabetico ordine per materias digestas, cura et Studio Salvatoris Pallottini* (17 vols., Romae: 1868-1893), s. v. *Matrimonium* XIV, n. 2 (hereafter cited *Collectio Resolutionum S.C.C.*); cf. Woeber, *The Interpellations,* pp. 22-23 regarding the importance of this response as the first explicit act of legislation on the necessity of the interpellations.

[24] *De Synodo Dioecesana,* lib. VI, cap. IV, n. 3.

[25] *Op. cit.,* lib. XIII, cap. XXI, n. 1.

[26] *Op. cit.,* lib. VI, cap. IV, n. 3.

[27] *Op. cit.,* lib. XIII, cap. XXI, n. 3, pars. 2.

[28] *Op. cit.,* lib. VI, cap. IV, n. 3.

[29] Benedictus XIV, ep. *In suprema,* 16 ian. 1745—*Fontes,* n. 353; *Coll. S.C.P.F.,* n. 2252; *Bullarium Sanctissimi Domini Nostri Benedicti Papae XIV* (4 vols. in 10, Venetiis, 1777-1784) I, 483-485.

In reviewing the cases contemplated in the Constitution *Populis* of Gregory XIII, Pope Benedict XIV readily granted that in his own day similar cases occured and that very often bishops and missionaries were forced to wait for the dispensation to come from Rome, so that the delay thus occasioned gave rise to notable inconvenience. Accordingly, he urged that they obtain the faculty of dispensing from the interpellations. In this way they would be prepared for the eventuality, and all inclination whatsoever to follow the opinion of Sanchez, which according to Pope Benedict could not safely be followed in practice, could be duly suppressed.[30] That opinion had proposed that without the obtaining of a dispensation the making of the interpellations could be foregone whenever in some particular case such action appeared impossible of accomplishment or altogether useless.[31]

Article II: The Nature and Juridical Effect of the Dispensation

A second problem followed inevitably from the first. If the Holy See allowed a dispensation from the making of the interpellations and permitted the convert to enter a second marriage without fulfilling this otherwise necessary requirement, what then was the exact nature and juridical effect of this dispensation? Did it merely serve to extend the scope of the Pauline privilege, or was it an actual dissolution of the matrimonial bond through a use of the apostolic power in favor of the Faith?

Section 1: Extension of the Scope of the Pauline Privilege

The first opinion contended that the Pope had no authority over and consequently could not dissolve the consummated marriages of infidels, and therefore in the cases proposed in the Papal Constitutions the Holy Father did not dissolve the marriages of the native converts but simply

[30] Laymann had made a similar suggestion more than a century earlier.—*Theologia Moralis*, lib. V, tract. X, pars. 2, cap. 3, n. 4.

[31] *De Synodo Dioecesana*, lib. XIII, cap. XXI, n. 6.

widened the scope and the extension of the Pauline privilege by allowing the omission of one of the formalities, namely, the interpellations, which, under normal circumstances, were demanded at least for the licit use of the privilege.

Pontius, one of the defenders of this position, listed several cases as relating to the problem here concerned, but he regarded them as unyielding to the authority of the Holy See in the matter of dissolving them, either because of the insoluble character of the marriage bond itself or in view of the Church's lack of jurisdiction over them.[32] Speaking explicitly of the Constitution of Gregory XIII, which indeed was the specific source that gave rise to the discussion, he questioned the opinion of Sanchez, and demanded the obtaining of a dispensation. The granted dispensation did not dissolve the bond of the consummated marriage of the two infidels, but exemplified the supreme authority of the Church in using its right to interpret the divine law, which law through the Pauline privilege afforded a means of dissolving the marriages of infidels upon the conversion of one of the parties. There was involved in this case simply a declaration that the essential conditions for the use of the privilege were verified, and that, accordingly, the convert was freed from the obligation of making the interpellations. In all other respects there was reflected a simple application of the Pauline privilege.[33]

Benedict XIV, who likewise insisted on the obtaining of a dispensation when it was impossible to make the interpellations according to the prescribed form, asserted that this dispensation did not in any way dissolve the legitimate marriage of the infidels, and that its effect was simply that of tempering the rigor of the canonical laws relative to the judicial and formal interpellations.[34] While referring to the

[32] *De Sacramento Matrimonii,* lib. IX, cap. II, nn. 8-11; lib. VII, cap. XLVIII, n. 22.

[33] *Op. cit.,* lib. VII, cap. XLVIII, n. 22.

[34] *De Synodo Dioecesana,* lib. XIII, cap. XXI, n. 4: "... nihil aliud egisse quam canonicarum legum rigorem temporare in eo quod pertinet ad iudicialem interpellationem."

Constitutions of Paul III and Pius V, neither of which required the making of the interpellations or the obtaining of a dispensation from them, Benedict stated:

> "Id autem est, quod in Apostolicis litteris, duo illi Romani Pontificis praestiterunt; admittendo scilicet, in favorem Fidei, loco formalis et rigorosae interpellationis, extrajudicialem illam notitiam, quod vel omnino ignoretur ubinam gentium degat infidelis coniux, vel saltem ratio non suppetat eumdem iudicialiter interpellandi, atque huic interpellationem praefatam notitiam subrogando. In quo profecto nullus extraordinariae illius potestatis usus apparet, qua vinculum matrimonii in infidelitatis statu consummati dissolvere in animo habuerint."[35]

According to Benedict XIV, then, all three constitutions merely mitigated the canonical requirements relative to the making of the interpellations, thus allowing the use of the Pauline privilege, through which the marriage that had been contracted in infidelity became dissolved in direct consequence of the divine authority.

In times approaching closer to the present this opinion was supported by Perronne (1794-1876). Citing Benedict as his authority and referring particularly to the Constitution of Gregory XIII, Perronne contended that the Pope, acting simply as interpreter of the divine law, decreed that these marriages came under the application of the privilege and were dissolved immediately by God.[36]

Substantially the same was the teaching of Heiss (1818-1890) who likewise aligned himself in support of Benedict XIV's doctrine by contending that the Holy Father did not dissolve the marriages of infidels since he had no such power over consummated marriages, but that he simply declared

[35] *Loc. cit.*

[36] *De Matrimonio Christiano Libri Tres* (3 vols., Romae: Typis S. Congregationis de Prop. Fide, 1858) II, 312; cf. also *op. cit.*, II, 318: "Ast non fit ex auctoritate Ecclesiae quae non potest dissolvere quod Deus coniunxit, neque ad id potestatem hanc a Deo est assecuta, sed immediate a Dei privilegio in Fidei favorem."

the Pauline privilege to be applicable, even though the interpellations could not be made.[37] Finally this teaching was supported also by Feije (1820-1894).[38] This author restated the arguments of Pontius and Benedict XIV, and summarized their defense of their position, namely, that Popes Paul III, Pius V, and Gregory XIII were merely asserting that the Pauline privilege was applicable in the cases under consideration, even though not all of the required formalities could be fulfilled. Accordingly, the marriages of the unbaptized as mentioned in the constitutions of these Popes were dissolved through the simple use of that privilege.

Section 2: Dissolution of the Marriage by Papal Authority

There were others who held that the privileges granted in these Papal Constitutions had no reference to the Pauline privilege, but pointed in fact to an application of a wider power which in favor of the Faith effected the dissolution of the marriage bond, contracted indeed and consummated in infidelity, but brought under the jurisdiction of the Church in consequence of the baptism of one or both of the parties. It is irrelevant to raise the question whether the Holy See has such power. The Roman Pontiffs are themselves the

[37] M. Heiss, *De Matrimonio Tractatus Usui Venerabilis Cleri Americani Accomodatus* (Monachi: Ex Typographia E. Stahl, 1861), p. 116, note 1, "Non solvitur tale matrimonium ex iure Pontificio, matrimonium enim consummatum non potest iure pontificio solvi, quamvis in infidelitate initum sit, saltem lege generali; sed dissolvitur ex privilegio Christi, id in fidei favorem concedentio, quod privilegium d Paulus, Cor. 7:15 explicuit in verbis allegatis, ita ab Ecclesia intellectis . . ."

"Quando evenit, coniugem infidelem in longinquas abiise regiones, aut ita latitare, ut interpellari nequeat, tunc dubitatur, an interpellatione omissa, fas sit converso alias inire nuptias; affirmant plerique; alii ex adverso in eo rerum statu necessariam putant dispensationem Summi Pontificis, cuius est declarare in quibusnam circumstantiis desinat obligare praeceptum divinum, quo praedicta interpellatio ante recissionem matrimonii videtur iniuncta." (hereafter cited *De Matrimonio.*)

[38] *De Impedimentis et Dispensationibus Matrimonialibus*, pp. 488, 494-496.

best interpreters of the extent of their power, and there is no longer any room for doubting the existence of such power on their part when *de facto* they have repeatedly exercised their supreme authority in the Church. Though the use of this power is something distinct from the application of the Pauline privilege, and though this power reflects an apostolic and therefore a human character, the power is principally and primarily divine in its source and nature, but rests ministerially and instrumentally in the hands of the Roman Pontiff for its use.[39]

The proponents of this opinion offered arguments in its support. First among these proponents was Martinus Azpilcueta (1493-1586), known commonly as Navarrus. He considered a case in which a Jew had been a party to a non-Christian marriage. Only after he had separated from his wife did the latter become a convert. He married again, and in time both he and his second wife became Christians. Navarrus asserted that this second marriage could not have been allowed unless the man had obtained a papal dispensation, since his first and legitimate wife was still living. He could not have used the Pauline privilege, since his first wife had also been baptized. He stated that upon the previous obtaining of a papal dispensation the second marriage could be valid, thus implying the absolute dissolution of the first marriage in consequence of the papal dispensation.[40]

Sanchez referred to this case also. Without specifically adverting to the Constitution of Gregory XIII, he defended the opinion that the marriages of infidels could be dissolved by papal authority. He based this contention on the fundamental premise that by reason of their sacramental char-

[39] G. Vromant, *Ius Missionariorum*, Tom. V, *De Matrimonio* (Louvain: Museum Lessianum, 1931) nn. 270-271 (hereafter cited *De Matrimonio*); Theodorus M. Vlaming, *Praelectiones Iuris Matrimonii* (3. ed., 2 vols., Bussum in Hollandia: Sumptibus Societatis Editricis Anonymae Olim Paulus Brand, 1919-1921) (hereafter cited *Praelectiones*); Payen, *De Matrimonio*, II, n. 2210.

[40] *Consilia seu Responsa*, lib. III, *de conversione infidelium*, consil. 2, n. 13; cf. Burton, *A Commentary on Canon 1125*, p. 73.

acter the ratified marriages of Christians are much more firm than are the consummated marriages of infidels. Since the Holy See could dissolve the ratified marriages of Christians, it could *a fortiori* dissolve the consummated marriages of the unbaptized upon the conversion of one of the parties. The Holy See could further dissolve such marriages after the conversion of both of the parties as long as the marriage remained unconsummated.[41]

Within a few years Laymann quoted Navarrus and Sanchez and stated explicitly that there were times when the first marriage of an infidel could not be dissolved by his entering a second marriage. Evidently Laymann contemplated here the non-applicable use of the Pauline privilege. But, so Laymann taught, in such a case a dispensation could be obtained, since relative to the matter of firmness the marriage between two infidels did not share in the perfection of a sacramental union.[42]

In his consideration of the general question regarding the dissolution of a ratified but subsequently non-consummated marriage, Pirhing (1606-1679) answered the objection that ratified marriages are by divine institution insoluble. He admitted that the Roman Pontiff does not and cannot directly and immediately dispense from the divine law, but only from the natural contract, but he also contended that this direct dispensation from the natural contract incidently implied a dispensation from the divine law contract.[43] He

[41] *De Sancto Matrimonii Sacramento*, lib. II, disp. XVII, n. 2; also lib. VII, disp. LXXIV, n. 4.

[42] *Theologia Moralis*, lib. V, tract. X, pars., II, cap. III, *de matrimonio infidelium*, n. 2.

[43] *Ius Canonicum* (ed. novissima, Dilingae, 1722), lib. IV, tit. I, sect. V, n. 4, obj. 143; Cf. Also: Bouscaren-Ellis, *Canon Law*, p. 433, "The Roman Pontiff cannot dispense from the *absolute* provisions of the *divine* law, natural or positive; that is, where the divine law is binding on persons independently of any act of their own free will; for example, in impotence, consanguinity in the first degree of the direct line. Within certain limits he can dispense from the so-called *conditional* provisions of the divine law; that is, where the divine law is binding only because of some act of the free will of the parties; for

later expressly stated that the Holy Father could dissolve the consummated marriages of infidels even if both of them afterwards became baptized. His proof for this statement he rested on the acknowledged power of the Roman Pontiff to dissolve the ratified marriages of Christians, to the bond of which there was attached an added firmness in view of the sacramental character of the contract.[44]

St. Alphonsus (1696-1787) added his authority to this opinion in his assertion that, although the marriages of infidels are naturally insoluble, they can, however, be dissolved upon the conversion of at least one of the parties, provided, of course, that the marriage has not been consummated after the baptism of the spouses, and that there is a sufficiently urgent cause. He then referred explicitly to the two declarations of Urban VIII,[45] in which the Pontiff stated: "Nos attendentes huiusmodi infidelium matrimonia, non ita censeri, quin necessitate suadente, dissolvi possunt." He furthermore pointed to the Constitution *Populis*. In it Pope Gregory XIII had left open a way for the dissolution of certain marriages contracted in infidelity, even when the spouses of the unions had both become converts to the Faith.[46]

Later pre-Code authors supported this theory as the more acceptable explanation of the nature of the grants given through the three papal constitutions of the 16th century. DeBecker (1857-1936), in defending the papal power to dissolve marriages contracted and consummated among the

---

example, an oath, a vow or a contract. This is not a dispensation in the strict sense, because it is not a relaxation of the law itself directly, but of a human act which brought the subject within the law. It is thus that the Roman Pontiff can dispense from solemn vows in religion, sacred orders, and even from the bond of a former marriage, provided it is not *ratum et consummatum*." Cf. further, Vermeersch-Creusen, *Epitome*, I, n. 187, p. 174; Wernz-Vidal, *Ius Canonicum*, I, n. 307, p. 463.

[44] *Loc. cit.*

[45] Briefs dated October 20, 1626, and September 17, 1627. Cf. Burton, *op. cit.*, p. 74.

[46] Alphonsus Liguori, *Theologia Moralis* (4 vols., ed. L. Gaudé, Romae: 1905-1912), lib. VI, *de matrimonio*, n. 897.

unbaptized, asserted that it was the application of this power that furnished the answer to the problem occasioned by these papal documents.[47] Gasparri (1852-1934), arguing from the practice of the Church, stated that the Holy See has dispensed in cases which cannot in any way be interpreted as cases that fall within the applicable use of the Pauline privilege. The extraordinary power postulated by this practice of the Church was given by God to the Church, and was used by Popes Paul III, St. Pius V, and Gregory XIII, in their Constitutions.[48]

Wernz (1842-1914) likewise felt that this theory furnished the more probably correct explanation, especially if the argument dealt exclusively with the actual wording of the constitutions themselves.[49] And here precisely he impugned the basic argument of those who held with Pontius and Pope Benedict XIV that the constitutions made provision solely for the application of the Pauline privilege as a means whereby the marriages of the native converts became dissoluble. For these had held that the Roman Pontiffs simply dispensed from the strict obligation of making the interpellations by substituting an extrajudicial knowledge of the infidel's evil and obstinate will in place of a judicial knowledge derived through interpellations. If this had been the intention of these Pontiffs, however, namely to interpret officially the applicable use of the Pauline privilege, then their constitutions could in their applicability not have been restricted to definite and limited localities as they actually were, but would have been as universal in application as was the privilege itself.[50]

[47] Julius DeBecker, *De Matrimonio* (ed. nova, Louvain: Establiss, Fr. Ceuterick, 1931), sect. X, *de dissolutione matrimonii,* p. 257.

[48] *De Matrimonio,* II, nn. 1165-1167.

[49] *Ius Matrimoniale,* n. 705, note 93: Wernz-Vidal, *Ius Matrimoniale,* n. 635, p. 834, "Quare non est recurrendum ad privilegium Paulinum a Gregorio XIII non allegatum, sed ad *plenitudinem* potestatis pontificiae *iustasque causas,* et *minorem firmitatem* vinculi istorum matrimoniorum, quibus R. Pontifex insistit."

[50] Other authors who supported this explanation of the nature of these papal Constitutions were: Ignaz Fahrner, *Geschichte der Ehe-*

Likewise, any other explanation seems wholly without support if one considers exclusively the actual grant as it is worded in the constitutions; only through an unwarranted distortion of the obvious sense of the wording could such an interpretation still stand as acceptable. In line with this concept is the following strong statement: "Re quidem vera, in vanum videntur laborare auctores sententiae contrariae, qui Constitutiones SS. PP. ad usum privilegium Paulini limitare conantur."[51]

The Constitutions *Altitudo* and *Romani Pontificis* made no mention of the interpellations. Inasmuch as it was not required to make the interpellations, the question of a dispensation was not a relevant matter. The convert was allowed to enter a second marriage even though his legitimate spouse was still living. Under the circumstances contemplated in the Constitution *Romani Pontificis* it frequently would not have been difficult much less impossible to meet the ordinary requirement of the making of the interpellations. The third Constitution, *Populis,* left room for a dispensation from the interpellations, but the granted dispen-

scheidung in kanonischen Recht, und Geschichte des Unauflöslichkeitsprinzips und der Vollkommenen Scheidung der Ehe im kanonischen Recht (Freiburg in Breisgau, 1903), p. 281; Joyce, *Christian Marriage,* pp. 479-480, 492, who mentioned a number of other authors; Feije, *De Impedimentis et Dispensationibus Matrimonialibus,* n. 488, who listed also the following Commentators whose works were not all available to the present writer for proper verification: Angelus Maria Verricelli, *Questiones Morales et Legales in Octo Tractatus Distributae* (Venetiis: apud Franciscum Bada, 1635), tract. II, q. XVII, n. 2; Dominicus Palmieri, *Tractatus de Matrimonio Christiano* (Romae, 1880) p. 221; Josephus Biederlack, *Institutiones Iuris Ecclesiastici de Fundamentali Ecclesiae Constitutione* (Romae, 1907), pp. 307, seq.; Augustinus Lehmkuhl, *Theologiae Moralis* (10. ed.; 2 vols., Friburgi Brisgoviae, 1902), II, nn. 707 seq., pp. 503 seq.; Ludovicus Billot, *De Ecclesiae Sacramentis Commentarius in Tertiam Partem S. Thomae* (6. ed., 2 vols., Romae, 1895), II, 395 seq.; Rudolph Ritter von Scherer, *Handbuch des Kirchenrechts* (2 vols., Graz, 1886-1898), II, 560 seq.

[51] Cl. Marc.-F. X. Gesterman-J. B. Raus, *Institutiones Morales Alphonsianae* (2 vols., Lugduni: Typis Emmanuelis Vitte, 1927-1928) II, n. 989, with reference to lib. VI, n. 897 in the *Theologia Moralis* of St. Alphonsus.

sation could hardly be interpreted as simply certifying the applicable use of the Pauline privilege, since in the Constitution it was explicitly stated that the second marriage of the convert was valid and remained absolutely indissoluble even though the separated spouse of the earlier union had been baptized before the second marriage was contracted. But, the Pauline privilege is never applicable once the partners of the marriage which was contracted by them in infidelity have both become Christians. From this it is evident that the three papal constitutions implied the use of a power distinct from and greater than that used in the Pauline privilege. In no way can they be limited within the scope of the Pauline privilege as understood in its truly limited extension.

CHAPTER IV

OFFICIAL INTERPRETATION THROUGH FACULTIES AND RESPONSES

Article I: Necessity of the Dispensation

THE Constitutions of Popes Paul III and St. Pius V provided for the actual and total omission of the interpellations under certain definite conditions. However, in the years preceding the codification and promulgation of the present Code the Holy See did not under these conditions allow in general the omission of the interpellations, for that privilege had effective validity only in those localities to which it had been originally granted or extended by specific decree. In accord with the Constitution of Gregory XIII the Apostolic See permitted and required the obtaining of a dispensation. This is substantiated by the overwhelming percentage of responses explicitly forbidding the omission of the interpellations and demanding that a previous dispensation be obtained from the competent ecclesiastical authority in warrant of their omission for any reason. The precedent for these later responses was set already in 1722. The Vicar Capitular of Florence referred this case to the Sacred Congregation of the Council. A convert from Judaism had been repudiated by her husband eleven years earlier. At the time of the divorce he had spoken very bitterly to her, and had made no attempt since that time to see her or their children. She now had the opportunity of marrying a Christian, but his early call to military service demanded that the ceremony be celebrated promptly.

The Sacred Congregation repeated in summary the two recognized opinions of the authors,[1] and then issued its own conclusions against those who had held that the interpellations could be omitted whenever it appeared impossible, extremely difficult, or altogether useless to make them. The

[1] Cf. Chapter III.

questions and answers may word for word be reproduced here:

His stantibus dignabuntur EE. VV. decernere:

I. An de iure necessaria sit interpellatio in casu? Et quatenus affirmative:

II. An, stantibus circumstantiis, indulgenda sit dispensatio ab interpellatione in casu? Ad utrumque: Affirmative.[2]

Following the principle enunciated in the answer to these questions, the Holy See demanded also in other cases that the interpellations be made. In one such case the infidel had consented to continue cohabitation after the conversion of his spouse but later changed his mind and attempted to lead the convert into sin. The Holy See demanded that the interpellations be repeated.[3] In a later answer to the Archbishop of Quebec, the Holy See demanded either the making of the interpellations or the obtaining of a dispensation when the formalities of the interpellations were impossible. The response quoted Benedict XIV and the response of the year 1722.[4]

In practice it was held not to be sufficiently safe to omit the interpellations, not even in those cases wherein great distances separated the two spouses or when their actual residence was unknown,[5] nor was it deemed allowable to

[2] S.C.C., Florentina, 17 ian. 1722—*Fontes*, n. 3237; *Thesaurus Resolutionum Sacrae Congregationis Concilii* (167 vols., Romae: 1718-1908) II, 116-119: *Collectio Resolutionum S.C.C.*, s.v. *Matrimonium*, n. 10, p. 612; *Canones et Decreta Concilii Tridentini ex Editione Romana* 1834, sess. XXIV, p. 286.

[3] S.C.C. Off. (Cochinchin.), 1 aug. 1759—*Fontes*, n. 810; cf. can. 1124.

[4] S.C.S. Off., instr. (ad Archiep. Quebecen.) 16 sept. 1824—*Fontes*, n. 866; *Coll. S.C.P.F.*, n. 784.

[5] S.C.S. Off., instr. (ad Archiep. Quebecen.), 16 sept. 1824—*Fontes*, n. 866; *Coll. S.C.P.F.*, n. 784; S.C.S. Off. (Siam), 4 iul. 1855—*Fontes*, n. 931; *Coll. S.C.P.F.*, n. 1114; *Acta Sancta Sedis* (Romae, 1865-1908) XXVI (1893-1894), 70-73 (hereafter cited *ASS*).

omit the interpellations in such cases where they evidently or at least in all likelihood were useless.[6]

This doctrine was held to be applicable even in the case wherein the first and legitimate spouse was held in captivity,[7] and in another case wherein the convert had been publicly and notoriously repudiated by her husband according to the civil statutes of the locality.[8] Thus in its practical policy the Church came to demand the obtaining of a dispensation.[9] This is evident not only from the great number of responses, but more conclusively from the fact that the Holy See refused to grant *sanationes in radice* when the interpellations had been omitted without the obtaining of a dispensation, and demanded a renewal of consent between the parties.[10] Such a *sanatio* was granted, however, in a case wherein the interpellations were not entirely omitted but were judged insufficient.[11]

Article II: Nature of the Dispensation

Section 1: Later Sources—Faculties

Very often the great distance that separated the missionaries from the Holy See worked a great handicap upon the

[6] S.C.S. Off., instr. (pro Vic. Ap. ad Gallos) 10 iun. 1866—*Fontes*, n. 994; *Coll. S.C.P.F.*, n. 1293; S.C.S. Off. (Portland), 18 iun. 1884—*Fontes*, n. 1088; *Coll. S.C.P.F.*, n. 1620.

[7] S.C.S. Off. (Siam), 4 iul. 1855—*Fontes*, n. 931; *Coll. S.C.P.F.*, n. 1114; *ASS*, XXVI (1893-1894), 70-73.

[8] S.C. de Prop. Fide (C.P. pro Sin. Tunkin. Occident.) 5 mart. 1816—*Coll. S.C.P.F.*, n. 704.

[9] S.C.S. Off., instr. (ad Archiep. Quebecen.), 16 sept. 1824, ad 3—*Fontes*, n. 866; *Coll. S.C.P.F.*, n. 784; S.C.S. Off., 8 iun. 1836—*Fontes*, n. 874; *Coll. S.C.P.F.*, n. 848; S.C.S. Off. (Siam) 4 iul. 1855, III, quaer. 2—*Fontes*, n. 931; *Coll. S.C.P.F.*, n. 1114; *ASS*, XXVI (1893-1894), 70-73; S.C.S. Off., 11 aug. 1859—*Fontes*, n. 954; *Coll. S.C.P.F.*, n. 1180; S.C.S. Off. (Tchely Orient.), 13 apr. 1859—*Fontes*, n. 951; *Coll. S.C.P.F.*, n. 1175; S.C.S. Off. (Mongoliae), 29 nov. 1882, ad 2—*Fontes*, n. 1075; *Coll. S.C.P.F.*, n. 1581; S.C.S. Off., 18 maii 1892—*Fontes*, n. 1156; *Coll. S.C.P.F.*, n. 1797.

[10] S.C.S. Off. (Coreae), 11 sept. 1878, ad 1—*Fontes*, n. 1057; *Coll. S.C.P.F.*, n. 1499.

[11] S.C. de Prop. Fide (Sutchuen.), 17 ian. 1836—*Fontes*, n. 4760; *Coll. S.C.P.F.*, n. 845.

efficient administration of their mission territories, and great inconveniences upon the native converts who had to wait for dispensations sought from Rome. Very early, then, it became evident that specific faculties would have to be given to the missionaries in alleviation of these emergencies. Burton in giving a resumé of the origin regarding the formulas of faculties in use before the Code points out that, although the faculties given to the missionary countries were very similar, they were not, however, drawn up in general formularies.[12] In 1637 the newly established Congregation on Faculties organized the many faculties that were in existence into five formulas. These were approved by Pope Urban VIII in that same year, 1637.[13]

Each of these formulas except the third contained a faculty similar to that granted by Pope St. Pius V, which permitted the various bishops and vicars apostolic to allow converts from polygyny or polyandry to choose whichever one of their spouses they wished, as long as he or she was willing to become a Christian, and provided that the first spouse refused to be converted. The faculty read:

> "Dispensandi cum gentilibus et infidelibus plures uxores habentibus, ut post conversionem et baptismum, quam ex illis maluerint, si etiam ipsa fidelis fiat, retinere possint, nisi prima voluerit converti."[14]

It is of interest to note that the wording of the faculty was used unchanged in a faculty dated June 10, 1915, only a few years before the promulgation of the present Code:

> SSmus D.N. Benedictus Div. Prov. PP. XV ... impertita R.P.D. Ordinario Daressalomensi facultatem benigne concedere dignatus est dispensandi cum gen-

[12] *A Commentary on Canon 1125*, pp. 98-101.

[13] A. Vermeersch, "Commentaria de Formulis Facultatum Quas S. Congr. de Propaganda Fide Concedere Solet," *Periodica de Re Canonica et Morali utilia praesertim Religiosis et Missionariis* (Brugis, 1905—) XI (1922), 33-144 (hereafter this publication will be cited as *Periodica*).

[14] Formula I and II, art. 11; Formula IV, art. 9; Formula V, art. 14; Vermeersch, "art. cit.", *Periodica*, XI (1922), 48, 51, 56, 60.

tilibus et infidelibus plures uxores habentibus, ut post conversionem et baptismum quam ex illis maluerint, se etiam ipsa fidelis fiat, retinere possint, nisi prima voluerit converti.

In singulis autem casibus expressa fiat mentio Apostolicae delegationis. Praesentibus valituris ad quinquennium.[15]

Besides the official grant of faculties, an important step in the development of the legislation on this dispensing power was the recognition by the Holy See of the Acts of the Synod of Suchow, a synod held in China at the beginning of the 19th century.[16] The legislators of this synod, taking their lead from the Constitution of Gregory XIII, insisted on the necessity of the interpellations, even in the face of physical danger to the convert or to the one making the interpellations. Only a dispensation could substitute for the interpellations, and no cause was to be considered sufficiently grave to excuse from the obtaining of this dispensation. On June 29, 1822, the Holy See approved the acts of this Synod, extending their application to all the provinces of China and even to neighboring countries.[17]

Section 2: Characteristics of the Dispensation

Slowly but definitely the official interpretation regarding the need of this dispensation was effected by means of the succeeding responses of the Holy See to numerous and varied questions from the missionaries, who were prompted

[15] S.C.S. Off., *Facultas Prima circa Privilegium Paulinum,* 10 iun. 1915—"Die neuen Missionsfakultäten von 1915," *Arkiv für katholisches Kirchensrecht* (Innsbruck, 1857-1861; Mainz, 1862—) XCVII (1917), 432 (hereafter cited *AKKR*).

[16] Synodus Sutchuensis, 2 sept. 1803, cap. IX, n. 8—J. D. Mansi, *Sacrorum Conciliorum Nova et Amplissima Collectio* (53 vols. in 60, Pariis-Arnhemii-Lipsiae, 1901-1927), XXXIX, 43 (hereafter this work will be cited as Mansi).

[17] S.C. de Prop. Fide, ep. 29 iun. 1822—*Acta et Decreta Sacrorum Conciliorum Recentiorum, Collectio Lacensis* (7 vols., Friburgi Brisgoviae: Sumptibus Herder, 1870-1892) VI, coll. 638-639 (hereafter cited *Coll. Lac.*)

by the circumstances of their missionary activity to use these privileges to their fullest. From the very beginning it was clear that certain antecedent conditions were to be verified before the dispensation could be granted. On the one hand one could not merely presume the existence of these conditions,[18] and yet, on the other, moral certitude sufficed.[19] This certitude was to be established in consequence of some form of summary and extrajudicial investigation. This kind of investigation was demanded by Gregory XIII in the original grant of the faculty for dispensing from the making of the interpellations.

Between these two extremes in the period of development this requirement of the dispensation was clarified and insisted on in numerous responses of the Holy See.[20] According to an answer of the Holy Office this extrajudicial investigation was to have a threefold purpose, namely, to determine whether the infidel party could be interpellated or not, and, if so, whether he could answer within the time prescribed, and finally, whether the interrogation would probably bring harm upon the Christian party or to other Christians.[21] The acts of the Synod of Suchow demanded that this investigation be made in writing and that it be preserved along with the other records pertaining to the marriage in question.[22]

In interpreting the words *plures uxores* in the Constitu-

[18] S.C.S.Off. (Chen-si et Chan-si), 23 nov. 1769 ad 1—*Fontes*, n. 825; *Coll. S.C.P.F.*, n. 425; S.C.S. Off., instr. (ad Archiep. Quebecen.), 16 sept. 1824, ad 3—*Fontes*, n. 866; *Coll. S.C.P.F.*, n. 784.

[19] S.C.S.Off. (ad Vic. Ap. Iaponiae Merid.), 4 febr. 1891—*Fontes*, n. 1130; *Coll. S.C.P.F.*, n. 1746.

[20] S.C.S. Off. (Mongoliae), 29 nov. 1882—*Fontes*, n. 1075; *Coll. S.C.P.F.*, n. 1581; S.C.B. Off. (Portland), 12 iun.1884—*Fontes*, n. 1088; *Coll. S.C.P.F.*, n. 1620; S.C.S. Off. (Chen-si et Chan-si), 23 nov. 1769—*Fontes*, n. 825; *Coll. S.C.P.F.*, n. 475; S.C.S. Off. (ad Vic. Ap. Iaponiae Merid.), 4 febr. 1891—*Fontes*, n. 1130; S.C.S. Off., 10 iun. 1915—*AKKR*, XCVII (1917), 433.

[21] S.C.S. Off. (Mongoliae), 29 nov. 1882—*Fontes*, n. 1075; *Coll. S.C.P.F.*, n. 1581; Faculty II and III, 10 iun. 1915—*AKKR*, XCVII (1917), 433.

[22] Synodus Sutchuensis, cap. IX, n. 6—Mansi, XXXIX, 43.

tions of Popes Paul III and Pius V, both of whom had acted in favor of converts from polygamy, the Holy See indicated that the words referred to the spouses who had been repudiated as well as those with whom the convert was still living, and that they pointed to both a simultaneous and a successive polygamy.[23]

Several responses clearly defined practical phases in the use of the faculty of dispensing. Thus the Holy Office refused a request to extend the power of dispensing from the interpellations to the case wherein the infidel was willing to resume cohabitation, but wherein the Christian, wishing to marry another person, was not willing to admit the infidel party.[24] The faculty to dispense in an individual case was declared to be devoid of validity if it had not been used within a year's time, and hence the grant had to be renewed if the faculty was to be used after that time limit.[25] Ordinarily the use of the faculty was limited to a determined number of cases; thus an individual grant of the Holy Office, approved by the Holy Father, was made available for use in ten cases,[26] another was valid for us in fifteen cases,[27] while the faculty which was granted in 1915 was restricted to five cases for its effective use.[28]

Section 3: Extent of the Dispensation

The juridical act of interpellating involved the asking of two questions of the infidel spouse after his partner had

[23] S.C. de Prop. Fide (C.P. pro Sin. Tunkin. Orient.), 14 ian. 1806—*Fontes*, n. 4686; Coll. *S.C.P.F.*, n. 685. This is vastly important for the proper interpretation of the application of canon 1125, for, although most countries do not allow simultaneous polygamy, they do, in the eyes of the ecclesiastical law, permit successive polygamy.

[24] S.C.S. Off. (Cochinchin. Orient.), 6 aug. 1856—*Fontes*, n. 939; *Coll. S.C.P.F.*, n. 1130.

[25] S.C. de Prop. Fide (C.P. pro Sin-Sutchuen.), 26 iun. 1820—*Fontes*, n. 4717; *Coll. S.C.P.F.*, n. 743.

[26] S.C.S. Off., (Portland), 10 iun. 1884—*Fontes*, n. 1088; *Coll. S.C.P.F.*, n. 1620.

[27] S.C.S. Off., instr. (ad Vic. Ap. Sutchuen. Orient.), 3 iun. 1874—*Fontes*, n. 1030; *Coll. S.C.P.F.*, n. 1415.

[28] Facultates II, III, 10 iun, 1915—*AKKR*, XCVII (1917), 433.

become a Christian: 1) whether he was willing to be converted and to receive baptism, and 2) whether he was willing to continue the conjugal life peacefully, that is, without offering offense to God or to the faith of the Christian.

Ordinarily the faculty to dispense was given without restriction in this regard. It looked to both interpellations to the extent that both could be foregone in consequence of the dispensation. But it is evident that the Supreme Pontiff could *a fortiori* dispense or grant the faculty of dispensing from either one of the two interpellations, and this has been recognized in practice by the Holy See.[29]

The law likewise required that the interpellations be made after the baptism of the convert, so that ordinarily they could not be made by a catechumen. However, the Holy See has again allowed exceptions to this general and common rule. Thus in a particular response the faculty was given not only for the case requested, but was accorded for use in the next fifteen cases. The faculty, however, carried the warning that it was to be used only in cases of great urgency, so that the convert could enter a Christian marriage immediately after the baptism.[30] An early response had required that those who sought to obtain the faculty of dispensing had carefully to list all of the circumstances that attended the case in question.[31]

Article III: Author of the Dispensation

In granting a faculty to dispense certain converts in

[29] S.C.S. Off. (Cochinchin.) 1 aug. 1759, ad 3—*Fontes*, n. 810; *Coll. S.C.P.F.*, n. 424; Synodus Sutchuensis, cap. IX, n. 8—Mansi, XXXIX, 43; S.C.S. Off. (ad Archiep. Quebenen.), 8 iun. 1836—*Fontes*, n. 874; *Coll. S.C.P.F.*, n. 848; S.C.S. Off. (Siam), 4 iul. 1855—*Fontes*, n. 931; *Coll. S.C.P.F.*, n. 1114; *ASS*, XXVI (1893-1894), 70-73; S.C.S. Off., instr. (pro Vic. Ap. ad Gallos), 20 iun. 1866—*Fontes*, n. 994; *Coll. S.C.P.F.*, n. 1293.

[30] S.C.S. Off., instr. (ad Vic. Ap. Sutchuen. Orient.), 3 iun 1874—*Fontes*, n. 1030; *Coll. S.C.P.F.*, n. 1415; S.C.S. Off. (Bengal), 21 nov. 1883—*Coll. S.C.P.F.*, n. 1607.

[31] S.C.S. Off. (Tchely Orient.), 13 apr. 1859—*Fontes*, n. 951; *Coll. S.C.P.F.*, n. 1175.

pagan countries from the obligation of making the interpellations, Pope Gregory named as the recipients of the power three separate and definite classes of persons, namely local ordinaries, pastors, and priests of the Society of Jesus who had been approved by the Superior of that Society for the hearing of confessions. Since there was, already in the 16th century, a wide intercommunication of privileges among the religious Orders, it is evident that confessors of these Orders, especially the Mendicants, soon participated in these privileges.[32]

Later responses, while making explicit mention of bishops and vicars apostolic, made it plain that those who dispensed by virtue of this faculty were acting as delegates of the Holy See,[33] and not with an ordinary power, and that they were to use this privilege only under urgent circumstances which did not leave time or opportunity for recourse to the Holy See.[34]

To ordinaries was accorded also the discretionary power of deciding what circumstances were sufficient to warrant the use of the faculty.[35] The decrees of the Chinese Synod of Suchow (1803) warned the missionaries who had this faculty that they were not to use it freely. They were to make us of it solely in cases of great urgency and on oc-

[32] Cf. Burton, *A Commentary on Canon 1125*, pp. 51-52; 70-71 and 174, who considers this intercommunication of favors among 16th century missionaries. Cf. also Raymond A. Matulenas, *Communication, a Source of Privileges*, The Catholic University of America Canon Law Studies, n. 183 (Washington, D.C.: The Catholic University of America Press, 1943) for a more detailed treatment of that question in general.

[33] S.C.S., Florentina, 17 ian. 1722—*Fontes*, n. 3237; S.C.S. Off., 11 aug. 1859—*Fontes*, n. 954; *Coll. S.C.P.F.*, n. 1180; S.C.S. Off. (Coreae), 10 sept. 1878—*Fontes*, n. 1057; *Coll. S.C.P.F.*, n. 1499; Facultates II, III, 10 iun. 1915—*AKKR*, XCVII (1917), 433.

[34] S.C.S. Off., 11 aug. 1859—*Fontes*, n. 954; *Coll. S.C.P.F.*, n. 1180; S.C.S. Off., (Tchely Orient.), 13 apr. 1859—*Fontes*, n. 951; *Coll. S.C.P.F.*, n. 1175.

[35] S.C.S. Off., instr. (ad Archiep. Quebecen.), 10 sept. 1824—*Fontes*, n. 866; *Coll. S.C.P.F.*, n. 784; S.C.S. Off. (Coreae), 10 sept. 1878—*Fontes*, n. 1057; *Coll. S.C.P.F.*, n. 1499.

casions of grave necessity exclusively.[36] Despite the continued insistence of the Holy See on the necessity either of making the interpellations or of obtaining a dispensation from them, the Holy Father on one occasion declared that, if without a dispensation the interpellations had been made before the catechumen's reception of baptism, and on another occasion that, if the interpellations were not made but were dispensed with by a missionary who did not have the faculty of dispensing, then the marriage in question was nevertheless to be regarded as valid and the parties were not to be disturbed.[37]

Article IV: Causes Valid for the Granting of the Dispensation

In the light of the many causes recognized by the Holy See, in the centuries before the Code, as sufficient grounds for the use of the faculty of dispensing, it is evident that no thorough consideration could be given to the validity or the applicable extent of the cause except in the measure in which the consideration was necessary for the interpretation of the cause itself. The Synod of Suchow indicated that it was not the wish of the Church that this faculty be used indiscriminately; there had to be grave reasons that urged its application. All these reasons somehow involved the notion of impossibility, physical or moral, or of futility, or of danger to the convert himself or to other Christians. It has always been noted that these conditions could not be presumed, but had to be clearly established by means of a summary and extrajudicial investigation.[38]

[36] Synodus Sutchuensis, cap. IX, n. 8—Mansi, XXXIX, 43.

[37] Pius VI, S.C. de Prop. Fide (C.P. pro Sin-Sutchuen.), 5 mart. 1787 ad 2—*Coll. S.C.P.F.*, n. 589; and Pius IX, S.C.S. Off., instr. (ad Vic. Ap. Sutchuen. Orient.), 3 iun. 1874—*Fontes*, n. 1030; *Coll. S.C.P.F.*, n. 1415.

[38] S.C.S. Off. (ad Vic. Ap. Iaponiae Merid.), 4 febr. 1891: "Iustae autem huiusmodi causae tunc aderunt cum ex processu saltem summario et extraiudiciali moraliter constet coniugem infidelem interpellari non posse, aut interpellationem vel iniutilem vel graviter periculosam futuram esse."—*Fontes*, n. 1130; *Coll. S.C.P.F.*, n. 1746; S.C.S.

Faculties granted to missionaries after the Code divided the causes for dispensation into ordinary and extraordinary,[39] but since this division was recognized at times even before the Code, it may serviceably be retained here for the sake of order and clarity.[40] Ordinary causes embraced those situations in which the making of the interpellations was impossible or useless, while extraordinary causes arose from predicaments in which the interpellations, though they could be made, would at the same time occasion serious harm, either physical or spiritual, to the Christian himself or to others.[41]

Section 1: Ordinary Causes

In the listing of these causes the successive order is dictated solely by the frequency with which the individual reason receives mention in the faculties and responses of the Holy See.

1. When the exact whereabouts of the infidel was unknown.[42]

Off. (Portland), 18 iun. 1884: "Quatenus vero saltem summarie et extraiudicialiter constet interpellationem vel impossibiliem vel inutilem fore utetur Episcopus facultate dispensandi, si ea polleat: sin minus supplicandum SSmo pro facultate pro decem casibus."—*Fontes*, n. 1088; *Coll. S.C.P.F.*, n. 1620.

[39] Xaverius Paventi, *Brevis Commentarius in Facultates S. Congregationis de Propaganda Fide* (Romae: Officium Libri Catholici, 1944) cap. III, *Facultates circa Matrimonium*, Facultates 22-28 (hereafter cited *Brevis Commentarius*); G. Vromant, *Facultates Apostolicae quas Sacra Congregatio de Propaganda Fide Delegare Solet Ordinariis Missionum* (Louvain: Editions de Museum Lessianum, 1926), pp. 78-87 (hereafter cited *Facultates Apostolicae*); G. Vromant, *De Matrimonio*, tit. I, cap. VI, *Dispensatio ab Interpellationibus*, art. II, Facultates a S.C. de Prop. Fide concessa, nn. 368-381; A. Vermeersch, "Commentaria de Formulis Facultatum, etc.", *Periodica*, XI (1922), 33-144.

[40] S.C.S. Off. (Mongoliae), 29 nov. 1882—*Fontes*, n. 1075; *Coll. S.C.P.F.*, n. 1581; Synodus Sutchuensis, cap. IX, n. 8—Mansi, XXXIX, 43.

[41] S.C.S. Off. (ad Vic. Ap. Iaponiae Merid.) 4 febr. 1891—*Fontes*, n. 1130; *Coll. S.C.P.F.*, n. 1746; Synodus Sutchuensis, 2 sept. 1803, cap. IX, n. 8—Mansi, XXXIX, 43.

[42] S.C.S. Off., instr., (ad Vic. Ap. Sutchuen. Orient.), 3 iun 1874—

2. When a long and difficult journey was necessary for the making of the interpellations, and great expense and serious inconvenience were both involved.[43] Although the Holy See persistently declined to give a general answer to the frequent query of the missionaries with reference to the length of the journey necessary in warrant of the use of the faculty, it did, in an answer for a particular case, acknowledge that a journey which consumed seven or eight days for the round trip had been considered sufficient by the Synod of Suchow.[44]

3. When communication with the infidel party was impossible because of the barbarous and warlike nature of the country where the infidel was residing.[45]

Fontes, n. 1030; *Coll. S.C.P.F.*, n. 1415; S.C. de Prop. Fide. (C.P. pro Sin.—Sutchuen.), 3 ian. 1777—*Coll. S.C.P.F.*, n. 517; S.C. de Prop. Fide (C.P. pro Sin.—Sutchuen.), 26 iun. 1821—*Fontes*, n. 4275; *Coll. S.C.P.F.*, n. 760; S.C. de. Prop. Fide (C.P. pro Sin.—Tunkin. Occident.), 5 mart. 1816—*Fontes*, n. 4698; *Coll. S.C.P.F.*, n. 705; Synodus Sutchuensis, 2 sept. 1803—Mansi, XXXIX, 43; Facultates II, III, 10 iun. 1915—*AKKR*, XCVII (1917), 433; S.C.S. Off. (Mongoliae), 29 nov. 1882—*Fontes*, n. 1075; *Coll. S.C.P.F.*, n. 1581. In this case the listed cause pointed out that street names and numbers, and also public announcements were unknown in the locality where the infidel was staying. In another case the wife, after having been divorced by her husband, had not seen him and had not heard from him for eleven years. Cf. S.C.C., *Florentina*, 17 ian. 1722—*Fontes*, n. 3237.

[43] Benedictus XIV, *In suprema*, 16 ian. 1745—*Fontes*, n. 353; *Coll. S.C.P.F.*, n. 2252; S.C.S. Off., instr., (ad Superior. Mission. Peguan.), 11 iun. 1760—*Fontes*, n. 811; S.C.S. Off. (Mongoliae), 29 nov. 1882—*Fontes*, n. 1075; *Coll. S.C.P.F.*, n. 1581; Synodus Sutchuensis, 2 sept. 1803—Mansi, XXXIX, 43; S.C.S. Off., instr. (ad Vic. Ap. Sutchuen. Orient.), 3 ian. 1874—*Fontes*, n. 1030; *Coll. S.C.P.F.*, n. 1415; S.C. de Prop. Fide (C.P. pro Sin.—Sutchuen.), 26 iun. 1821—*Fontes*, n. 4725; *Coll. S.C.P.F.*, n. 760; S.C. de Prop. Fide (C.P. pro Sin.—Sutchuen.), 3 ian. 1777—*Fontes*, n. 4572; *Coll. S.C.P.F.*, n. 517.

[44] S.C. de Prop. Fide (C.P. pro Sin.—Sutchuen.), 26 iun. 1821—*Fontes*, 4725; *Coll. S.C.P.F.*, n. 760; S.C.S. Off. (Mongoliae), 29 nov. 1882—*Fontes*, n. 1075; *Coll. S.C.P.F.*, n. 1581; Synodus Sutchuensis, 2 sept. 1803—Mansi, XXXIX, 43.

[45] Gregorius XIII, Const. *Populis*, 25 ian. 1585—*Codex Iuris Canonici*, Documentum VIII; Synodus Sutchuensis, 2 sept. 1803, cap. IX, n. 8—Mansi, XXXIX, 43; S.C.S. Off. (Mongoliae), 29 nov. 1882—

4. When the convert did not know who among his many wives was the first and, therefore, the legitimate one.[46]

5. When he was not certain that he had given true matrimonial consent to any of the women with whom he had cohabited.[47]

6. If the infidel could not furnish an answer within a reasonably limited period of time,[48] or if he was impeded from answering either in consequence of the laws of his land, or in view of customary traditions or conventions, or as a result of his own timidity,[49] or if he could have answered within the time limit but actually had not.[50]

7. When the infidel had deliberately gone into hiding to avoid being confronted with the interpellations.[51]

8. When the making of the interpellations gave rise to an occasion for a wave of bigotry or persecution against the Christians of the community where the infidel lived.[52]

Fontes, n. 1075; *Coll. S.C.P.F.*, n. 1581; S.C.S. Off. (ad Vic. Ap. Iaponiae Merid.), 4 febr. 1891—*Fontes*, n. 1130; *Coll. S.C.P.F.*, n. 1746.

[46] Paulus III, const. *Altitudo*, 1 iun. 1537—*Codex Iuris Canonici*, Documentum VI; S.C.S. Off. (Siouxormen.) 18 maii 1892—*Fontes*, n. 1155; *Coll. S.C.P.F.*, n. 1796;*ASS*, XXIX (1896-1897), 641; S.C.S. Off., 8 iun. 1836—*Fontes*, n. 874; *Coll. S.C.P.F.*, n. 848.

[47] S.C.S. Off., 8 iun. 1836—*Fontes*, n. 874; *Coll. S.C.P.F.*, n. 848; S.C.S. Off., (Siouxormen.), 18 maii 1892—*Fontes*, n. 1155; *Coll. S.C.P.F.*, n. 1796.

[48] S.C.S. Off. (Natal.), 11 iul. 1866—*Fontes*, n. 996; *Coll. S.C.P.F.*, n. 1295; Synodus Sutchuensis, 2 sept. 1803, cap. IX, n. 8—Mansi, XXXIX, 43; Facultates II, III, 10 iun. 1915—*AKKR*, XCVII (1917), 433.

[49] S.C. de Prop. Fide, instr. (ad Vic. Ap. Siam), 20 mart. 1836—*Coll. S.C.P.F.*, n. 2265; *Fontes*, n. 4762.

[50] S.C.S. Off., 11 aug. 1859—*Fontes*, n. 954; *Coll. S.C.P.F.*, n. 1180; S.C.S. Off. (Mongoliae), 29 nov. 1882—*Fontes*, n. 1075; *Coll. S.C.P.F.*, n. 1581; S.C. de Prop. Fide (C.P. pro Sin.—Tunkin. Occident.), 5 mart. 1816—*Fontes*, n. 4697; *Coll. S.C.P.F.*, n. 704.

[51] A. L. Eloy, *Variae Institutiones Practicae ad Matrimonium et ad Causas Matrimoniales Spectantes* (Hongkong, 1915), n. 170, cited by Winslow, *The Pauline Privilege*, n. 102, p. 36.

[52] S.C.S. Off. (Chen-si et Chan-si), 23 nov. 1769, ad 4—*Fontes*, n. 825; *Coll. S.C.P.F.*, n. 475.

9. When the Christian feared that she would be sold into slavery, as had been other wives of her pagan husband.[53]

10. When the only available intermediaries were unaware of the importance of the interpellations, so that they would not fulfill their office conscientiously.[54]

11. When the Christian had been publicly repudiated by her husband.[55]

12. When the Christian feared that she would be accused before the civil court.[56]

13. When war or persecution was an attendant factor.[57]

14. When in cases of extreme necessity all possibility of recourse to the Holy See was precluded.[58]

15. It was likewise allowable to grant a dispensation when the making of the interpellations was judged useless.[59] Two commonly suggested examples of cases in which the

[53] Synodus Sutchuensis, 2 sept. 1803, cap. IX, n. 8—Mansi, XXXIX, 43; S.C.S. Off. (Chen-si et Chan-si), 23 nov. 1769—*Fontes*, n. 825; *Coll. S.C.P.F.*, n. 425; S.C. de Prop. Fide (ad Vic. Ap. Sutuchen.), 17 ian. 1836, ad 2—*Fontes*, n. 4760; *Coll. S.C.P.F.*, n. 845; S.C. S. Off. (Mongoliae), 29 nov. 1882—*Fontes*, n. 1075; *Coll. S.C.P.F.*, n. 1581; S.C.S. Off. (Portland), 18 iun. 1884—*Fontes*, n. 1088; *Coll. S.C.P.F.*, n. 1620.

[54] S.C.S. Off. (Mongoliae), 29 nov. 1882—*Fontes*, n. 1075; *Coll. S.C.P.F.*, n. 1581.

[55] S.C. de Prop. Fide (C.P. pro Sin.—Tunkin. Occident.), 5 mart. 1816—*Fontes*, n. 4697; *Coll. S.C.P.F.*, n. 704.

[56] S.C. de Prop. Fide (C.P. pro Sin.—Sutchuen.), 3 ian. 1777, ad 2—*Coll. S.C.P.F.*, n. 517.

[57] S.C.S. Off. (Coreae), 11 sept. 1878—*Fontes*, n. 1057; *Coll. S.C. P.F.*, n. 1499.

[58] S.C.S., *Florentina*, 17 ian. 1722—*Fontes*, n. 3237; S.C.S. Off., 11 aug. 1859—*Fontes*, n. 954; *Coll. S.C.P.F.*, n. 1180.

[59] S.C.S. Off., instr. (pro Vic. Ap. ad Gallas), 20 iun. 1866, in resp. ad primam dubiorum classem, "Quod autem pertinet ad interpellationem, duo praeterea adnotanda sunt ... alterum, cum infidelibus quibuscumque ad fidem conversis posse ex eisdem Apostolicae Sedis auctoritate dispensari ut interpellationem utramque omittant, quoties haec aut fieri reipsa nequeat, aut, si fieret, nullius utilitatis fore reputatur."—*Fontes*, n. 994; *Coll. S.C.P.F.*, n. 1293; S.C.S. Off. (ad Vic. Ap. Iaponiae Merid.), 4 febr. 1891—*Fontes*, n. 1130; *Coll. S.C.P.F.*, n. 1746; Benedictus XIV, *de Synodo Dioecesana*, lib. XIII, cap. XXI.

making of the interpellations was thought to be useless or of no avail were the following: 1) when the infidel had become permanently insane, and 2) when, after having obtained a civil divorce, he had remarried.[60]

Section 2: Extraordinary Causes

The extraordinary causes embraced those situations wherein the infidel could indeed be reached and the interpellations made without any great difficulty, but in which there was a substantiated fear that the making of the interpellations would occasion serious harm. The situation could obtain whether the harm was directed against the Christian convert himself[61] or against other Christians individually or as a community.[62] Again there were certain conditions that needed to be verified. The threatened harm could be of a character either temporal or spiritual, as in one case when the Holy Father granted the dispensation in favor of a young Christian woman, whose former husband had treated her with physical cruelty and at the same time had refused to allow her to practice her faith.[63] Winslow points out that it was not necessary for the impending harm certainly to follow; what was postulated was the established danger that serious harm would result.[64] This proof was

[60] S.C. de Prop. Fide (C.P. pro Sin.—Sutchuen.), 5 mart. 1787—*Fontes*, n. 4615; *Coll. S.C.P.F.*, n. 589; S.C.S. Off. (Portland), 18 iun. 1884—*Fontes*, n. 1088; *Coll. S.C.P.F.*, n. 1620; S.C.S. Off. (ad Vic. Ap. Iaponiae Merid.), 4 febr. 1891—*Fontes*, n. 1130; *Coll. S.C.P.F.*, n. 1746.

[61] S.C. de Prop. Fide (C.P. pro Sin.—Sutchuen.), 3 ian. 1777—*Fontes*, n. 4572; *Coll. S.C.P.F.*, n. 517; S.C.S. Off. (Mongoliae), 29 nov. 1882—*Fontes*, n. 1075; *Coll. S.C.P.F.*, n. 1581; Faculty II, 10 iun. 1915—*AKKR*, XCVII (1917), 433.

[62] S.C.S. Off. (Mongoliae), 29 nov. 1882—*Fontes*, n. 1075; *Coll. S.C.P.F.*, n. 1581; S.C.S. Off. (Chen-si et Chan-si), 23 nov. 1769—*Fontes*, n. 825; *Coll. S.C.P.F.*, n. 475; Synodus Sutchuensis, 2 sept. 1803, cap. IX, n. 8—Mansi, XXXIX, 43; S.C. de Prop. Fide (C.P. pro Sin.—Sutchuen.), 26 iun, 1821—*Fontes*, n. 4725; *Coll. S.C.P.F.*, n. 760.

[63] S.C. de Prop. Fide (Sutchuen.), 17 ian. 1836—*Coll. S.C.P.F.*, n. 845; *Fontes*, n. 4760.

[64] *The Pauline Privilege*, p. 39.

required by the Holy See, for it implied that the fear or the presumption of danger was not sufficient to warrant a dispensation; furthermore, the dispensation could not be granted if the danger could be avoided in any way.[65] Finally, the harm had to arise from the actual making of the interpellations itself, and not from some other source. Thus, if the danger occasioned by the formal and judicial interpellations could be avoided through the use of the summary or private form, this was to be done in preference to the granting of a dispensation.[66]

The Holy See refused to grant the faculty when the cause as proposed in the case gave indication that the interpellations would endanger the reputation of the infidel, or when the threats in the case were raised solely against the person of the intermediary who had been sent into the hostile country to make the interpellations.[67]

Article V: Juridical Effect of the Dispensation

No more far-reaching effect could follow from these dispensations than that given by Pope Gregory XIII in his Constitution *Populis,* for there the Supreme Authority of the Church declared that, when a dispensation had been granted from the making of the interpellations in accordance with the norms of the same Constitution, the convert was to be permitted to enter a second marriage with a Christian even though the first spouse was still living and was willing, although unknown to the convert, both to receive baptism and to cohabit in peace with the convert. This second marriage was to be considered valid and indissoluble

[65] S.C.S. Off. (Chen-si et Chan-si), 23 nov. 1769—*Fontes*, n. 825; *Coll. S.C.P.F.*, n. 475; S.C.S. Off. (Natal), 11 iul. 1866; *Fontes*, n. 996; *Coll. S.C.P.F.*, n. 1295.

[66] S.C.S. Off. (Mongoliae), 29 nov. 1882—*Fontes*, n. 1075; *Coll. S.C.P.F.*, n. 1581.

[67] Woeber, *The Interpellations*, p. 34, and Winslow, *The Pauline Privilege*, n. 2, p. 40, listed this cause as being sufficient, but neither of them gave any ruling of the Holy See in support of this contention.

under all conditions, so that it could not be dissolved even if later it was proved beyond all doubt that the convert's first spouse had also become a Christian, and had, in fact, been baptized before the second marriage was contracted. The same doctrine was supported by Pope Benedict XIV in unmistakable terms in his letter *In suprema*, and also as a private author in his work, *De Synodo Dioecesana*, in these words:

> Primum enim matrimonium eo ipso momento et quidem irrevocabiliter, solutum remanet, quo coniux conversus ad alias nuptias cum fideli transivit sive quia in hanc libertatem vindicatus fuerit *Iure Divino*, propterea quod infidelis coniux, iudicialiter interpellatus, evangelicae veritati, aut innocuae cohabitationi se denegaverit; sive quia peculiares rerum circumstantiae viam aperuerint *Indulto Apostolico*, quo sublata fuit interpellandi necessitas quod quidem Indultum, cum nulli conditioni sit alligatum, secundi matrimonii validitatem et firmitatem perpetuo asserit, et reditum intercludit ad prima connubia, etiamsi quis probare contenderet, primo coniugi interpellato non fuisse liberum respondere, vel eum iam tunc Christianae Religioni amplectendae paratum fuisse, immo ante illum diem, qua secundum matrimonium a coniuge converso celebratum fuit, ipsum quoque Christo nomen dedisse, et baptismum suscepisse.[68]

Much more recently the Holy See in an Instruction to the Vicar Apostolic of Japan reiterated the extraordinarily extensive effect that follows from a dispensation from the interpellations:

> Matrimonium vero eius cum quo dispensatum fuerit, etiamsi postea innotuerit coniugem infidelem suam voluntatem iuste impeditam declarare non potuisse, et ad fidem etiam tempore initi matrimonii conversum fuisse,

[68] *De Synodo Dioecesana*, lib. XIII, cap. XXI, n. 5.

nihilominus numquam rescindi, sed validum esse debebit.[69]

In the event that a dispensation had been obtained, but the convert had not entered the second marriage within a year, then the dispensation had to be renewed before the convert could enter the second union.[70]

[69] S.C.S. Off. (ad Vic. Ap. Iaponiae Merid.), 4 febr. 1891—*Fontes*, n. 1130; *Coll. S.C.P.F.*, n. 1746; *ASS*, XXVI (1893-1894), 62-64.

[70] S.C. de Prop. Fide (C.P. pro Sin.—Sutchuen.), 26 iun. 1820—*Fontes*, n. 4717; *Coll. S.C.P.F.*, n. 743.

PART TWO

INTERPRETATION AND APPLICATION OF THE CONSTITUTIONS TODAY

CHAPTER I

VARIOUS INTERPRETATIONS ACCORDED THE CONSTITUTIONS

Article I: Restrictive Interpretations

Canon 1125 states that whatever pertains to marriage in the three papal constitutions of Popes Paul III, St. Pius V, and Gregory XIII is now included in the universal law of the Church. It further states that all such provisions, *"quaeque pro peculiaribus locis scripta sunt, ad alias quoque regiones in eisdem adiunctis extenduntur."* Certain provisions of these constitutions dealt with the Pauline privilege and the interpellations; it is in them that one finds the only basic grant of power for dispensing from the interpellations. The first two provided for the absolute omission of the interpellations; the third granted the power of dispensing from them under certain prescribed conditions. These constitutions, which were originally written for particular and restricted localities, have now been extended with their privileges by the universal law. The exact extension of the privileges centers about the precise meaning of the words, *"in eisdem adiunctis."*

Do these words mean that the canon has application only in the countries where the circumstances of social conditions are identical with those which existed in the countries to which the constitutions were originally directed and which had, in fact, occasioned the original grant? Or are they to be understood in the sense that the canon has application in any country to a particular case, the circumstances of which are similar to those which had prompted the constitutions in the 16th century?

Although now there is a uniform interpretation of this phrase of the canon, it was not so from the beginning. In the years immediately subsequent to the promulgation of the Code the phrase, and consequently the entire canon, was given a most restrictive interpretation.

This interpretation is indeed rejected in its entirety today, yet it deserves attention here as background for the practical use of the privileges which the canon contains. But in all justice credit must be given to these early commentators for their work. There is a tendency to be unjustly critical of their opinions. The main fault lay simply in that they lived at a time too near the enactment of the Code and consequently lacked the overall vision gained through the perspective of time and distance.

According to the first opinion, canon 1125 has application only in those countries of the world today in which the circumstances of the entire country are identical with those of the countries to which the constitutions were originally directed, for then only can these regions be said to be *"in eisdem adiunctis."*[1]

Augustine (1872-1943) required that the circumstances be identical and not merely similar to those of the 16th century countries.[2] De Becker (1857-1936) also demanded a very strict interpretation of the word *adiuncta,* to the extent namely that the Constitution of Gregory XIII has no application in the United States today, for there is no question here of people being held in captivity.[3] This is

[1] H. A. Ayrinhac, "Indissolubleness of Non-Catholic Marriages," (*The American Ecclesiastical Review* [*AER*], Vols. I-XXXII, Philadelphia, 1889-1905; *The Ecclesiastical Review* [*ER*], Vols. XXXIII-CIX, Philadelphia, 1905-1943; from 1944: *The American Ecclesiastical Review* [*AER*], Vol. CX—, Washington, D.C., 1944—), LXXII (1925), 408.

[2] Charles Augustine, *A Commentary on the New Code of Canon Law* (8 vols., Vol. V, 2 ed., B. Herder Book Company, 1920), Vol. V, *Marriage Law,* p. 364 (hereafter cited *A Commentary*).

[3] Julius De Becker, Recensiones: "Criticism of Augustine's *Commentary,*" *Ephemerides Theologicae Lovanienses* (Lovanii-Brugis, 1924—), II (1925), 445.

evidently also the opinion of Ramstein. Although he omits entirely any commentary on canon 1125, he states quite simply in comment on an earlier canon (1121) that the Ordinaries of the United States have no faculties to dispense from the interpellations by law. Obviously he must feel that the explicit grant of Gregory XIII has no application whatsoever in this country.[4]

If this be true, then the privileges of these constitutions are restricted practically to non-use. For where in the civilized world today could one possibly find a single country or even locality in which the circumstances of everyday life are so identical. One will remember that the Constitution of Pope Paul III was directed to the so called West and South Indies, where polygamy was so common that men and women could no longer remember accurately who was their first spouse. Pope Pius V directed his constitution to a class of people called 'Indi', in circumstances similar to those referred to by Paul III. The third constitution, that of Gregory XIII, was directed to infidels specifically in Angola, in Africa, Ethiopia and in Brazil. It was occasioned by the capture and forceful separation in the slave trade of many husbands and wives who lost all hope of ever finding their legitimate consorts.

In truth, there is no place in the world where such identical circumstances are common and universal, not even in the countries, e.g., in South America, which were included in the original grants of Gregory XIII.[5]

Before the Code these privileges were extended to many countries and localities which were not mentioned in the original grants and in which the circumstances were not identical with those of the countries envisioned at the time the constitutions were written.[6]

[4] Matthew Ramstein, *A Manual of Canon Law* (Hoboken, N.J., Terminal Printing and Publishing Company, 1947), p. 504.

[5] A. Vermeersch, "De Canone 1125 eiusque vi extensiva," *Periodica*, XX (1932), pp. 1*-5*, p. 2, sect. 'd'; Woods, *The Constitutions of Canon 1125*, p. 75.

[6] S.C.S. Off. (Siam), 22 nov. 1871—*Fontes*, n. 1019; *Coll. S.C.P.F.*,

A second restrictive interpretation holds that the constitutions have practical value in all countries in which there are regions or sections of the country that are under the same social conditions that obtained in the 16th century countries mentioned in the constitutions. This variation of the interpretation does not demand that the entire country be in these circumstances, but consider it sufficient if definite localities fall under a similarity of conditions. Illustrative of this interpretation was Gregory (1903-1947) who required that the similarity "prevail in the region rather than merely among persons." He thought that the Indian reservations in the West and the Negro colonies of the South in the United States could be classified as "regions," and consequently that the privileges of the constitutions applied to these sections of our country. Gregory recommended that the Ordinaries in these territories, "should not hesitate in applying canon 1125."[7]

These interpretations are reduced to absurdity if one but only consider the almost impossible obstacles that would have to be overcome before the constitutions would have any valid practical application under these restrictions. As Woods[8] well points out, it would be necessary to undertake a lengthy and necessarily precise study, not only of the circumstances of the countries of those days, but also of the fact whether or not those circumstances correspond identically to the circumstances now existing. Such a restriction would but prepare the way for scruples, and either for a non-use or possibly an invalid use of the privileges, and in that way it would destroy the purpose and nature of this new legislation, which was intended to be a privilege and not a burden.[9]

n. 1377; Burton, *A Commentary on Canon 1125*, p. 115; Woods, *The Constitutions of Canon 1125*, pp. 74-75.

[7] *The Pauline Privilege*, p. 87.

[8] *The Constitutions of Canon 1125*, pp. 75-76.

[9] Joannes Chelodi, *Ius Matrimoniale* ([ed. 3, Tridenti: Libri. Edit. Tridentum, 1921], n. 160, p. 175), also seems to restrict the use of the constituions in that he quotes the canon and comments, "quod hucusque erat prohibitum."

Article II: Extensive Interpretation

Section 1: Meaning of the Texts of the Constitutions

It is evidently clear that the phrase, *"in eisdem adiunctis,"* cannot be restricted to the extent that, before canon 1125 can be applied, one must find an entire country or even a section of a country in which the social conditions are identical with or even similar to those which occasioned the original grant of the constitutions mentioned in the canon. There remains but a third possibility which may serve as a basis for the use of the privileges, namely the similar nature of the individual case. This interpretation states simply that the canon has practical value and is applicable when the circumstances of an individual case are similar to those envisioned in the constitutions. Thus canon 1125 extends the privileges of these constitutions throughout the entire Church, in all countries, civilized and uncivilized, to every section of every country throughout the world as long as there are individual cases similar to those for which the constitutions were given.[10]

Canon 18 explicitly states the various norms which are to be followed in the interpretation of any ecclesiastical law, and at the same time posits a definite priority in which these norms are to be considered. One must first consider the actual meaning of the text in the commonly accepted meaning of the words. The ultimate solution of the meaning of the canon depends entirely on the sense in which the phrase, *"in eisdem adiunctis,"* is accepted.

It is true that an earlier reading of the canon seemed to be clearer. In canon 402 of the 1913 schema the words

[10] Cappello, *De Matrimonio*, "Verba canon 1125, 'ad alias quoque regiones', intelligenda sunt universim de omnibus regionibus, etiam extra loca missionum sive regiones sunt catholicae sive non-catholicae. Verba, 'in eisdem adiunctis' significant peculiares casus sive circumstantias, de quibus fit mentio in praefatis constitutionibus, ita ut istae hodie *ubique locorum* valleant modo verificentur adiuncta in illis expresse memorata." n. 787, p. 778, note 70; cf. Woods, *The Constitutions of Canon 1125*, p. 78.

read, *"ad universam ecclesiam extenduntur."*[11] Yet, even the final choice of words as they stand in the Code today, if carefully analyzed, demand an extensive interpretation. As Burton[12] points out, the universal extension of the law seems to be intended by the very position of the phrase in the Latin sentence structure. The phrase under discussion, *"ad alias quoque regiones,"* stands in direct opposition to the earlier clause, *"quae pro peculiaribus regionibus scripta sunt."* Such a juxtaposition of the clauses can reasonably be interpreted only as meaning that what had been intentionally particular has now become intentionally universal.[13] And if these words are to be interpreted as implying a universal extension, they can only refer to circumstances of fact, for if they referred to circumstances of place, then they too would be equally particular.[14]

Furthermore, if the legislator wished to restrict the application of the canon to definite places, he could easily have done so with a more specific choice of words. As examples Vermeersch suggested, *"ad alias regiones quarum adiuncta sint eadem"* or *"quae in iisdem adiunctis versantur."*[15]

[11] *Schema Codicis Iuris Canonici* (Sub secreto pontificio publicata) *Codex Iuris Canonici cum notis Petri Card. Gasparri* (Romae: Typis Polyglottis Vaticanis, 1913): Rayanna ("De Constitutione S. Pii Papae V, *Romani Pontificis," Periodica,* Vol. XXVIII [1939]) states that the change led to more confusion, but that the opinion which states that the circumstances refer only to particular cases must be preferred, p. 127.

[12] *A Commentary on Canon 1125,* p. 115.

[13] Vermeersch, "De Canon 1125 eiusque vi extensiva," *Periodica,* XX (1931), p. 2, n. 'b': "Dum verbis 'quae pro peculiaribus regionibus scripta sunt' verbis 'ad alias quoque regiones' opponit, legislator negat constitutiones iam pro peculiaribus vigere, sed valere pro non-peculiaribus affirmat, seu quod perinde est iis iam vim universalem inesse declarat."

[14] Woods, *The Constitutions of Canon 1125,* p. 79; Vermeersch-Creusen, *Epitome,* II, n. 436, note 2, "Verba 'in iisdem adiunctis' non verbis 'ad alias regiones' sed verbo 'extenduntur' unienda esse demonstrat P. Vermeersch in *Periodica,* XX, 1* ff."

[15] Vermeersch, "De Canone 1125 eiusque vi extensiva" *Periodica,* XX (1931), p. 2*; Burton, *A Commentary on Canon 1125,* p. 115; Woods, *The Constitutions of Canon 1125,* p. 79.

In a similar vein, if the codifiers had intended to restrict the use of the canon, they might well have substituted the word *"restringuntur"* for the word *"extenduntur"* that is used in the Code, for then they would have left little doubt as to the fact that the privileges were to be applied only in countries where the common circumstances are similar to the social conditions that existed in the countries of the original destination.[16]

Section 2: Historical Background of Canon 1125

The background of the canon as it now stands in the Code gives an insight into the precise meaning of the phrase, *"in eisdem adiunctis."*

Already before the promulgation of the Code in 1918 the Sacred Congregations had extended the privileges of these constitutions to countries other than those which had been the recipients of the grants of Popes Paul III, St. Pius V, and Gregory XIII. At the same time it was clear that these new local beneficiaries could in no way be said to be in the same particular circumstances in which had been the countries in whose favor the 16th century Popes had legislated so wisely. Thus the Constitution, *In suprema,* of Pope Benedict XIV essentially is nothing more than a concession of the Brief of Pope Gregory XIII to Benedict's nuncio in Venice. Evidently the conditions in Venice were not identical with or even similar to those in Ethiopia two centuries earlier.[17] In the same way Pope Paul V had granted the privileges to the Bishop of Naples.[18]

[16] Vermeersch, *loc. cit.*, "Dum consuetam rationem scribendi servavit si verbis 'ad alias quoque regiones' vim generalem tribuas, ut in canone 1125 hoc attendas, ut de specie facti adiuncta eadem comprobentur. Egregio latinae linguae cultori, quem interrogavimus, id manifestum videbatur." Cf. Burton, *A Commentary on Canon 1125*, p. 115; Louis Chaussegros de Léry, *Le Privilège de la Foi* (Montréal: Ex Typis Collegii Maximi Immaculatae Conceptionis, 1938), n. 86.

[17] Cf. *De Synodo Dioecesana*, lib. XIII, cap. XXI, nn. 3-6; Const. *"In Suprema,"* 16 ian. 1745—*Bullarium Benedicti XIV*, II, 183-184.

[18] S.C.S. (Neapolitana), 21 iun. 1611—Benedictus XIV, *De Synodo Dioecesana*, lib. XIII, cap. XXI, n. 6; cf. also S.C.S. Off. (Siam), 22

This favorable interpretation of the use of the privileges found expression in the work of the Commission of Cardinals who had been appointed to work out the final reading of the canons. In the first draft of the canon edited in 1913, canon 402 read: "Ea quae matrimonium respiciunt in Constitutionibus ... quaeque pro peculiaribus locis scripta sunt, *ad universam Ecclesiam extenduntur.*" In the second edition of the schema in 1916[19] the canon was numbered 1128, but read the same as it had in the first edition. In yet another, but undated, edition one finds the same wording as in the two previous editions. And yet, when the final and approved draft of the canon appeared in the Code, the words, *"ad universam Ecclesiam,"* had been changed to read, *"ad alias quoque regiones in eisdem adiunctis."*

This complete variation of the text in its final edition prompts one to ask why such a change was made, a change which does in fact seem to restrict the application of the canon in comparison with what had been suggested as the text of the canon. The wording of the various schemata, covering a period of five years, makes it certain that the Cardinals who served on the Commission clearly intended that the Papal Constitutions be extended to the entire Church without any restrictions whatsoever. The final choice of words has actually prompted an altogether contrary interpretation.[20]

Since one cannot contend that the Cardinals intended to confuse the issue, it but remains to conclude that the final selection of words was made for the sole purpose of clarification, for that was, in fact, the purpose of the Code itself.[21]

---

nov. 1871—*Fontes*, n. 1019; *Coll. S.C.P.F.*, n. 1377; Woeber, *The Interpellations*, p. 121.

[19] For these later drafts of the Schema the writer refers to material cited by Woods, *The Constitutions of Canon 1125*, p. 80, to whom the later editions were available.

[20] Rayanna, "De Constitutione S. Pii Papae V, *Romani Pontificis,*" *Periodica*, XXVIII (1939), 127.

[21] *Codicis Iuris Canonici, Praefatio;* cf. section 3 of this article, pp. 60-66.

Rayanna indicates that such a clarification has actually been gained by the approval of the phrase as it now reads in that it designedly produces a logical order and balance in the canon.[22] This balance was gained by means of the juxtaposition of the phrase with the one immediately preceding in the canon. The interpretation of the words themselves is made in the light of this purposeful grammatical opposition.[23] This effect could not have been obtained with the words as employed in the various earlier schemata, for the phrase, "*Ecclesia Universa,*" would have included the "*loca peculiaria,*" and the effect of the opposition would have been destroyed.[24]

Woods offers a more reasonable explanation for the change in the text.[25] Perhaps the original phrase, "*ad universam Ecclesiam,*" was altogether too general to be clear, so that the wording as then contemplated could have led to an indiscriminate use (or abuse) of the privileges. The final reading was intended as an assurance that the privileges would be used according to the mind of the original grantors of the constitutions. The text, as it now stands, is intended therefore to restrict the use of the privileges to those individuals who are converts and now find themselves in the same conditions that affected those in whose favor the Constitutions were originally given.

The very fact that the constitutions are in the Code argues for their practical value, for surely the Commission would not have given so much time and consideration to the canon, if the application of it had been meant to be restricted almost to non-use. But such would have been more the rule than the exception if the applicable use of the Constitutions were to be restricted to countries where the general condition of the people is identical with or similar to that of 16th century Ethiopia or Brazil.

[22] Rayanna, *ibid.*, p. 128.
[23] Cf. *supra*, p. 56.
[24] Rayanna, *loc. cit.*
[25] *The Constitutions of Canon 1125*, p. 81.

Section 3: Purpose of the Constitutions and Canon 1125

Although canon 18 states that the purpose and circumstances of a law and the intent of the legislator are the last norms to which reference is made, they are, however, recognized as valid norms for the interpretation of law. In cases of doubt and obscurities they may well be the only or at least the principal means of understanding a specific law.[26]

The doubt which formerly existed concerning the precise meaning of the words of the canon has been admittedly solved. Yet it seems that canon 1125 can best be understood in the light of the purpose of the original constitutions and of the Code itself. From the very outset it was clear that the Constitutions mentioned in this canon were meant to be privileges. They were given at a critical time in the history of the spread of the Faith, and they came as an answer to the pleas of missionaries who knew at first hand the problems that confronted the Church in mission fields.

At the close of the 15th and the opening of the 16th century territorial exploration and discovery opened vast and rich fields for the spread of the Faith. With an attraction born of its divine institution, the Faith spread in every known land. The missions of the new world, however, presented problems threatening, so it seemed, to stifle the cause of Christianity. Wholesale polygamy and divorce among the natives prepared the way for multiple invalid marriages; and because of these invalid unions many natives were prevented from embracing the Faith except under almost impossible conditions. It was in answer to this crying need of the Church that the Popes granted the unusual and far-reaching privileges of their constitutions.

Nothing is more explicit than the words of Pope Gregory XIII in the preamble introducing his Constitution *Populis*:

For the future:

"It is advisable to be lenient (*expedit indulgere*), in the matter of freedom to contract marriage, toward the

[26] C. 6, X, *de verborum significatione*, V, 40; cf. Burton, *A Commentary on Canon 1125*, p. 39.

peoples and nations recently converted from paganism to the Catholic Faith, lest men, unaccustomed to continence, might less willingly persevere in the Faith and deter others from receiving it by their example."[27]

Note well those words. Pope Gregory explicitly stated that the express purpose of the privileges which he was granting was to make it easier for converts to accept the Faith and likewise to prepare the way for the conversion of others who would not otherwise be able to embrace Christianity.

Popes Paul III and St. Pius V were not as explicit, but the tenor of their Constitutions clearly indicates that their intention was solely to help the natives, and thus open the way for their conversion.[28]

The purpose of these constitutions and the expressed intention of the legislators then can only mean that these grants were meant to be, and in fact are, privileges. Any interpretation which intends to or does destroy this notion of privilege cannot be accepted. For such an interpretation, be it in theory or in practice, violates the provisions of the law itself[29] and betrays a timidity unknown to the original legislators who acted for the good of the Church and for the salvation of countless souls.[30]

For the constitutions of canon 1125, together with canon 1127 and the Pauline privilege, is a law which in a very special way favors the Catholic Faith. And as Kearney states, "It is, therefore, to be interpreted widely, for such laws even though they establish exceptions to the common

[27] Translation from Burton, *A Commentary on Canon 1125*, p. 164.
[28] Burton, *op. cit.*, pp. 38, 52.
[29] Canons 50 and 68.
[30] Vromant, "De Dispensatione ab Interpellationibus in Ordine ad Privilegium Fidei—Applicationes Practicae Canonis 1125," *Periodica*, XX (1931), 108*, "Constitutiones extenduntur ad omnes regiones in iisdem casibus, attento praesertim textu canonis et mente legislatoris; cui sententiae astipulamur eo magis quod agitur de lege late interpretanda nisi aliud clare appareat, siquidem canon citatus rationem habet privilegii, et favorem praestat pro 'utilitate publica' ad fidem et religionem catholicam dilatandam."

law are considered favorable, not odious, and are not to be given a strict interpretation. From the very nature of the principle involved the desirability of a broad interpretation is evident. Narrow interpretation could hardly be reconciled with the terms and intent of the canon."[31]

In much the same vein the purpose of the codification of Canon Law was not simply that of gathering into one the many collections of approved canons, but also that of constituting as certain and definite many extant doubtful and disputed laws, and of clarifying in this way much of the confusion that commonly arose in the interpretation and application of legislation that was to continue in effect.

This purpose was expressed by Cardinal Gasparri in the preface to his edition of the Code.[32]

And since that was the expressed purpose of the Code, namely to substitute manifest and clear laws in the place of difficult and uncertain ones, it certainly seems alien to burden canon 1125 with any obnoxious interpretation. For if one were required before applying this canon to make an ethnological and historical study of the conditions existing in remote and uncivilized lands in the sixteenth century, thus to ascertain whether the same or similar conditions exist today in any country to which we might wish to apply the provisions of the canon now in question, as some would have us do, would be to frustrate the very purpose inherent in the canon. For one can scarcely believe that the legislators wished this one canon to be an exception to the general rule of simplifying ecclesiastical laws.[33]

[31] Francis P. Kearney, "The Privilege of the Faith," *The Jurist* (The Catholic University of America, Washington, D.C., 1941—), VII (1947), p. 282.

[32] "Id fuit constans catholicae Ecclesiae propositum, ex quo potissimum tempore imperii romani leges sunt in Corpus Iuris redactae, ut sacri item canones in unum colligerentur, sicque eorum scientia et usus et observantia facilior unicuique fieret." Cf. Burton, *A Commentary on Canon 1125*, p. 114.

[33] Vermeersch, "De Canone 1125 eiusque vi extensiva", *Periodica*, XX (1931), p. 3*; Bouscaren, "An Inquiry into the Practical Application of Canon 1125 Outside of Mission Territories," *Miscellanea Ver-*

Woods further points out that in the past the missionaries to whom the privileges were later extended were not required to study these conditions before validly using the privileges,[34] and Coronata states that it was entirely unnecessary to make such an investigation.[35]

Thus an unduly restrictive interpretation of the canon would manifestly not only violate the purpose of the law, but militate also against the mind of the legislator.[36]

And finally the fact that not only are the privileges included in the canon, but also that the pertinent parts of the constitutions are themselves quoted in the Code, offers incontestable proof that the Commission of Cardinals considered the privileges to be of definite practical value.[37] These excerpts are found in Documents VI, VII, VIII appended to the Canons of the Code.[38]

Their inclusion in the Code was approved by the Commission in formal session after a motion of the Bishop of Panama had urged that this would be in accord with the overall plan of the Commission for the sake of clarity. Since the

---

meersch (2 Vols., Romae: Pontificia Universita Gregoriana, 1935), Vol. I, p. 285; Rayanna, "De Constitutione S. Pii Papae V, *Romani Pontificis*," *Periodica*, Vol. XXVIII (1939), 127; Burton, *A Commentary on Canon 1125*, p. 115.

[34] *The Constitutions of Canon 1125*, p. 82.

[35] *De Matrimonio*, n. 646, p. 903.

[36] Cappello, *De Matrimonio*, n. 787, p. 778, note 70, "Sine fundamento nonnulli restringunt sensum verborum 'ad alias regiones', quatenus intelligantur tantum de locis missionum seu de regionibus infidelium. Hac quippe admissa hypothesi, favor vi can. 1125 concessus maxime coarctatus foret, contra mentem legislatoris et finem legis, ut manifestum videtur."

[37] Doheny, *Informal Procedure*, p. 549, "That excerpts from these same constitutions should be included among the documents officially appended to the Code indicates that they must have some value even today."

[38] P. Nicolaus Farrugia, *De Matrimonio et Causis Matrimonialibus* (Taurini, Romae: Marietti, 1924), n. 324, p. 475, "Citatae Constitutiones, quae leguntur in appendice Novi Codicis Iuris Canonici inter documenta VI, VII, VIII, hodie extenduntur ad universum orbem, ubi eadem rerum adiuncta habentur."

exact provisions of the constitutions were not entirely familiar to all, other bishops made the same suggestions after they had received and studied copies of the earlier schemata sent under secrecy to all the Bishops in the Church.[39]

The constitutions, however, are a part of the Code, and since they carry the same approbation as do the canons they have the force of law.[40]

Though these privileges were given primarily for the good of individual converts, they looked also to the good of the Faith.[41] In their original particular grant they were privileges in the strict sense of the word, for they were private laws granting an exception from the general laws of the Church, and thus were to be interpreted strictly. Now that they are included in the Code and thereby have been extended to the whole Church they are privileges in the wide sense of the term.[42]

In accord with the general norms of interpretation as stated in canons 50 and 68, therefore, canon 1125 is to be

[39] *Riassunto delle Osservazione dei Vescovi e Superiori Regolari ad libro III del Codice*, canon 402, p. 174 as cited in Woods, *The Constitutions of Canon 1125*, p. 29. Cf. Amleto G. Cicognani, *Canon Law*, (2 revised edition, authorized English version, translated by J. M. O'Hara and F. Brennan, Philadelphia: Dolphin Press, 1935), who states that these were minutes of the meetings of the Commission and so were not included in the canon itself. n. 134, p. 464. Cf. also Coronata, *De Matrimonio*, n. 646, p. 903, who writes, "Concessiones factae a Constitutionibus Pauli III et Gregorii XIII ad abundantiam videntur expresse insertae in codice."

[40] Armandus Gougnard, *Tractatus de Matrimonio* (ed. 7, Mechlinae: H. Dessain, 1931), p. 299, "Cum ergo illa indulta transierint in ius commune Codicis, habemus ex iure communi Codicis ... in casibus Const. Greg. XIII ubique terrarum concessam facultatem ad interpellationibus dispensandi." V. Heylen, *Tractatus de Matrimonio* (9 ed., Mechlinae: H. Dessain, 1945), p. 349, where the same wording is retained.

[41] Vromant,"De Dispensationibus ab Interpellationibus", *Periodica*, XX (1931), p. 108*, "... cui sententiae astipulamur eo magis quod agitur de lege late interpretanda nisi aliud clare appareat, siquidem canon citatus rationem habet privilegii, et favorem praestat 'pro utilitate publica' ad fidem et religionem catholicam dilatandam."

[42] Woods, *The Constitutions of Canon 1125*, p. 31.

interpreted widely for the favors contained therein *"concessi sunt pro utilitate publica ad fidem et religionem catholicam facilius dilatandem."*[43] At any rate no interpretation of a privilege may ever be so strict as to make its application burdensome, for some benefit must accrue from every privilege.[44]

Therefore it is concluded that the phrase, *"in eisdem adiunctis,"* was and is intended to refer certainly not to countries or localities but to individual cases, so that canon 1125 can be used when the circumstances of an individual case are similar to those considered in the original constitutions. One may go even further and say that, if the conditions are truly verified in a particular case, then the privileges not only can but should be used, particularly when their application will pave the way for conversions to the Faith.

Post-Code commentators point out that the constitutions, by virtue of their inclused mention in canon 1125, have become part of the universal Church law, and are placed on the same basis as any other canon in the Code, no matter whither they may look for their source. Cappello expresses the common teaching when he writes that the provisions of these constitutions, though originally granted for particular localities and simultaneously to be considered as privileges, are now extended to the Church everywhere by canon 1125, and therefore today constitute universal law.[45] Woeber states simply that the promulgation of the present Code has made the provisions of these constitutions a part of the Church's universal law.[46] Blat writes that Pope Pius X instigating the codification of the Code and Pope Benedict XV promulgating it have given their Supreme approbations to the constitutions so that everywhere in the future they have the force of canon law.[47]

[43] Vromant, *De Matrimonio*, n. 354, p. 278.

[44] Canon 68.

[45] *De Matrimonio*, n. 787, § 2, p. 776.

[46] *The Interpellations*, p. 123.

[47] Albertus Blat, *Commentarium Textus Codicis Iuris Canonici* (5

This extensive interpretation is further evident from the recent promulgation of a matrimonial code for the Oriental Church.[48] This discipline, binding on all Oriental Catholics from the second day of May, 1949, gives force to this interpretation by including among its canons the same papal Constitutions extended to the universal Latin Church. Canon 114 of the Oriental Code is identical with canon 1125 of the Code of Canon Law.

This approbation of the privileges of these papal constitutions and their further extension in this canon of the Oriental discipline can only be understood as further evidence of the Holy See's desire that the privileges themselves be given widest application, conditioned only upon the specific requirements of the individual grants.

From all of this—the original intent of the constitutions, the purpose of the Code, and the inclusion of these papal documents in the canons of both the Latin and Oriental discipline—one conclusion alone is evident: the constitutions were originally granted after the manner of privileges, and are to be given an extensive interpretation today.

Section 4: Argument from Authority

As was indicated earlier, the overwhelming weight of authority urges the extensive interpretation of the privileges listed in canon 1125. In the years closely following the promulgation of the Code there was a tendency to demand a restrictive interpretation of the canon. The passing of time and the development of post-Code canonical study shifted the weight of authority so completely to the other opinion that today it stands as certain.

Vermeersch in an article on the extensive force and ap-

---

vols. in 6, Romae: Ex Typographia Pontificia in Instituto Pii IX, 1919-1927), lib. III, Pars I. *De Sacramentis*, n. 536, p. 685 (hereafter cited *De Sacramentis*); Burton, *A Commentary on Canon 1125*, pp. 114-115; Bouscaren, "An Inquiry into the Practical Application of Canon 1125 outside of Mission Territories," *Miscellanea Vermeersch*, I, 293.

[48] *Acta Apostolicae Sedis, Commentarium Officiale* (Romae, 1909—), XLI (1949), 89-119 (hereafter cited *AAS*); *The Jurist*, Supplement, April 1949; canon 114.

plication of Canon 1125[49] outlined the arguments which have now merited universal approval. The meaning of the words, the grammatical construction of the canon, the purpose of the constitutions, the plan of the Code, all argue for the universal application of canon 1125 and the privileges given in the constitutions mentioned therein.

Many authors base their support of this extensive application of the constitutions on the fact that, although granted originally for particular places, they are now part of the universal ecclesiastical law, and as such pertain to the Church universal without exception. Among these authors may be numbered: Gasparri,[50] Wernz-Vidal,[51] Heylen,[52] Blat,[53] De Smet,[54] Farrugia,[55] Gougnard,[56] Merkelbach,[57]

[49] "De Canone 1125 eiusque ci extensiva," *Periodica,* XX (1931). 1*-5*.

[50] "Constitutiones..., datae pro peculiaribus locis, postea per Codicem (rel. can. 1125) extensae fuerunt ad alias quoque regiones in eisdem adiunctis."—*De Matrimonio,* II, n. 1160, p. 235.

[51] "In iure Codicis can. 1125 ad universum orbem extenduntur declarationes et dispensationes, quas olim pro peculiaribus locis dederant Paulus III..., St. Pius V..., et Gregorious XIII."—*Ius Matrimoniale,* n. 633, p. 828.

[52] "Cum ergo illa indulta transierint in ius commune Codicis, habemus ex iure commune Codicis concessam facultatem ab interpellationibus dispensandi."—*Tractatus de Matrimonio,* p. 349.

[53] "...in can. 1125, quem commentamur, praedicta omnia generaliter 'in eisdem adiunctis extenduntur' quoad loca, ut *ubilibet* in posterum vim habeant iuris canonici."—*De Sacramentis,* n. 536, p. 685.

[54] "Et quidem a favore can. 1125 ad universum orbem extenduntur declarationes et dispensationes, quas olim pro peculiaribus locis concesserunt Paulus III..., Pius V..., et Gregorius XIII."—*De Sponsalibus et Matrimonio,* (4. ed., Brugis: Carolus Beyaert, 1927), n. 351, 3°, p. 299.

[55] "Citatae Constitutiones quae leguntur in appendice novi Codicis Iuris Canonici inter Documenta VI, VII, VIII, hodie extenduntur ad universum orbem, ubi eadem rerum adiuncta habentur."—*De Matrimonio et Causis Matrimonialibus,* n. 324, p. 475.

[56] "In iure codicis can. 1125 ad universum orbem extenduntur declarationes et dispensationes, quae olim pro peculiaribus locis dederant Paulus III, St. Pius V, et Gregorius XIII,"—*Tractatus de Matrimonio,* p. 299.

[57] Benedictus Merkelbach, *Summa Theologiae Moralis* (Vol. III, (Parisiis, 1933), "Nunc vi can. 1125 iam extensae fuerant ad universalem Ecclesiam," n. 796.

Schaff,[58] Vromant,[59] Vermeersch-Creusen,[60] Cappello,[61] Bouscaren-Ellis,[62] Woeber,[63] Doheny,[64] Cerato,[65] Léry,[66] Knecht,[67] Sipos,[68] and Cicognani.[69]

[58] "Finally, it must be remembered that the three Constitutions at the end of the Code (Documents VI, VII, VIII) have been extended to the whole world, by canon 1125," "Dispensation from the Interpellations," *ER*, LXXXVI (1932), 537.

[59] "... ut in gratiam cleri sacro ministerio addicti, magis distincte appareant favores qui super hac materia, beneficio Codicis Iuris Canonici, pro universo orbe ab Ecclesia benigne hodie sunt consessi," "De Dispensatione ab Interpellationibus," *Periodica*, XX (1931), 108*.

[60] "Canone 1125 monemur ius antiquum particulare de privilegio fidei ad totum orbem extendi,"—*Epitome*, II, n. 427, p. 295.

[61] "Dispositiones contentae in his Constitutionibus, quae pro peculiaribus locis latae erant, et quae proinde tamquam indulta seu privilegia censebantur, nunc ex can. 1125 ad universas regiones in eisdem adiunctis extensae fuerunt ideoque *ius commune* hodie constituunt,"—*De Matrimonio*, n. 787, p. 776.

[62] "In the words of the Code, these constitutions which were written for particular places are extended also to other regions in the same circumstances,"—*Canon Law: A Text and Commentary* (Milwaukee: The Bruce Publishing Company, 1946), p. 555.

[63] "By the promulgation of the present Code, this provision was made a part of the Church's universal law,"—*The Interpellations*, p. 123.

[64] "However, according to the generally accepted opinion, the provisions of the Apostolic Constitutions cited in canon 1125 have been extended by the Code to the entire world wherever the individual cases are found to be the same,"—*Informal Procedure*, p. 550.

[65] "Canone praesenti indulta apostolica huiusmode esse possunt *ubique locorum*, si eadem videantur contingere rerum adiuncta,"—*Matrimonium a Codice I.C. Integre Desumptum* (4 ed., Patavii: Libreria Gregoriana edidit Typis Seminarii, 1927), n. 125, p. 214 (hereafter cited *Matrimonium*).

[66] "Originairement destinées à certains pays, ces constitutions sont étendues par le Code à tout l'univers,"—*Le Privilège de la Foi*, n. 84, p. 109.

[67] "Viele der früheren Zweifel in der Anwendung des Paulinischen Privilegs hat der C.I.C. durch eine Reihe von klaren Sätzen in can. 1120 bis 1127 und durch die ausdrückliche Ausdehnung der oben besprochenen partikular-rechtlichen Konstitutionen Pauls III, Pius V, und Gregors XIII, auf andere Gegenden mit gleichen Verhältnissen beseitigt,"—*Handbuch des katholischen Eherechts* (Freiburg im Breisgau: Herder and Company, 1928), p. 711.

Other authors, however, simply quote the words of the canon and state that the constitutions with their privileges are extended to the whole world or to the universal Church. Some of these are: Burton,[70] Ayrinhac-Lydon,[71] Badii,[72] and Vermeersch.[73]

And still other commentators affirm that the canon has extensive application because the conditions required for its use refer not to countries but to individual cases, no matter where they are found. Representative of this thought are: Bouscaren,[74] Rayanna,[75] Joyce,[76] Petrovits,[77] Boggiano-

[68] "Canon 1125 extendit in eisdem adiunctis seu sub iisdem quoad substantiam conditionibus 'ad alias regiones' ",—*Enchiridion Iuris Canonici* (2. ed., Pécs: ex Typographia "Haladas R. T.,"), n. 140, p. 622.

[69] "By virtue of Canon 1125 [these three documents] are extended to all places (where, it is understood, there are converts placed in the same circumstances),"—*Canon Law,* p. 425.

[70] *A Commentary on Canon 1125,* pp. 114-115.

[71] "The provisions of these Constitutions are now applied to the other parts of the world in the same circumstances,"—*Marriage Legislation in the New Code of Canon Law,* "The provisions of these Constitutions are now applied to the other parts of the world in the same circumstances," (New revised edition, New York: Benziger Brothers, 1946), pp. 320-321. (Hereafter cited *Marriage Legislation*).

[72] "Huiusmodi concessiones nunc ad universum orbem 'iisdem in adiunctis' extenduntur. Haec documenta ad calcem Codicis invenies," *Institutiones Iuris Canonici,* (3 ed., 2 vols., Florentiae: Libreria Editrice Florentina, 1922), II, p. 96, note 1.

[73] "Dum verba 'quae pro peculiaribus regionibus scripta sunt' verbis 'ad alias quoque regiones' opponit, legislator negat Constitutiones iam pro peculiaribus tantum regionibus vigere, sed valere pro non-peculiaribus affirmat; seu, quod perinde est, iis iam vim universalem inesse declarat," "De Canone 1125 eiusque vi extensiva," *Periodica,* Vol. XX (1921), 2*.

[74] "Hence it is safe to assume that the phrase, 'in iisdem adiunctis' was intended to refer not to the country in general but to a particular case," "An Inquiry into the Practical Application of Canon 1125," *Miscellanea-Vermeersch,* Vol. I, p. 284.

[75] "Mox tamen praevaluit sententia quae docet adiuncta tantum singulorum casuum eadem esse debere," "De Constitutione Pii V, Romani Pontificis," *Periodica,* vol. XXVIII (1939), p. 127.

[76] *Christian Marriage,* p. 494.

[77] "These three foregoing Constitutions contain the most important

Pico,[78] Chelodi,[79] and Nau.[80]

Besides these general classifications Payen[81] states that the constitutions are extended to any region of the world where the necessary conditions are fulfilled, but he points out the important fact that it is not necessary to demand a similarity of those historical or sociological conditions which occasioned the original grants of these privileges.

Coronata[82] likewise asserts that the constitutions are applicable to all cases in the world without any territorial restriction, as long as the personal circumstances required by the constitutions are verified, and therefore it is not necessary that the regional or territorial circumstances found in the countries to which the Constitution were directed be demanded now as a condition for the use of the privileges.

In addition to the authorities mentioned above, Woods[83]

---

legislation regarding the extensive interpretation of the Pauline privilege. In the former discipline it was questionable whether these decrees were to be applied to all places or only to those places for whose special benefit they were issued. The new law dispels all doubt on this subject by declaring that they are not conditioned on territory but on circumstances. Should the conditions which they relate be present in all parts of the world, the law they enforce would be opperative everywhere," *The New Church Law on Matrimony,* (The Catholic University of America Canon Law Studies, n. 6, Washington, D.C., The Catholic University of America, 1919), pp. 412-413.

[78] "Una spiegazione dene aggiungersi, del canon 1125, che estende l'applicazione di alcuni antichi provvedimenti di SS. Pontefici, emanati da questi per determinate contrade, a tutto il mondo, quando si verifichino le medesime circostanze in essi previste," *Il Matrimonia nel Diritto Canonico* (Torino: Unione Tipografico-Editrice Torinese, 1936), n. 861, p. 560.

[79] "Huc spectant Constitutiones quae pro peculiaribus locis scriptae sunt, nunc ad alias regiones in eisdem adiunctis extenduntur (c. 1125)," *Ius Matrimoniale,* n. 160, p. 175.

[80] "Canon 1125 extends to the whole world certain privileges formerly granted only to certain countries ... Thus the privileges are granted whenever the conditions exist," *Marriage Laws of the Code of Canon Law* (New York: Frederick Pustet Co., Inc., 1933), n. 146, p. 184.

[81] *De Matrimonio,* II, n. 2404, p. 734.

[82] *De Matrimonio,* n. 646, pp. 902-903.

[83] *The Constitutions of Canon 1125,* pp. 76-78.

lists the following commentators whose works were not available to this writer for reference or verification: Ubach,[84] Michel,[85] Raus,[86] Piscetta-Gennaro,[87] Wouters,[88] Pruemmer,[89] Bouvaert-Simenon,[90] and Genicot-Salsmans.[91]

Burton[92] objects to the use of many of these references on the grounds of ambiguity. He refers evidently to those quotations particularly which repeat the words of the Code verbatim or only paraphrase the thought of the text. Thus many authors, as quoted above, give as their reason for the extensive interpretation of the canon the fact that the constitutions have now been "extended to other parts of the world," or the "privileges which were formerly and originally particular have now become universal."

Vermeersch, however, notes that this repetition of the words of the canon, *"in eisdem adiunctis,"* does not destroy the value of these authorities. For whoever admits a universal extension of these constitutions can only admit that

[84] "... nunc per novi iuris Can. 1125 ad omnes regiones extenduntur," *Compendium Theologiae Moralis* (2 vols., Friburgi Brisgoviae, 1927), n. 880, p. 608.

[85] "... le canon 1125 etend a tous les pays ou elles trouvent leur application les concessions," *Ce qu'il y a de plus pratique pour le pretre dans le nouveau Code Canonique* (ed. 2, Alger, 1919), n. 298.

[86] "... nunc vi codicis ac modo citati canonis 1125 in specie iam eadem dispositio ad matrimonium infidelium in genere extenditur dummodo eadem occurrunt adiuncta," *Institutiones Canonicae* (2. ed., Lugduni, Parisiis, 1931), n. 319, p. 493.

[87] "... quae canon 1125 ad universum orbem extenduntur," *Elementa Theologiae Moralis* (7 vols., Vol. VI, Torino, 1929), n. 5, p. 173.

[88] "... dicitur ad alias regiones', i.e., ubique terrarum in eisdem adiunctis," *Manuale Theologiae Moralis,* (2 vols., Brugis, 1933), cap. II, art. III, n. 721, p. 556.

[89] "... pro omnibus regionibus si eadem adiuncta adsunt," *Manuale Theologiae Moralis* (2. ed., 3 vols., Friburgi Brisgoviae: Herder, 1922), Vol. III, n. 680, p. 473.

[90] "... iuxta communem interpretationem universum orbem," *Manuale Iuris Canonici ad Usum Seminariorum* (3. ed., 3 vols., Vol. II, Gandae et Leodii, 1931), II, n. 327, p. 4.

[91] *Institutiones Theologiae Moralis* (11. ed., 2 vols., Bruxellis: Alb. Dewit, 1927.

[92] *A Commentary on Canon 1125,* p. 114.

the conditions required by the constitutions refer to cases and not to whole territories. For to profess such a universal extension and then limit the application of the privileges to only a few, isolated cases would indeed be contradictory.[93]

This weight of authority added to the intrinsic arguments for the extensive nature of the privileges of the papal constitutions mentioned in canon 1125 only serves to make overwhelmingly certain the doctrine which argues for the universal application of these privileges in every case in all parts of the world without exception where their use will make it easier for some convert from infidelity to accept the Faith. That is why they were granted in the first place, and that is why they are included in the Code of Canon Law today.

Article III: Apostolic Faculties as Interpreters of the Constitutions

A very practical point arises in the consideration of the Formulas of Faculties granted by the Sacred Congregation for the Propagation of the Faith after the promulgation of the Code.

It was evident that the former faculties would need revision in view of the faculties granted in the law contained in the Code. Two such revisions have been issued, the first in 1919, the second in 1941.

The 1919 Formula contained the following faculty under number XXIV of *Formula Tertia Maior*:

> Dispensandi cum gentilibus et infidelibus plures uxores habentibus, ut post conversionem et baptismum, quam

[93] Vermeersch, "De Canone 1125 eiusque vi extensiva," *Periodica*, XX (1931), p. 3, "Neque vim istius suffragationis infirmari existimes, quia plures formaliter vel aequivalenter repetunt limitationem 'in eisdem adiunctis.' Qui enim extensionem universalem profitetur non potest adiuncta aliter intelligere quam adiuncta causae." Cf. Woods, *The Constitutions of Canon 1125*, p. 78.

ex illis maluerint, si etiam ipsa fidelis fiat, retinere possint, nisi prima voluerit converti."[94]

The faculty herein granted is basically identical with that given in the Constitution *Romani Pontificis* of Pope St. Pius V and conceded *iure communi* in canon 1125. Although the faculty had long been in use, its utility after the Code was justly questioned, and in the formulas of faculties issued in 1941 this faculty is no longer listed except as a footnote to Faculty XXV, and makes reference to canon 1125, which amply covers the possibilities formerly covered in Faculty XXIV.[95]

Formula XXIV was actually more strict than the Constitution *Romani Pontificis,* which now supplants it. The Constitution permitted the convert to choose any one of his wives who was willing to be or had already been converted; the faculty, however, limited this choice if the first wife was willing to be converted, and thus it became necessary in such a case to interpellate her. Actually the constitution nowhere makes mention of such an obligation.

The suppression of the Faculty, therefore, is a clear indication that the Holy See desires that the privileges of this Constitution be given their original and wider interpretation. This return to the genuine sense of the Constitution had already been anticipated by the First Chinese Council in 1924.[96]

The Council, in proposing the contradiction between the Faculty and the original grant of the privilege by Pope St. Pius V, asked the Holy See whether it was lawful to allow the converts to make their choice without regard to the wishes of the first wife. The Sacred Congregation for the

[94] "Facultates P. F. Facultates Formulae III," *Periodica,* XI (1922), p. (138).

[95] Winslow, *The Pauline Privilege,* pp. 69-70.

[96] *Primum Concilum Sinense, Acta-Decreta et Norma-Vota,* etc. (Tou-see-we, Zi-ka-wei, Shanghai: Typographia Missionis Catholicae, 1929), Votum XII; Winslow, *op. cit.,* p. 63, note 22; Payen, *De Matrimonio,* II, n. 2407 bis, p. 740.

Propagation of the Faith answered in the affirmative,[97] so that it is not required to make any attempt to interpellate the first and legitimate wife or husband.

The revision of 1941, however, did not suppress Faculty XXV of the 1919 revision. This faculty, together with Faculty XXVI of the 1941 Formulas grants the power of dispensing from the interpellations in the so-called ordinary and extraordinary cases.

Since the first of these possibilities is clearly covered by the Constitution, *Populis,* of Gregory XIII and the universal law in canon 1125, it is to be wondered that it too was not dropped from the Formulas of Faculties, particularly in the light of the suppression of Faculty XXIV. It is to be noted further that the new Formulas of Faculties issued after the Code through the Consistorial Congregation by the various other Congregations, each within its own competency, contains nothing relative to the dispensation from the interpellations.[98]

From a comparison of the texts it is certain that the faculty given by the Congregation for the Propagation of the Faith is definitely the same as that which is given to all local Ordinaries, Pastors and Jesuit Confessors by canon 1125.[99]

[97] *Primum Concilium Sinense,* Votum XII; cf. Winslow, *op. cit.,* pp. 64-65; Burton, *A Commentary on Canon 1125,* pp. 156-157.

[98] George Eagleton, *The Diocesan Quinquennial Faculties, Formula IV,* The Catholic University of America Canon Law Studies, n. 248 (Washington, D.C., The Catholic University of America Press, 1948), cf. Chapter VI, pp. 48-85; Hubert Louis Motry, *Diocesan Faculties According to the Code of Canon Law,* The Catholic University of America Canon Law Studies, n. 16 (Washington, D.C., The Catholic University of America, 1922).

[99] Vermeersch, "Commentaria de formulis Facultatum Quas S. Congr. de Propaganda Fide Concedere Solet," *Periodica,* Vol. XI, (1922), "Nn. 24 et 25 conceduntur facultates quae omnibus competere videntur in c. 1125 qui ad alias regiones extendit CC. Pauli III, St. Pii V, et Gregorii XIII de lato usu Privilegii Paulini," p. 139 (hereafter cited "Facultates Prop. Fide."); Xaverius Paventi, *Brevis Commentarius,* p. 44, "Casus ordinarius certae impossibilitatis in facultate n. 25 est ipsissima facultas concessa a Constitutione Gregorii, c.

The Constitution gave the power of dispensing from the obligation of making interpellations "dummodo constet etiam summarie et extraiudicialiter, coniugem, ut praefertur, absentem moneri legitime non posse, aut monitum intra tempus in eadem monitione praefixum suam voluntatem non significasse."

Under number XXV of the Formulas conceded by the Congregation for the Propagation of the Faith the faculty is granted:

> "Dispensandi super interpellatione coniugum in infidelitate relictorum pro omnibus *casibus ordinariis,* quando scilicet adhibitis antea omnibus diligentiis, etiam per publicas ephemerides ad reperiendum locum ubi coniux infidelis habitat, iisque in irritum cessis, constet ex processu saltem summario et extraiudicialiter coniugem absentem moneri legitime non posse aut monitum intra tempus in monitione praefixum suam voluntatem non significasse."[100]

This identity is openly evident from the choice of words in the faculty, which is clearly quoting the Constitution in declaring the conditions for its use, namely whenever it is clear from a summary and extrajudicial investigation that the infidel party cannot be interpellated, or, if interpellated, cannot possibly get an answer back within the time limit determined in the interpellation.

Although several explanations have been offered for the practicality of the faculty in the light of the more universal grant of canon 1125 nothing is of more paramount importance than the fact that the Sacred Congregation in the Faculty is identifying the conditions of the Constitution with the *casus ordinarii* of earlier faculties. Long before the Code, faculties to dispense from the interpellations were

1125", p. 44; Payen, *De Matrimonio,* II, n. 2410, "Et forte hac de causa S.C. de Prop. Fide tribuit hanc facultatem, quae in iure communi seu in praedicta constitutione certe existit." Léry, *Le Privilège de la Foi,* n. 94, p. 121, "La faculté ici concédée pour les cas d'*impossibilité* ne diffère pas du pouvoir accordé par la Constitution de Grégoire XIII."

[100] *Formula Tertia Maior,* n. 25.

distinguished into those which were to be used in the ordinary cases and those given for extraordinary cases.[101]

Pre-Code responses of the Holy See have explained that ordinary cases were those in which the interpellations were impossible or evidently useless, while the extraordinary cases were those in which the interpellations could indeed be made, but not without occasioning harm to the convert or danger to Christians in general.[102]

This distinction is recognized even today,[103] and therefore the privileges of the Constitution, *Populis,* are applicable in all cases of proven impossibility and inutility of making the interpellations. Cases of impossibility are clearly those in which "coniugem absentem moneri legitime non posse," while inutility is identified with the cases in which "(coniugem absentem) monitum intra tempus in monitione praefixum suam voluntatem non significasse."[104]

[101] S.C.S. Off. (Mongoliae), 29 nov. 1882—*Fontes,* n. 1075; *Coll. S.C.P.F.,* n. 1581.

[102] S.C.S. Off. (Coreae), 11 sept. 1878—*Fontes,* n. 1057; *Coll. S.C.P.F.,* n. 1499; S.C.S. Off. (Mongoliae), 29 nov. 1882—*Fontes,* n. 1075; *Coll. S.C.P.F.,* n. 1581; S.C.S. Off. (ad Vic. Ap. Iaponiae Merid.), 4 febr. 1891—*Fontes,* n. 1130; *Coll. S.C.P.F.,* n. 1746.

[103] Vermeersch, "Commentaria de Formulis Facultatum," *Periodica,* XI (1922), (139), "Iam ante codicem distinguebatur ordinaria facultas dispensandi in interpellatione. Ordinaria describitur ipsis verbis formulae. Ex ipsis S. Officii responsis, collegimus, n. 77 opusculi de *Casu Apostoli,* facultatem istam exerceri posse quotiescumque interpellatio cernatur ob absentiam et distantiam coniugis, vel ignoratam residentiam (adhibitis tunc diligentiis ad eam inveniendam) impossibilis aut certo inutilis fore. Atque, ex canone 1125, norma Brevis *Populis ac Nationibus* tuto applicari potest." Léry, *Le Privilège de la Foi,* n. 93, p. 121, "On distingue entre cas ordinaries, quand l'interpellation est impossibile, an inutile, et cas extraordinaires, quand elle est dangereuse. Le Saint-Office veut que l'on distingue avec soin entre ces deux espèces de cas." Winslow, *The Pauline Privilege,* p. 35; Woeber, *The Interpellations,* pp. 111-114; Payen, *De Matrimonio,* II, nn. 2413-2414, pp. 750-752; Vermeersch-Creusen, *Epitome,* II, n. 435, p. 301; Doheny, *Informal Procedure,* pp. 531-532.

[104] Léry, *Le Privilège de la Foi,* n. 95, p. 122, "De plus, les derniers mots *dummodo ... constet ... coniugem monitum ... suam voluntatem non significasse* donnent un exemple d'interpellation inutile."

Vermeersch,[105] further sees in the faculty a practical guide for the interpretation of the concessions of canon 1125. For the interpretation of the formulas by the Holy See will also serve as a safe norm to judge the extent of the power granted through the Papal Constitutions.

Commentators on the Apostolic Faculties generally acquiesce in this explanation of the continued grant of this faculty, even though the faculty seems to be altogether unneeded in view of the faculty granted through canon 1125 itself.

Winslow, likewise, finds in the faculty a norm that will be conducive to a prudent use and application of the constitutions.[106]

Vromant sees in it a practical application of the constitution, and states that its primary advantage consists in that it serves to clarify the power granted to the missionaries by canon 1125, in that it gives a rule by which one may more definitely determine the means of establishing the impossibility of interpellating the infidel.[107] In another work Vromant says that the extensive interpretation of the Constitution is based in a very special way on these faculties which are themselves adapted to the provisions of the common law.[108]

Paventi,[109] Payen[110] and Léry[111] likewise find in this faculty a means of more accurately determining the conditions required for the use of the privileges of Gregory XIII, namely the impossibility or inutility of making the interpellations.

105 "Facultates Prop. Fide," *Periodica*, XI (1923), (139).

106 *The Pauline Privilege*, p. 21; *A Commentary on the Apostolic Faculties* (New York: The Field Afar Press, 1946), p. 151.

107 *Facultates Apostolicae* (3. ed., Paris: Desclee de Brouwer, 1947), p. 79.

108 *De Matrimonio*, n. 354, p. 279.

109 "Facultas n. 25 tantum pressius determinat modum quo constare debet impossibilitas vel inutilitas interpellandi," *Brevis Commentarius*, p. 44.

110 *De Matrimonio*, II, n. 2410.

111 *Le Privilège de la Foi*, n. 94, p. 121.

When the Synod of Suchow in 1803 interpreted a faculty to dispense from the interpellations identical with that of Faculty XXV it reminded the missionaries that they were to use the faculty to dispense only in accord with the norms of the Constitution of Pope Gregory XIII.[112]

Faculty XXV is recognized, then, as being identical with the grant of Pope Gregory as now extended to the universal Church by reason of the law contained in the Code. Since, from practical circumstances, it is evident that the privileges will naturally be of more frequent application in missionary countries, this faculty was granted by the Sacred Congregation for the Propagation of the Faith as a guide to these missionaries in the use of the privileges, especially in setting up norms for determining the impossibility or futility of the interpellations.

Although Bouscaren formerly agreed with this interpretation,[113] he has admittedly changed his stand. Acknowledging that the opinion to which he formerly subscribed "is not devoid of probability, yet upon re-examination of the question, it seems better to keep the faculties granted to Ordinaries by special indults distinct from those which are given by canon 1125."[114]

His change of attitude seems to be based on a strict reading of the text of the Papal Constitution of Gregory XIII without considering any of the interpretations given by the Sacred Congregations in the years both preceding and following the Code in their general faculties and particular responses. He is correct in seeking the first interpretation of the Constitution, not from some extrinsic source such as the faculty, but from the text itself.

As reason for his change of opinion he concludes it to be the common opinion of the authors that the moral impos-

[112] *Coll. Lac.* Vol. VI, Cap. IX, n. VIII, p. 623; Cf. Winslow, *The Pauline Privilege*, p. 81; *A Commentary on Apostolic Faculties*, p. 151; *Coll. S.C.P.F.*, n. 2265.

[113] "An Inquiry into the Practical Application of Canon 1125," *Miscellanea-Vermeersch*, I, 279.

[114] Bouscaren-Ellis, *Canon Law: A Text and Commentary*, p. 558.

sibility of interpellating the infidel offers a sufficient reason for granting a dispensation in virtue of the Constitution, *Populis,* while their inutility or resulting danger of harm is not sufficient. The writer agrees that the danger of harm that might arise from the making of the interpellations is not covered by the Constitution of Gregory XIII; in the light, however, of the obvious meaning and purpose of the faculty he feels that the proven inutility of making the interpellation is not excluded by the Constitution as a sufficient cause for a dispensation.[115]

Actually this faculty merely grants explicitly what is implicitly contained in the Constitution, and thus the earlier opinion of Vermeersch, followed today by Vromant, Winslow, Paventi, Payen and Léry quite surely seems to be the more valid one.[116]

[115] This particular point shall be the subject of a more thorough consideration in Article II of Chapter V, pp. 171-178.

[116] Léry, *Le Privilège de la Foi,* "La faculté vise explicitement les cas où l'interpellation est impossibile, et implicitement les cas où elle est *inutile.* Car le Saint-Siège a déclaré plusieurs fois qu'on pouvait dispenser de l'interpellation, quand elle était impossibile ou inutile. De plus, les derniers mots *dummodo . . . constet . . . coniugem monitum . . . suam voluntatem non significasse* donnent un exemple d'interpellation inutile." n. 95, p. 122.

CHAPTER II

APPLICATION OF CANON 1125 TO THE UNITED STATES TODAY

In view of the arguments for the extensive and universal interpretation of canon 1125, an interpretation which is today acknowledged as certain, one may be tempted to abstract very precisely from the question whether or not the canon has any application in the United States today. Why should this country be excepted, for the use of the canon depends not upon place or time but upon the circumstances of individual cases which alone are the criteria.[1]

The privileges will cease to be applicable only when this canon of the Code is revoked or when there are no more infidels anywhere in the world to use these favors to the advantage of the Faith in preparing the way for their conversion.

And yet, as Woeber frankly indicates,[2] there is an unfounded hesitation on the part of those who have the right and duty, conceded by the law itself, to apply the constitutions when the prescribed conditions are verified. Since these privileges were granted not in favor of ecclesiastical superiors, but in favor of the Faith and for the benefit of individual converts, these same superiors cannot refuse to apply the privileges without doing harm to the Faith and oftentimes impeding the eternal salvation of the souls of those who can accept the Faith only by using these privileges.[3]

It may well be that the hesitation and confusion is based upon the failure to make a proper distinction between the reasons for which the original grant of favors was made,

[1] Bouscaren-Ellis, *Canon Law: A Text and Commentary*, p. 555.

[2] *The Interpellations*, p. 137, conclusions: "... it appears to the writer that the Ordinaries of the United States are either unaware of their power or are loath to use the extraordinary faculty to dispense given to them in the common law by reason of canon 1125."

[3] Bouscaren-Ellis, *Op. Cit.*, p. 558, n. 4.

and the occasions which merely prompted these grants. The prime motive cause of the constitutions is the same and must remain so even today, namely a desire to aid converts to the Faith, while the occasions or mere impelling circumstances cannot be verified literally and need not be the same.[4] Thus, for example, one need not look for cases of slavery or of forceful abduction of husbands and wives, for these were merely the occasions, not the motives, for the papal grants of the privileges.[5]

In a study of the extensive application of these privileges Bouscaren answers unhesitatingly that these conditions are not required to be present before the powers granted through canon 1125 may be used both licitly and validly. He observes that this is true because Pope Gregory spoke of this forceful separation of husband and wife only in the preamble of his Constitution, *Populis,* which merely recites the occasion for the enactment. Such a requisite is not mentioned in the dispositive part of the Constitution, and its mention occurs quite separately from the *dummodo* clause, in which are enumerated the essential conditions.[6] For the use of the privilege it is sufficient therefore that the two spouses be in such a way separated that it is impossible for the one to find the other, or that it is impossible or evidently useless to make the interpellations for any one of a

[4] Vromant, *De Matrimonio,* n. 354, p. 280, "Sed prudenti discretione distinguendae sunt *causae motivae primae* concessionis Summorum Pontificum et causae mere impulsivae vel occasiones concessionis. Causae motivae eadem esse et manere debent etiam hodie; dum causae impulsivae et occasiones impune abesse quin propterea applicatio impediatur." Vermeersch, "De Canone 1125 eiusque vi extensiva", *Periodica,* XX (1931), 1*-5*; Payen, *De Matrimonio,* II, n. 2404, p. 734; Ayrinhac-Lydon, *Marriage Legislation,* p. 321.

[5] Benedictus, XIV, *De Synodo Dioecesana,* lib. XIII, cap. XXI, n. 3, "Circumstantiae locales abductio nempe coacta et inde exorta difficultas priorem coniugem reperiendi, fuerunt occasio concessionis pontificiae." Vermeersch, *Op. Cit.,* 4*, "Si, e.g., exigas pro applicatione ut conversi fuerint vi abducti, vix hodie erit locus isti privilegio." Payen, *De Matrimonio,* II, n. 2409, p. 745.

[6] "An Inquiry into the Practical Application of Canon 1125," *Miscaellanea-Vermeersch,* I, 287.

number of approved reasons.[7] As has been indicated, there were a few authors in the years immediately following the Code who held that the favors of canon 1125 had no or only a very restricted application in the United States. Of course, this country in 1918, or at any time in its history for that matter, was never in the same social circumstances that were prevalent in 16th century African and South American countries.

Augustine excluded all possible use in this country of the provisions contained in canon 1125,[8] while others, like Gregory[9] and De Becker[10] felt that the Indians of the Western reservations and the Negroes on Southern plantations could possibly be considered as potential recipients of the privileges granted in the Papal Constitutions. Ayrinhac-Lydon[11] mention the possibility of using the power in deal-

[7] Vermeersch-Creusen, *Epitome*, II, n. 436, "Censemus cum Payen n. 2409, satis esse ut coniux fidelis coniugem infidelem interpellare non possit, non autem requiri ut vi fuerint separati." Ayrinhac-Lydon, *Marriage Legislation*, p. 321, "It will scarcely be necessary, however, that a man be carried off by force; it will suffice that the couple be separated and that it is impossible to find one of the parties." Coronata, *De Matrimonio*, n. 646, p. 903; Payen. *op. cit.*, II, n. 2405, note 1, "Sic Constitutio *Populis* Gregorii XIII non spectat tantummodo ad eum coniugem fidelem qui compartem, vi raptam, interrogare non potest, sed pertinet etiam ad coniugem baptizatum qui coniugem infidelem *qualibet de causa* interpellare nequit." Gasparri, *De Matrimonio*, II, n. 1160, p. 235, "Constitutiones ... extensae fuerunt ad alias quoque regiones in eisdem adiunctis, quae, singulas pontificias constitutiones resumentes, adnotavimus, *omissis circumstantiis quae doctrinam non afficiunt.*" (Italics inserted.)

[8] *A Commentary*, Vol. V, "These circumstances must affect the countries, not merely persons ... we scarcely believe that the United States, or even our Indian reservations could claim to be in that category." p. 364. In a later work, *The Rights and Duties of Ordinaries According to the Code and the Apostolic Faculties*, (St. Louis: B. Herder Book Company, 1924), p. 296, Augustine, although he does not speak explicitly of the United States, clearly adopts a more extensive view of the application of the Canon.

[9] *The Pauline Privilege*, p. 87.

[10] "Recensiones," *Ephemerides Theologicae Lovaniensis*, II (1925), 445.

[11] *Marriage Legislation*, p. 321.

ing with converts among polygamous Indian tribes, but do not specifically limit its application to this instance. Ramstein offers no commentary on canon 1125, but evidently alludes to it when he states that the Ordinaries of the United States have no faculties by law to dispense from the interpellations; if this be so, then he must necessarily admit that the faculty of Gregory XIII, extended by common law to the Church universal, has no application in the United States.[12]

Since Woywod in the foreward of his commentary states that his work is intended chiefly for the clergy of the United States[13] one cannot help but feel that his interpretation of canon 1125 is too strict, certainly misleading. For he states that these constitutions are applicable only where and when the circumstances are the same as those outlined in the constitutions. "Wherefore they are not very practical in Christian nations, although they are of practical utility in the missions of heathen countries."[14]

Today, however, commentators literally without exception acknowledge that the argument against the *local* interpretation is so strong that there seems to be little room for prudent doubt as to the nature of the extensive force of canon 1125, so that in consequence the privileges are to be deemed applicable to the United States, as also they are to any other part of the Church throughout the world.[15] Schaaf was explicit when he stated that there can be no doubt that in numerous cases the conditions contemplated in the different constitutions are really present, with the result that one or the other can quite frequently be employed with the result that a convert can become dispensed from the obligation of making the interpellations.[16]

[12] *A Manual of Canon Law,* p. 504.

[13] *A Practical Commentary on the Code of Canon Law,* p. viii.

[14] *Op. cit.,* I, p. 713.

[15] Francis Patrick Kearney, *The Principles of Canon 1127,* The Catholic University of America Canon Law Studies, n. 163 (Washington, D. C.: The Catholic University of America Press, 1942), p. 127, note 85.

[16] "Dispensation from Interpellations," *ER,* LXXXVI (1932), 537.

The Constitution *Altitudo* of Pope Paul III, and also the Constitution *Romani Pontificis* of St. Pius V were granted in favor of converts from polygamous infidel unions, while the Constitution *Populis* of Pope Gregory XIII was directed to converts from paganism regardless of what had been their marital status. It is evident, therefore, that the provisions of this latter constitution can more frequently become of practical use. The first two, however, are not without value even in the United States today.

In the first place, these constitutions were directed to countries entirely or overwhelmingly pagan and in which polygamy was the common and accepted practice of the majority of the people. Is it possible then that these general conditions are verified in the United States?

There is a rather general conviction that ours is a Christian nation; yet facts prove definitely that this conviction lacks a sound basis. The estimated population of the United States on July 1, 1948, according to the Government Bureau of Census, was 146,571,000.[17] At the same time the estimated religious affiliation in this country was a mere 76,058,849 and of this number over 40,000,000 were listed as members of the various 223 Protestant sects. Of this latter group many certainly never received baptism at all, and many received it only invalidly. In the light of these figures there is a conservative estimate of almost 100 million people in the United States who are possible beneficiaries of these privileges.

But there is a further pre-requisite for the use of the favors granted by Pope Paul III and St. Pius V, for these considered converts who had been living in simultaneous polygamy. That would, upon first consideration, seem to eliminate the use of the privileges of these two Papal grants in this country, for none of the states permit simultaneous polygamy. The ever increasing number of divorces and remarriages among the American people, however, opens the

[17] Reported in the *1949 Information Please Almanac* (New York: Farrar, Straus & Co., 1949), pp. 216, 742.

way to another form of multiple marriages—successive polygamy.[18]

This successive marrying of men or women after the obtaining of a civil divorce may not be considered polygamous in the eyes of the civil authorities, but it most certainly is so far as the law of God is concerned, which law does not recognize civil divorces even when granted in favor of two infidels.[19]

In the use of the privileges of canon 1125 polygamy includes not only the simultaneous kind but also successive polygamy, i.e., when a non-baptized man has obtained a civil divorce, perhaps several times, from unbaptized women and then remarried.[20]

That successive polygamists are not excluded from the privileges is certain from an authentic interpretation of the words, *"qui plures habent uxores."* The Sacred Congregation for the Propagation of the Faith has answered that the privileges granted to polygamists in general are granted also to those who practice successive polygamy.[21] It is to be pointed out further that the favors granted to men in these constitutions are, by equity of law, extended to women also.[22]

[18] The Federal Security Agency reports an increase from 195,000 divorces in 1930 to 264,000 in 1940, and 471,000 in 1947—*1949 Information Please Almanac*, p. 240.

[19] Nau, *The Marriage Laws of the Code of Canon Law*, n. 146, p. 184, "These concessions of St. Pius V can be applicable to our country. Simultaneous polygamy does not exist, at least not to any extent, but on account of the laxity of our divorce laws, successive polyandry and [polygyny] do exist to such an extent legally by civil law that it can be said successive [polygyny] and polyandry are a recognized custom."

[20] Vromant, *De Matrimonio*, n. 355, p. 281; Ayrinhac-Lydon, *Marriage Legislation*, p. 321; Bouscaren-Ellis, *Canon Law: A Text and Commentary*, p. 559.

[21] S.C. de Prop. Fide (C.P. pro Sin-Tunkin Orient.), 14 ian. 1806—*Fontes*, n. 4686; *Coll. S.C.P.F.*, n. 685; Cf. Payen, *De Matrimonio*, II, n. 2420; Winslow, *The Pauline Privilege*, p. 58, n. 101.

[22] S.C.S. Off. (ad P. A. Thibeten), 5 sept. 1855—*Fontes*, n. 933; *Coll. S.C.P.F.*, n. 1117; Payen, *De Matrimonio*, II, n. 2405.

In consideration of the individual constitutions it is evident that these will not be of equally frequent application. The Constitution *Altitudo* requires that the convert be unable to remember which of his many wives—or many husbands—was the first and legitimate one. Evidently, such a case would indeed be rare today despite the extant laxity and indifferent attitude toward the unity and indissolubility of marriage. If, however, the conditions actually are verified, the convert is allowed in virtue of the privileges of this constitution to contract marriage, according to the canonical form, with any one of his former wives without being obliged to interpellate any of the other spouses, and no dispensation from the impediment of disparity of cult is necessary when that impediment exists in the case, for this dispensation is implicitly granted through the very use of the privilege itself.

The privileges of the Constitution *Romani Pontificis* were granted in favor of converts who likewise were parties to polygamous unions. To these converts is granted the right to contract marriage, by means of a renewal of consent with any of their former wives who already have received or will receive baptism with them. Again, they are exempted from the obligation of making the interpellations even though their first wives are known and can easily be interpellated.

The Constitution *Populis* of Gregory XIII was not limited to former polygamists, as were the two preceeding constitutions, but was directed to any and all converts from paganism who were parties to infidel marriages and who wished to marry Catholics, but were in consequence of circumstances prevented from using the Pauline privilege in its ordinary procedure. As soon as it was proved with at least moral certainty that it was impossible or useless to make the interpellations which are normally required, the privileges of this papal grant became applicable. When this certainty was had on grounds approved by the Holy See, all local ordinaries, pastors and Jesuit confessors were empowered to dispense the convert from the obligation of making one or the other, or even both, of the interpellations. These authorized agents acted with ordinary power. In no case was any recourse to any higher authority necessary, and the latter could not in any way validly limit these agents in the use of the power that had been granted to them.[23]

[23] For a comprehensive consideration of this question the reader can most profitably consult two works written specifically on the interpretation and application of these papal constitutions. Burton, *A Commentary on Canon 1125*, pp. 138-180; and Woods, *The Constitutions of Canon 1125*. Confer also Doheny, *Informal Procedure*, pp. 551-565; Winslow, *A Commentary on The Apostolic Faculties*, pp. 149-152; Léry, *Le Privilège de la Foi*, nn. 74-92, pp. 100-120.

PART THREE

CANONICAL COMMENTARY AND ANALYSIS

CHAPTER I

THE INTERPELLATIONS

Article I: Purpose of the Interpellations

In the midst of his advice on marriage St. Paul spoke of the obligation of a converted spouse toward his or her partner who had remained in infidelity. It is this text that gives the basis for the Pauline privilege.[1] St. Paul himself meant it to be a privilege, "But if the unbeliever departs, let him depart, for a brother or a sister is not under bondage in such cases, but God has called us to peace." Any discussion of this teaching or any phase of its application which does not consider the apostolic grant in the nature of a privilege does violence to the text and to the mind of St. Paul.[2]

The text quite explicitly stated that the only necessary condition for the use of the privilege was the departure of the unbeliever. When an unbaptized partner had deserted his converted consort, that convert was thereby, and without any further formalities, free to separate.

In the historical and doctrinal evolution of the practical application of the privilege new corollaries to the doctrine became evidently necessary. These were at once the result of that evolution as well as the solution to ever increasing and complicating circumstances. Slowly it was determined what precisely constituted a departure, physical or moral. Inevitably there arose a need to establish in some way that this essential condition of departure had been actually verified.[3]

[1] I Cor., 7:12-15.

[2] Gregory, *The Pauline Privilege*, p. 48; Doheny, *Informal Procedure*, p. 509.

[3] *Supra*, p. 16, Note 1.

In the early years some quite general proof was required. This was generally derived through the form of some *monitio*[4] by which the infidel was assured that his attitude toward his converted spouse would have to be peaceful and accompanied with due respect for the convert's new Faith. The development of a definite means of determining the will of the infidel in this respect was so gradual as not to cause any comment among pre-18th century commentators. Actually it was not until the early part of that century that there was enacted the first explicit act of legislation demanding the interpellations as they are known today.[5]

The interpellations are therefore considered as a corollary of the doctrine of St. Paul, as the means of investigating the mind of the infidel.[6] Today the interpellations are the legitimate means of fulfilling this investigation for the purpose of verifying whether or not the condition of departure on the part of the infidel, which St. Paul necessarily postulated, has actually taken place.[7]

The purpose of the interpellations is to ascertain in the external forum, formally and officially, the presence of this prescribed condition. Burton summarizes the object and purpose of the interpellations:

> In the use of the Pauline privilege the separation of the infidel party—the *discessus*—is a fundamental condition and cannot be presumed but must be demonstrated. The normal way in which the demonstration will be made is by the formal declaration of the infidel

[4] Prior to the 17th Century the words *monere, admonere, monitio, admonitio* were in use to signify what is now understood by the terms, *interpellare* and *interpellatio*.

[5] Woeber, *The Interpellations*, p. 22, quotes a response issued by the Sacred Congregation of the Council on January 23, 1603. The reader may well consult this dissertation for the general historical background and development of the interpellations.

[6] Innocentius III, ep. *Gaudemus in Domino*, 22 apr. 1201—c. 8, X, *de divortiis*, IV, 19; Wernz-Vidal, *Ius Matrimoniale*, n. 632, p. 822, note 68. Woeber, *The Interpellations*, p. 46.

[7] Coronata, *De Matrimonio*, n. 630, p. 881. Payen, *De Matrimonio* II, n. 2345.

> party in answer to the interpellations, first as to whether he desires to be converted and receive baptism, or at least whether he will cohabit with his convert spouse peacefully and without insult to the Creator.[8]

This is the substance of the canonical legislation of the Code.[9]

It is necessary, in the light of further consideration, to emphasize this fundamental characteristic of the interpellation, namely that it is a means and not an end in itself. With only a few exceptions all recent commentators on the Pauline privilege have insisted on this distinction, and then immediately seem to confuse or disregard it in their commentary.[10]

This insistence on the notion of the interpellations as means and not as ends in themselves is not principally or primarily pure theory, as it may seem to be, for it is precisely this consideration that gives the basis for allowing the omission of the interpellations. For if the interpellations are means to an end, then it may well be that that end can, at times, be attained by more effective means. To our point —the purpose of the interpellations is to definitely determine the departure of the infidel partner; now, if that de-

[8] Burton, *A Commentary on Canon 1125*, p. 91.

[9] *Canon 1121.*

[10] Vermeersch-Creusen, *Epitome*, II, n. 434, p. 300: "Interpellationes ... immo sunt medium quo regulariter haec certitudo acquirenda est." Payen, *De Matrimonio*, II, n. 2341, p. 663: "Prior et primarius finis [interpellationis] est ut conjugi converso ac baptizato *certe et legitime*, seu ad normam legis, constet *de discessu* partis non baptizatae." Gougnard, *Tractatus de Matrimonio*, p. 296: "Solo iure divino spectato requiritur quidem interpellatio regulariter, utpote quae ordinarium medium sit ut constet de partis infidelis discessu." Bouscaren-Ellis, *Canon Law: A Text and Commentary*, p. 550: "For proving this condition (*discessus*) the normal *means* are the interpellations." De Smet, *De Sponsalibus et Matrimonio*, n. 351, p. 299, note 1: "Ius divinum regulariter exigere interpellationem, utpote quae ordinarium medium est ut constet de coniugis infidelis discessu." Doheny, *Informal Procedure*, p. 518.

parture is clearly known from some other means, then the interpellations are not only not necessary but they become entirely useless. There is a rule of law which gives force to this reasoning.[11]

St. Paul has clearly postulated the departure of the infidel as necessary, but he in no way determined the means for the establishment of the necessary proof.[12] Thus the departure, not the proof of it, is the all important fact.[13] And if this fact is clearly established by any means whatever, the interpellations, would of their nature, be of little use.[14]

Summarily, then, it is clear that the essential condition for the use of the Pauline privilege, namely, the departure of the unbaptized party, must have been in some way or other definitely determined and proved. The Church in practice has acknowledged the interpellations as the accepted means of establishing this condition.[15] Yet it was and is commonly agreed that the interpellations are essen-

[11] Reg. 31, R.J. in VI°: "Eum, qui certus est, certiorari ulterius non oportet."

[12] Gougnard, *Tractatus de Matrimonio,* p. 296: "Quod necessaria requiritur est discessus partis infidelis, sed non determinatur a S. Paulo quomodo debeat constare de hoc discessu." Coronata, *De Matrimonio,* n. 631, p. 884: "Quippe S. Paulus de interpellationibus qua talibus non loquitur, et ad usum privilegii fidei quod ipse concedit vel promulgat nihil amplius requirit quam discessus partis infidelis."

[13] Chelodi, *Ius Matrimoniale,* n. 158, p. 173: "Secundum matrimonium validum consideratur quia conditio privilegii est discessus non eiusdem probatio." Cappello, *De Matrimonio,* n. 777, p. 767: "... conditio privilegii obiective spectati est discessus coniugis infidelis, non autem eius probatio." Cf. Wernz-Vidal, *Ius Matrimoniale,* n. 632, § 3, note 68, p. 824.

[14] Chelodi, *Ius Matrimoniale,* n. 160, p. 175: "Si enim mala voluntas infidelis certa est ... interpellatio ex natura rei videtur supervacanea." The same reference is found in Payen, *De Matrimonio,* II, n. 2403, p. 733, and Cappello, *De Matrimonio,* n. 781, p. 283. Cf. also, Cappello, *De Matrimonio,* n. 776, p. 278: "Si discessus coniugis est certus, ex iure divino seu ex natura rei procul dubio nec ad validitatem nec ad licitum usum privilegii requiritur interpellatio." See also Léry, *Le Privilège de la Foi,* n. 73, p. 99.

[15] Sylvius Romani, *Institutiones Iuris Canonici,* Vol. II, pars altera, *De Matrimonio* (Romae: Editrice 'Iustitia', 1945), n. 1149, p. 781.

tially means, and that their purpose can at times be supplied in some other way.[16]

Long ago the Church had recognized that under such conditions theoretically the interpellations could be omitted entirely without prejudice or hazard to the valid use of the Pauline privilege; however, the Holy See has warned that that theory cannot be safely followed in practice.[17] And yet Popes Paul III and St. Pius V envisioned conditions under which the interpellations could be legitimately omitted in their entirety.[18] These grants are even now recognized in the Code.[19]

It is generally agreed that in those cases wherein the *discessus* of the infidel or his refusal to continue cohabitation is certain, then the Holy See will readily grant a dispensation from the interpellations, which are no longer necessary.[20]

It is pertinent to note here that actually the law of the Church itself recognizes this situation, for nowhere in the Code does any canon unconditionally demand the making of the interpellations whether for the valid or for the licit use of the privilege. In both paragraphs of canon 1121, as also in canon 1123, the law deals with the necessity of the interpellations, but in each instance the general command is not without qualification or reservation.[21] And, furthermore, the Code itself[22] states with sufficient clarity in canon

[16] De Smet, *De Sponsalibus et Matrimonio*, n. 351, p. 299.

[17] Benedictus XIV, *De Synodo Dioecesana*, lib. XII, cap. XXI, n. 6. Cf. *Supra*, p. 23 of this dissertation.

[18] Paulus III, const. *Altitudo*, 1 iun. 1537—*Codex Iuris Canonici*, Documentum VI; St. Pius V, const. *Romani Pontificis*, 2 aug. 1571—*Codex Iuris Canonici*, Documentum VII.

[19] Canon 1125.

[20] Vermeersch-Creusen, *Epitome*, II, n. 430, p. 297.

[21] De Smet, *De Sponsalibus et Matrimonio*, n. 353, p. 299: "Necessitas interpellandi *non est insupplebilis* nec *indispensabilis*, uti liquet e canone 1121, § 2, et canone 1123; sed a facienda interpellatione una, vel etiam utraque, *dispensari potest* a S. Sede, et de facto dispensari non raro contingit." Cf. also Coronata, *De Matrimonio*, n. 631, p. 885; Wernz-Vidal, *Ius Matrimoniale*, n. 632, note 68, p. 825.

[22] Canon 1124.

1124 that the right of the convert to enter a new marriage depends not on the interpellations but rather upon the actual *discessus* of the infidel party.[23]

Article II: Origin of the Obligation to Make the Interpellations

An argument of purely theoretic value centers about the origin of the obligation to make the interpellations.[24] The solution of the problem depends ultimately on whether or not the Pauline privilege itself is of immediate or mediate divine origin. Even today the argument remains unsolved in the face of equal authority upholding either view.[25]

Section 1: The Divine Origin Theory

Those who support the immediate divine origin of the Pauline privilege contend that the privilege was directly and immediately instituted by Christ, promulgated by St. Paul, and then extended to the entire Church by St. Peter.[26] They

[23] Coronata, *De Matrimonio,* n. 631, pp. 884-885; Chelodi, *Ius Matrimoniale,* n. 158; Wernz-Vidal, *De Matrimonio,* n. 632, Note 68, in fine, p. 825: "Quare si quis attendat in canone 1124, existente conditione discessus infidelis, coniugi fideli asseri ius ad novas nuptias, non facile admittet iure Codicis non solum conditionem discessus sed etiam *modum* probationis illius requiri ad valorem secundi matrimonii." Arturus Vermeersch, *Theologicae Moralis* (4 vols., Vol. III, 3. ed., Roma: Pontificia Università Gregoriana, 1933), III, n. 755.

[24] Gasparri, *De Matrimonio,* II, n. 1135; Payen, *De Matrimonio,* II, n. 2210, p. 533; Cappello, *De Matrimonio,* n. 768, p. 758: "Ceterum, sive theoretice sive practice ista quaestio est profecto minoris momenti."

[25] Cf. Gregory, *The Pauline Privilege,* pp. 48 ff., for a thorough and comprehensive consideration of this problem.

[26] Sanchez, *De Sancto Matrimonii Sacramento,* lib. VII, disp. 74, n. 4; Benedictus XIV, *De Synodo Dioecesana,* lib. VI, cap. IV, n. 3; Wernz, *Ius Matrimoniale,* n. 702.

Cf. Woeber, *The Interpellations,* pp. 49-57. In footnote n. 46 on p. 50 Woeber lists Gasparri and Vermeersch-Creusen as holding the opinion of the divine origin of the obligation to make the interpellations. In this he does an injustice to these authors. Gasparri, (*De Matrimonio,* II, n. 1166) clearly holds otherwise; Vermeersch-Creusen (*Epitome,* II, n. 430, p. 297; n. 434, p. 300) explicitly quality their statement in this regard and (*ibid.,* in note 3 under n. 427, p. 295) consequently contend, in line with their argumentation, that the origin of the obligation to interpellate the infidel spouse is also of immediate divine origin. Wernz-Vidal[27] hold strictly that the obligation is of divine origin, while Vermeersch-Creusen,[28] Coronata[29] and Payen[30] qualify their stand. Vermeersch-Creusen hold that the obligation is of divine origin when there is doubt of the infidel's intentions. Coronata seems to affirm that the obligation to make the interpellations arises from the divine law only in those cases wherein the interpellations are the one and only means for verifying the departure of the infidel. Payen gives as his reason for holding this theory the fact that it seems to be the common opinion, but he immediately adds that he sees little difference between the two.

Those who support the divine origin theory can and do cite to their advantage an Instruction of the Holy See.[31] In citing this document they reflect a tendency to maximize its importance. The document is simply an Instruction and cannot in any way, as Wernz-Vidal admit, be understood to be definitive or final.[32]

Section 2: Origin from the Ecclesiastical Law

A second opinion contends that Christ gave to His Vicar complete power over the marriages of the unbaptized, even

---

indicate their support of the mediate divine origin of this necessity. Moreover, in his appraisal of the opinions (p. 56), Woeber states: "The common opinion undoubtedly favors the divine authorship of the privilege and the necessity of proposing the interpellations by divine precept," yet two pages earlier (p. 54) he had affirmed that the opinion supporting the mediate divine origin of the privilege "appears to have the stronger arguments in its favor and is upheld by the majority of modern canonists."

[27] *Ius Matrimoniale*, n. 631, note 56.

[28] *Epitome*, II, n. 430, p. 297, and n. 434, p. 300.

[29] *De Matrimonio*, n. 632, p. 886.

[30] *De Matrimonio*, n. 2210, p. 535.

[31] S.C.S. Off., (Natal), 11 iul. 1866—*Fontes*, n. 907. Cf. Payen, *De Matrimonio*, II, n. 2210.

[32] *Ius Matrimoniale*, n. 631, note 56, p. 812.

to the point of dissolving them when a sufficiently just reason demands this course of action. Only consummated ratified marriages were excepted from this power. In the light of this reasoning the Pauline privilege is, then, only a special application of a much more extensive power.[33]

In support of their stand the proponents of this theory find a basis in the words of St. Paul, "Ceteris ego dico, non Dominus,"[34] and in the general principle that recourse to a higher immediately divine law is never necessary when a mediately divine law suffices. Thus no special, immediate and direct intervention of Christ is necessary when the solution of the bond is sufficiently explained in virtue of the extraordinary power granted by Christ. As De Smet writes: "If . . . the Church has of itself more than sufficient power, there is no apparent reason for the intervention of immediate divine power in the case of the Apostle."[35]

[33] Ayrinhac-Lydon, *Marriage Legislation*, n. 300; Woeber, *The Interpellations*, pp. 55-56; Gregory, *The Pauline Privilege*, pp. 48ff; Burton, *A Commentary on Canon 1125*, p. 85, "Moreover, in itself, the controversy is not of great moment, since the privilege from the nature of the matter must be of at least mediate divine origin." Woods, *The Constitutions of Canon 1125*, p. 18; Winslow, *The Pauline Privilege*, p. 1, n. 1; Cappello, *De Matrimonio*, n. 768, pp. 757-758; Gasparri, *De Matrimonio*, II, n. 1166, "Putamus Apostolum iis verbis non excludere potestatem a Domino receptam, quod foret absurdum, sed dicere receptam potestatem, propria apostolica auctoritate, applicare ad casum particularem iniustae derelictionis coniugis fidelis." Cf. Coronata, *De Matrimonio*, n. 632, p. 886; Vermeersch-Creusen, *Epitome*, II, n. 430, p. 297; Wernz-Vidal, *Ius Matrimoniale*, n. 636, p. 836; Payen, *De Matrimonio*, II, n. 2210, p. 534.

[34] I Cor. VII: 12; Cf. Woeber, *The Interpellations*, p. 54; Payen, *De Matrimonio*, II, n. 2210, p. 534; Cappello, *De Matrimonio*, n. 768, p. 757; Gasparri, *De Matrimonio*, II, n. 1166.

[35] *Betrothment and Marriage* (2 ed. translated from 3rd Latin edition of 1920, 2 vols., by W. Dobell and A. Owens [Brugis: Beyaert, 1923-1925]), I, n. 341; Cappello, *De Matrimonio*, n. 786, p. 757, "Semel admissa, ut admittenda est in R. Pontifice potestate solvendi matrimonium etiam consummatum infidelium, necessarius non est specialis interventus immediatus et directus Christi D., et solutio vinculi optime explicatur vi potestatis extraordinariae ab ipso Christo concessae." Burton, *A Commentary on Canon 1125*, p. 85.

The value of the first opinion rested primarily on the Instruction of the Sacred Congregation, but, as was there indicated, the Instruction had no decisive or peremptory value, nor was it even an official interpretation of the Church. Cappello states[36] that in the Instruction the Pauline privilege was said to be divine only in a very general sense, namely insofar as it is found in the Sacred Scripture, and is, admittedly, in some way derived from Christ.

The admission of the validity of this second opinion makes it much easier to solve some very practical difficulties that would otherwise arise in trying to explain the actions of the Popes who have actually dissolved marriages which cannot in any way be brought within the limits of the Pauline privilege.[37] Writers who defend this Apostolic origin of the Pauline privilege hold, therefore, that objectively the obligation of making the interpellations is a formality demanded by ecclesiastical law, which can consequently give way to a dispensation under given circumstances.[38]

Both opinions are certainly probable, since they are both defended with solid arguments and by respected authorities. Although the opinion which favors the immediately divine origin of the privilege is still held by many authors today, the second thesis, namely that St. Paul both instituted and promulgated the privilege which bears his name, is supported with more convincing arguments and, so it appears to this writer, must rank as the preferable doctrine.

Section 3: Variation by d'Annibale

An exception to these two opinions is reflected in a third proposal offered exclusively by its author, d'Annibale (1815-1892), who, in considering the origin of the obligation to make the interpellations, made a distinction between the first and second interpellation. The first interpellation,

[36] *De Matrimonio*, n. 768, p. 758.

[37] Woeber, *The Interpellations*, p. 55; Cappello, *De Matrimonio*, n. 768, p. 757; Payen, *De Matrimonio*, II, n. 2210.

[38] Woeber, *op. cit.*, p. 55; Rudolph Ritter von Scherer, *Handbuch des Kirchensrechts* (2 vols., Graz, 1886-1898), II, n. 563.

relative to whether or not the infidel wished to receive baptism, was required by the divine law, and the other question, whether he wished to and intended to cohabit peacefully, was imposed only as an ecclesiastical precept.[39]

One can see little reason for the distinction; if, however, any distinction is to be made, then it seems more correct to reverse the order, for the very text of St. Paul postulates the departure of the infidel as a basis for the use of the privilege, not his unwillingness to be baptized. In fact, the Christian was obliged to accept his unbaptized spouse if the latter wished to continue peaceful cohabitation.[40] It appears, then, that the necessity of the second interpellation rather than that of the first should have to be considered as rooted in an immediately divine origin.[41]

Although the controversy is admittedly of little moment even theoretically, it does serve a practical advantage in that it furnishes a basis for determining the distinction in the terminology used with reference to the legitimate omission of the interpellations. It also will help in understanding the precise nature of the pontifical power involved in the dissolution of legitimate marriages through a dispensation from the interpellations in the cases considered in the papal constitutions mentioned in canon 1125.

Article III: Necessity of the Interpellations

In any consideration regarding the necessity of making the interpellations one ventures into a field of yet unsolved controversy. A history of the Pauline privilege shows that the dispute was raging already in the early 18th century, for it was then that a response of the Sacred Congregation of the Council acknowledged the opinion of those who held that there are times when the interpellations are not necessary either for the valid or for the licit use of the privilege.

[39] *Summula Theologiae Moralis* (5 ed., 3 vols., Romae, 1908), III, n. 476, p. 405; cf. Doheny, *Informal Procedure*, p. 517. See also Gregory, *The Pauline Privilege*, p. 67, for a critique of this theory.

[40] I Cor., VII: 12-13.

[41] Wernz-Vidal, *Ius Matrimoniale*, n. 632, note 68, p. 822.

The Congregation, however, urged the seeking of a dispensation in such circumstances.[42]

Shortly afterwards Pope Benedict XIV required either the making of the interpellations or the obtaining of a dispensation from them.[43] From that time onwards the Holy See has issued a series of responses and the canonists have offered a list of commentaries which in their number were rivaled only by the variety of opinions expressed. Post-Code commentators are equally unagreed, and one can safely say that there are no two writers who are even in substantial agreement on all points.

In any consideration regarding the necessity of making the interpellations it is essential to bear in mind the fundamental nature of the interpellations as outlined in Article I above, namely that they are essentially means and not ends, and to remember the distinction that has been made in Article II regarding the origin of the obligation to make the interpellations. All observations of the writer relative to the necessity of the interpellations will be made in the light of these two pre-requirements.

More proximately it is necessary to indicate certain distinctions under which the disputed necessity can be judged. One must distinguish between a valid and a licit use of the privilege; between the divine and the ecclesiastical law; between the one and the other of the two interpellations, as well as between the various canonical methods approved for the making of the interpellations. Furthermore, one must acknowledge the various sources of certitude relative to the intent or the departure of the unbaptized, and lastly determine whether or not the departure has *actually* taken place, irrespective of any knowledge regarding this fact on the side of the parties.

Does then the law which calls for the making of the interpellations urge always for the valid or at least for the licit use of the privilege? The answer will depend primarily on

[42] S.C.C., *Florentina,* 17 ian. 1722—*Collectio Resolutionum S.C.C.,* v. *Matrimonium,* § XIV, n. 3. Cf. Woeber, *The Interpellations,* p. 47.

[43] Const., *Apostolici ministerii,* 16 sept. 1747— *Fontes,* n. 381.

one's convictions regarding the origin of the obligation, whether, namely, it derives through the divine or the ecclesiastical law.

Section 1: For the Licit Use of the Pauline Privilege

A. Required by the Divine Law.

It is certainly not proved as a requirement of the divine law that the interpellations must always be made. No proof based on the nature of the Pauline privilege, or otherwise supported by solid reasoning, can be offered in this regard.[44] A number of authors, however, and primarily those who support the divine origin theory, contend that the interpellations are *ordinarily* required by the divine law. They base their proof principally on the assumption that regularly the employment of the interpellations furnishes the only way of establishing the required proof of the departure of the infidel, whether that departure be moral or physical.[45] This argument would be valid, if, *de facto*, their assumption were true.

As a proof from authority they offer a response of the Holy Office. In answer to the question whether the nonmalitious departure of the infidel wife gave the convert the right to enter a second marriage, the Sacred Congregation responded that under the given condition the convert was bound '*ex divino praecepto*' to make the interpellation.[46]

No objection can be drawn, so they say, from the fact that the Supreme Pontiff can dispense and has dispensed from the interpellations, so that thereupon one may conclude that

[44] Payen, *De Matrimonio*, II, n. 2350, p. 673; Doheny, *Informal Procedure*, p. 518.

[45] Doheny, *loc. cit.*; Payen, *De Matrimonio*, II, n. 2350, p. 674.

[46] S.C.S. Off. (Cochinchin. Occident.), 12 iun. 1850, "Conversum de quo agitur, si non est legitime ab Apostolica Sede dispensatus, teneri ex divino praecepto ad faciendam in praesenti casu una vice interpellationem ... Expleta autem a converso hac divinitus iniuncta conditione, si pagana uxor ad ipsum non redierit intra iustum aliquod et rationabile temporis spatium, posse praefatum conversum, licite et valide alias inire nuptias ..." *Fontes*, n. 910.

they do not derive from the divine law. Wernz-Vidal stated that such an objection is not valid, since the Popes can in many ways dispense from obligations which are divine in origin, e.g., from vows, or from ratified marriages.[47]

In this regard it is agreed that the interpellations here demanded need not be formal, but that only some private form is required and accordingly suffices.[48] The authors here state that at least some private form of interpellations is required by the divine law for the licit use of the privilege. In no way do they specify what they mean by the divine law. To this writer it seems clear that they are not referring to the divine positive law as laid down in the Epistle of St. Paul, but that they refer to a basic principle of the natural divine law, which gives to every person the right to be heard when his fundamental rights are under attack. In the case of the Pauline privilege two parties are involved in a contract, namely in the marriage contracted in infidelity. Before one of the parties can by means of the privilege dissolve that contract, the natural law requires that the other party be given the opportunity to defend or express his intent in this regard.

It was said that the interpellations are *generally* required for the licit use of the privilege, for these same authors are in common agreement that the obligation is not *always* binding. If the departure or the evil intent of the unbaptized consort is certain, then the same divine natural law or natural equity has been satisfied, and the interrogation is no longer required from this source.[49]

As main support for this position the argument is based on the very nature of the privilege, which postulates the deliberate departure of the infidel as the essential condition for its application, and natural justice is satisfied if it is known in some way that the infidel has made known his

[47] *Ius Matrimoniale*, n. 632, note 68, p. 823.

[48] Cappello, *De Matrimonio*, n. 776, p. 766; Doheny *Informal Procedure*, p. 518.

[49] Cappello, *De Matrimonio*, n. 776, p. 766; Payen, *De Matrimonio*, II, n. 2350, p. 674; Doheny, *Informal Procedure*, p. 518.

position. If this departure is not only a fact but is even proved externally, then certainly one need not by divine law seek the additional proof that is gained by means of the interpellations.

Payen, admittedly strict in this regard, is slow to indicate that the interpellations are not always a *sine quo non medium* for the proving of the departure of the infidel. When real certainty and not mere presumption of this desertion is had from the words or actions of the infidel, the interpellations are no longer required by the divine law.[50] Payen further admits that the response of the Holy Office quoted earlier in his support can hardly be interpreted to mean that the interpellations, divinely enjoined, are *always* of divine obligation.[51]

On the other hand the same Holy Office has explicitly stated that there are circumstances in which the interpellations are not binding:

> "... etiam in casu quod coniux infidelis in longinquas abierit regiones, aut ita latitet ut interpellari nequeat, adhuc opus esse dispensatione Summi Pontificis, cuius est declarare in quibusnam circumstantiis desinat obligare praeceptum divinum quo praedicta interpellatio videtur iniuncta."[52]

The making of the interpellations, at least in a private, informal manner, is required by the natural divine law for the licit use of the Pauline privilege in those cases wherein the departure of the infidel has not been made clear by some other means. This *departure* can result not only from the fact of the physical separation of the parties to the marriage contracted in infidelity, but also from the state of mind of the infidel regarding his intentions toward his converted

[50] *De Matrimonio*, II, n. 2350, p. 674; Wernz-Vidal, *Ius Matrimoniale*, n. 632, note 68, p. 823.

[51] *Loc. cit.*; cf. *supra*, pp. 94, 99.

[52] S.C.S. Off., instr. (ad Archiep. Quebecen.) 16 Sept. 1824, ad 3—*Fontes*, n. 866, quoted in Payen, *De Matrimonio*, II, n. 2350, and Doheny, *Informal Procedure*, p. 519.

spouse specifically relative to the possibility of resumed cohabitation. As the above-quoted Instruction of the Holy See indicates, it pertains to the Holy See to determine the cases in which that state of mind may be considered as sufficiently established.

B. Required by the Ecclesiastical Law

The universal law of the Church states explicitly that the interpellations must always be made, except in those cases wherein the Holy See has declared otherwise.[53] The ecclesiastical law is, therefore, of a disjunctive character. For the licit use of the Pauline privilege it requires either that the interpellations be made, or that a dispensation from them be obtained in those cases in which there is a sufficient cause approved by the Church.[54] This is the overwhelming concensus of authority.[55]

In the consideration of whether or not the interpellations were required by the divine law for licitness in the procedure a distinction was made between the cases in which the departure and evil intent of the infidel were already well established, and the cases in which such proof was not yet certain. No such distinction is made in Church law, and this stand has been the constant teaching since the time of Pope Benedict XIV, who in 1747 declared that in practice there could no longer be safely held the opinion which al-

[53] Canon 1121, § 1,—Hae interpellationes fieri semper debent, nisi Sedes Apostolica aliud declaraverit.

[54] Payen, *De Matrimonio*, II, n. 2351, p. 675.

[55] Woeber, *The Interpellations*, p. 58; Gasparri, *De Matrimonio*, II, n. 1142; Burton, *A Commentary on Canon 1125*, pp. 91, 92, 97; Coronata, *De Matrimonio*, n. 631, p. 883; Doheny, *Informal Procedure*, p. 519; Cappello, *De Matrimonio*, nn. 776-777; Wernz-Vidal, *Ius Matrimoniale*, n. 632; Winslow, *The Pauline Privilege*, p. 16; Vermeersch-Creusen, *Epitome*, II, n. 430, p. 297; Bouscaren-Ellis, *Canon Law: A Text and Commentary*, p. 551; Chelodi, *Ius Matrimoniale*, n. 158; De Smet, *De Sponsalibus et Matrimonio*, n. 351, p. 298; Petrovits, *The New Church Law on Matrimony*, n. 560; G. Vromant, *Ius Missionariarum*, Tom. V, *De Matrimonio*, n. 327, p. 253.

lowed the omission of the interpellations.[56] Later on Pope Clement XIV (1769-1774) warned against indulging frivolous presumptions to the end that the interpellations might be omitted.[57]

From that time it is certain from many decrees and responses that there is no cause sufficiently grave to allow the omission of the formality of making the interpellations. In the words of Burton, "however great the distance or the difficulty of making the interpellations, whatever the danger involved or whatever persuasion or certainty may exist that it will be useless to make the interpellations, their omission will not be *licit* without the declaration of the Holy See."[58] Thus neither impossibility, nor danger, nor inutility suffices to allow the licit omission of the interpellations.[59]

Authors are just as generally agreed that the obligation binds even when the deliberate departure of the infidel consort is not only known but proved. Vermeersch-Creusen wrote: "Ideoque ... etiam si de facto discessus constet, non omittenda est [interpellatio]."[60] Cappello teaches: "Sancta Sedes urget instanter necessitatem interpellationis, etiam pro casu quo haec inutilis videtur vel difficilis aut moraliter impossibilis, itemque quando constat aliunde de partis infidelis discessu."[61] De Smet stated: "Omnes in hac conveniunt, ad licitum usum privilegii omnino requiri interpellationem ... etiam pro casu quo ... constat de discessu

[56] "Missionarios ... non satis tutam in praxi appellare opinionem illam quae ponit iudicialem interpellationem licite omitti posse quoties aut fieri reipsa nequit, aut, si fierit, nullius utilitatis fore reputatur." *De Synodo Dioecesana,* lib. XIII, cap. XXI, n. 6, Cf. Chapter III, Article I of this dissertation. Also, S.C.S. Off. (ad Archiep. Quebecen.), 16 sept. 1824, ad 3—*Fontes,* n. 866.

[57] S.C.S. Off. (Chen-si et Chan-si), 23 nov. 1769—*Fontes,* n. 825.

[58] *A Commentary on Canon 1125,* p. 92.

[59] Vromant, *De Matrimonio,* n. 327, p. 253: "... neque per se excusat impossibilitas, inutilitas, vel periculum;" Payen, *De Matrimonio,* II, n. 2351, p. 675; Doheny, *Informal Procedure,* p. 519; Cappello, *De Matrimonio,* n. 776, p. 766.

[60] *Epitome,* II, n. 430, p. 297.

[61] *De Matrimonio,* n. 776, p. 766.

compartis infidelis."[62] Woeber considers a very practical case when he considers the question in point: "One may state, therefore, that even if there is a presumption born of facts which offers moral certainty of departure, as for example, when there exists a civil divorce procured by the unbeliever and a second attempted marriage already effected by him, the interpellations must nevertheless be made for the licit use of the Pauline privilege, or a dispensation from them must be obtained."[63]

Although Bouscaren-Ellis[64] are in agreement with this common teaching, they conclude that the contrary doctrine as defended by several authors is probable. They list Wernz-Vidal as holding that the ecclesiastical law allows the omission of the interpellations if the departure is sufficiently proved. In the passage to which Bouscaren-Ellis refer, Wernz-Vidal answered a question proposed in the preceding paragraph, in which they had discussed the obligation arising from the *divine* law. In the immediately following paragraph they asserted that the interpellations are to be made or a legitimate dispensation obtained; they were in harmony with the common teaching when they wrote: "... porro in canone 1121, tamquam unica causa excusans ab interpellatione ponitur *declaratio* in contrarium S. Sedis."[65]

De Smet indicates that the obligation to make the interpellations is satisfied if they are made privately. It is not necessary that they be formal or judicial.[66]

The Code today recognizes this in that it allows the private interpellations for the valid and licit use of the privilege as long as the formal, extrajudicial interpellations

[62] *De Sponsalibus et Matrimonio*, n. 351, p. 298.

[63] *The Interpellations*, p. 59; cf. also Gasparri, *De Matrimonio*, II, n. 1142; Coronata, *De Matrimonio*, n. 631, p. 883; Burton, *A Commentary on Canon 1125*, p. 97.

[64] *Canon Law: A Text and Commentary*, p. 551.

[65] *Ius Matrimoniale*, n. 632, note 68, p. 824; cf. Canon 1121, § 2.

[66] *De Sponsalibus et Matrimonio*, n. 351, p. 298; cf. Cappello, *De Matrimonio*, n. 776, p. 766.

cannot be made.[67] However, the obligation extends to the making of both interpellations to the extent that both must be made for the sake of lawfulness in the procedure.[68]

The only exceptions to the rule are the cases in which the Holy See has declared that the interpellations need not be made. One such case is explicitly excepted from the universal law which otherwise requires the interpellations, and that is the provision of canon 1125, which provides for the omission of the interpellations or for a dispensation from them. This canon shall receive considerable attention throughout this dissertation.

An important and practical reason for requiring the interpellations under pain of illicitness is the consideration of due order and control in the use of the privilege. For, otherwise, there would always be the danger of omitting the interpellations without sufficient proof of the *discessus* of the infidel,[69] with the constant danger of subsequently invalid marriages.[70]

Since the departure of the infidel is the absolute condition for the use of the Pauline privilege, the Holy See has reserved to itself the final judgment on what is and what is not sufficient proof of departure, and consequently on what is and what is not a sufficient cause for the requesting and the granting of a dispensation from the interpellations.[71]

[67] Canon 1122, § 2.

[68] Vromant, *De Matrimonio,* n. 327, p. 253.

[69] "Finis quoque legis praescribendo et urgendo interpellationes, est praecise ut indubie et authentice, absque periculo hallucinationis, constet circa conditionem 'discessus' divinitus impositam ad usum privilegii."—Vromant, *De Matrimonio,* nn. 328-329, nn. 254-256.

[70] "Quod praeceptum ecclesiasticum interpellationes praescribens etiam pro casibus in quibus aliunde de discessione partis infidelis constare potest, latum est ad evitandum periculum ne certus dicatur discessus infidelis, qui de facto certus non est et forte non exsistit, cum periculo contrahendi invalide novi matrimonii." Coronata, *De Matrimonio,* n. 631, p. 883.

[71] "Proinde, licet cesset per se necessitas interpellandi a) si de obstinatione infidelis certo moraliter constet; b) si fieri nequeat absque gravi difficultate aut periculo gravi, v.g. fidelium aut interpellantis, vel si omnino fieri non possit; tamen haec in aestimatione R. Pontificis

Thus, although the interpellations are required by the universal law of the Church for the licit use of the privilege in all cases, the Holy See may, and does, declare that in certain circumstances the interpellations need not be made, and the licit omission depends on such a declaration.[72]

Section 2: For the Valid Use of The Pauline Privilege

A. Required by the Divine Law

There is an even greater disagreement among commentators as to whether the interpellations are required for the valid application of the Pauline privilege. This diversity is carried over even from pre-Code authors. It relates likewise to whether the necessity of the interpellations arises from the divine or the ecclesiastical law.

By way of introduction it is to be noted that the distinction between the first and the second interpellations is clearly insisted on at this point. The omission of only the first interpellation, "whether the infidel wishes to be converted and receive baptism," does not invalidate the use of the Pauline privilege as long as the unbaptized consort has answered negatively to the second question regarding the continuance or the resumption of peaceful cohabitation.[73] This would be true also in the case wherein the second interpellation had been legitimately dispensed with.

This distinction is reasonably based on the nature of the privilege, for nowhere did St. Paul require the conversion of the infidel; for the use of the privilege he postulated simply the fact of the infidel's deliberate departure. The great controversy, therefore, centers about the omission of

---

esse debent, qui in re tam gravi iudicium facti sibi reservat; quod cum prodiit, improprie dispensare dicitur. Unde iudicium facti etiam in hisce casibus reservatur Sedi Apostolicae." Cappello, *De Matrimonio*, n. 776, pp. 766-767; cf. De Smet, *De Sponsalibus et Matrimonio*, n. 351, p. 298.

[72] Burton, *A Commentary on Canon 1125*, p. 94.

[73] Vromant, *De Matrimonio*, nn. 328-329, pp. 254-6; Doheny, *Informal Procedure*, pp. 519-520.

that interpellation which seeks to reveal the intention of the infidel concerning this necessary point, namely, whether or not the infidel is willing to cohabit peacefully with the convert without giving offense to God, and without jeopardizing the newly won Faith of that convert.

This departure of the infidel, as it was contemplated by St. Paul, could be physical or moral, as has been indicated. The separation is obviously physical if the infidel refuses to or actually cannot cohabit. If he is willing to cohabit, but will do so only maliciously by blaspheming God or tempting the convert, the latter is no longer bound to keep his infidel partner, who then has in effect separated morally. It is evident that this second kind of separation is a factor that is more difficult to prove.

There are three opinions as to whether the divine law demands the making of the second interpellation as a requirement for the valid use of the privilege.

The first opinion simply states that the interpellation is *never* required for the validity. Granted that a marriage has been contracted by two unbaptized people, and that one of them has subsequently received baptism, then only one other condition is required for the convert validly to enter a second marriage, and that condition is the fact of the deliberate and malicious desertion of the party remaining in infidelity. No proof is required as long as the departure has actually taken place after the baptism of the convert party. Payen here made a comparison with a parallel case recognized in Canon Law. Just as the validity of a new marriage which without the use of the Pauline privilege has been contracted upon the dissolution of an earlier valid marriage does not depend on the proof of the death of the former spouse, whether that proof was actually furnished or altogether neglected, but upon the objective and true fact of death, so also the validity of a new marriage contracted with the use of the Pauline privilege does not depend on the proof but upon the objective fact of the departure.[74]

[74] Payen, *De Matrimonio*, II, n. 2353, pp. 677-678.

This opinion is strongly defended by other authors, among whom are Wernz-Vidal,[75] Cappello,[76] Vromant,[77] Chelodi,[78] Vermeersch-Creusen,[79] Bouscaren,[80] and likewise Bouscaren-Ellis,[81] Woeber[82] and Coronata.[83]

In this regard Burton[84] has summarized the teaching of this opinion in the words, "as long as it is clear, either from adequate questions privately asked or from other evidence, that the *discessus* has certainly taken place after the baptism of the convert party, divine law does not require the formal interpellation." In other words, St. Paul required only one condition for the valid use of the privilege, namely, the *discessus* of the infidel. The proof of this departure

[75] *Ius Matrimoniale,* n. 632, note 68: "Quo in casu valor matrimonii non pendet a probatione mortis bene facta vel neglecta, sed ab obiectiva veritate mortis."

[76] *De Matrimonio,* n. 777, p. 767: "Si discessus coniugis infidelis est certus, et interpellatio illegitime omissa fuerit, secundum matrimonium partis fidelis invalidum videtur, et quidem, ut opinamur, ex *solo iure positivo Ecclesiae."*

[77] *De Matrimonio,* nn. 328-329, pp. 254-6: "Etsi, attento solo iure divino, condicio privilegii Paulini sit *discessus,* non eiusdem probatio, propter ius tamen *ecclesiasticum,* omissis interpellationibus, usus privilegii nobis videtur invalidus, ac matrimonium subsequens irritum declarandum."

[78] *Ius Matrimoniale,* n. 158, p. 173; Payen (*De Matrimonio* II, n. 2353, note 3) lists also d'Annibale (*Summula,* II, n. 476, p. 405), as do also Doheny (*Informal Procedure,* p. 520, n. 15) and Wernz-Vidal (*Ius Matrimoniale,* n. 632, note 68, p. 824), but this important work of d'Annibale was not available to the writer for consultation.

[79] *Epitome,* II, n. 430, p. 297.

[80] "An Inquiry into the Practical Application," *Miscellanea-Vermeersch,* I, p. 289: "If the departure of the infidel is morally certain *aliunde,* it is certain that the divine law does not demand the interpellation."

[81] *Canon Law: A Text and Commentary,* p. 551.

[82] *The Interpellations,* p. 61.

[83] *De Matrimonio,* n. 631, p. 884: "Quippe S. Paulus de interpellationibus qua talibus non loquitur et ad usum privilegii fidei quod ipse concedit vel promulgat nihil amplius requiret quam discessus partis infidelis."

[84] *A Commentary on Canon 1125,* p. 95.

is a factor that pertains to the licitness, but not to the validity, of the use of the privilege.

The second opinion states that the second interpellation is *regularly* necessary for validity, for it is ordinarily the prescribed means for determining and proving the departure of the infidel. It is argued that not only the fact but also some proof of the departure of the infidel is understood in the words of St. Paul: "Quod si infidelis discedit, discedat."[85]

By these words St. Paul did not grant the right of validly entering a second marriage unless the convert was certain of the departure of which the words spoke. For St. Paul certainly did not wish to grant this tremendous privilege to the convert who would act temerariously and thus run the risk of entering an invalid marriage.

Held earlier by Sanchez,[86] this theory was later supported by Gasparri when he wrote:

> "Nam ex verbis Apostoli evidens est fidei privilegium esse *conditionatum*: coniux enim conversus potest ad alias transire nuptias *si* coniux infidelis renuat converti ad fidem aut saltem pacifice cohabitare sine contumelia Creatoris. De impleta igitur conditione constare debet, ut coniux conversus possit ad alia vota convolare."[87]

De Smet[88] expressly stated that the interpellation is *regularly* required by the divine law as the prescribed ordinary means of determining the necessary condition for the privilege, but he just as clearly stated that it is *not always* required. Though Vlaming (d.1935) appeared somewhat indefinite, it seems that one may consider him as having supported this second opinion.[89] Doheny lists Vermeersch and Burton as subscribing to the opinion.[90] Actually these

85 I Cor., VII: 15.

86 *De Sancto Matrimonii Sacramento,* Lib. VII, disp. LXXIV, nn. 12-13.

87 *De Matrimonio,* II, n. 1140, p. 212.

88 *De Sponsalibus et Matrimonio,* n. 351, p. 299.

89 *Praelectiones,* II, n. 722, p. 322, note 1.

90 *Informal Procedure,* p. 520, note 16.

two authors in the passages referred to in the reference are speaking of the obligation arising not from the divine but from the ecclesiastical law. This is evident from the fact that in the context both are speaking explicitly of the obligation imposed by the canons of the Code. On the other hand, when he speaks of the divine law obligation, Burton explicitly states that the interpellation is not required when it is clear that the *discessus* has taken place.[91] And Vermeersch does not professedly speak of the divine law in his consideration of the obligation.[92] But in the *Epitome* with Creusen he also states expressly: "Ubi discessus vel detrectata honesta cohabitatio *certa* sunt, S. Sedes a lege ecclesiastica interpellationum, *quae iure divino tunc non sunt necessariae,* dispensare potest."[93] According to this second opinion the interpellation must be made whenever there is doubt as to the fact of the departure of the infidel, for this interpellation is the ordinary means of solving that doubt.[94]

The third opinion claims that the divine law demands the interpellation *in every case* under pain of nullity, so that it must *always* be made without any exceptions. This theory, too, according to its defenders, has its basis in the text of St. Paul, and Rosset (1830-1902) claimed that this "opinion is certain and common."[95]

Basically, the opinion is held by those who insist that the privilege itself is of an immediate divine origin. Consequently they hold that not only the departure of the infidel but the proof of that departure through the use of the interpellations is required by the divine law and the nature of the privilege for the valid use of that privilege. As before, so now they quote responses of the Holy See[96] for their sup-

[91] *A Commentary on Canon 1125*, p. 95.

[92] *Theologia Moralis*, III, n. 755, p. 691.

[93] II, n. 430, p. 297.

[94] Woeber, *op. cit.*, p. 60.

[95] Rosset, cited in Payen, *De Matrimonio*, II, n. 2353, note 3, p. 678, notes 1 and 2, p. 679.

[96] S.C.S. Off. instr. (ad Archiep. Quebecen.) 16 sept. 1824, ad 3—*Fontes*, n. 866; (Siam), 14 iul. 1855—*Fontes*, n. 931; (Portland), 18 iun. 1884—*Fontes*, n. 1088.

port, but now, as then, it is certain that these documents are not definitive nor do they even "treat of this question *ex professo*,"[97] nor is it beyond question whether the responses speak of the divine or the ecclesiastical law.

De Becker stated that the interpellation is required by divine law for validity, but he does not any more qualify his statement in order to determine precisely under what conditions it is so required.[98]

Petrovits, writing shortly after the promulgation of the Code, is in his comment typical of the early post-Code commentators:

> "Ballerini maintains that the interpellation is prescribed for the purpose of ascertaining the will of the unconverted consort, but that the validity of the second marriage depends exclusively on the willingness or unwillingness of the infidel spouse to cohabit with the converted spouse *sine contumelia Creatoris*. This opinion can no longer be advocated, for even the former discipline inculcated the necessity of the interpellation as a duty originating from the divine precept and insisted on it, even if the infidel party publicly repudiated the converted consort."[99]

Although he does not speak explicitly of the divine law, yet it is sufficiently clear from the context that Gregory also demands that the interpellation be made always regardless of what mitigating circumstances may exist.[100] Again, Doheny[101] lists De Smet in this category; actually, as has been noted above, this author expressly stated that the interpellation is not always required for validity.[102]

[97] Woeber, *The Interpellations*, p. 60; cf. also *ibid.*, pp. 27 and 51.

[98] "A Criticism of Wernz-Vidal, *Ius Matrimoniale*," in *Ephemerides Theologicae Lovanienses*, II (1925), 271-275.

[99] *The New Church Law on Matrimony*, n. 560, p. 403.

[100] *The Pauline Privilege*, p. 67.

[101] *Informal Procedure*, p. 520, note 17.

[102] "... non autem exigere jus divinum ut interpellatio fiat *semper*, etiam ubi aliunde probe constat de conditionis verificatione." *De Sponsalibus et Matrimonio*, n. 351, p. 299.

Each of the three opinions concerning the problem of whether or not the divine law requires the second interpellation for validity has supported arguments. In this summary critique the writer reverses the order previously followed in the presenting of the arguments.

The third opinion states that the interpellation is *always* required for the valid use of the Pauline privilege. If, then, this is true, Wernz-Vidal ask how the Holy Father could possibly grant a *sanatio in radice* in any event to validate a second marriage entered into upon a supposed use of the Pauline privilege without the making of the interpellation.[103]

This evidently could not be done unless the marriage validly contracted in infidelity had been dissolved in some way or other. Therefore, if the omission of the interpellation even in a case wherein the pertinacious obstinacy of the infidel was known stood in the way of the validity of the second marriage, how can one explain that in such a case the Holy See has answered that the parties in the second and invalid marriage were not to be disturbed?[104] Surely the interpellation could not be easily set aside if it were required absolutely by the divine law or in very consequence of the nature of the privilege. It seems, therefore, that one cannot demand that the interpellation be always required by the nature of the Pauline privilege or from the text of St. Paul.

The second opinion asserts that the interpellation is ordinarily necessary for validity since it is the regular means of establishing moral certitude concerning the fact of the unbeliever's ill will and departure. Payen pointed out that the authors who hold this opinion are confusing the issue by using the same arguments to prove that the interpellation is necessary for validity that they used to prove its re-

[103] *Ius Matrimoniale*, n. 632, note 68, p. 824.

[104] S.C. de Prop. Fide (C.P. pro Sin-Sutchuen) 5 mart. 1787: "Quaestio: Num validum sit matrimonium cum secunda uxore initum ubi omissa fuit interpellatio? ... Resp: Attentis circumstantiis, de quibus agitur, non esse inquietandos."—*Fontes*, n. 4615; cf. Burton, *A Commentary on Canon 1125*, p. 96.

quirement for licitness. Their argument does indeed prove that the interpellation is required for licitness, but it does not prove that the same requirements exist for validity.[105] And Wernz-Vidal added, "Isti auctores non satis distinguunt *factum obiectivum* discessus ab eius *probatione* per interpellationem, neque ex textibus allegatis efficaci modo probant absolutam nullitatem actus."[106] This was also stated by Ballerini-Palmieri: "Tota ratio adversariorum consistit in confusione: confundunt enim *existentiam* conditionis cum *scientia huius* existentiae."[107]

The first opinion which demands only the fact of the departure of the infidel for the valid use of the Pauline privilege seems by far to be the most probable; Payen, quoting Pesch, calls it "most reasonable."[108] And if one considers objectively the words of St. Paul, it is the most consistent and logical interpretation, and in the light of the great support of the authors it is both common and certain that the divine law *never* demands either of the two interpellations for the valid application of the Pauline privilege.[109]

B. Required by the Ecclesiastical Law

As was indicated in an earlier article, the Church certainly demands the interpellations for the licit use of the Pauline privilege, yet it is not equally certain that the Church requires them for validity. The teaching of the Church on the necessity of making the interpellations is to be found in the decrees and responses of the Sacred Congregations as well as in the codified law of the Church in the sacred canons. First, then, there are to be investigated these sources, which offer a first hand knowledge of the Church's stand, and then there is to be undertaken an analysis of them in the light of the commentators.

[105] Payen, *De Matrimonio*, II, n. 2353; cf. also *ibid.*, n. 2350.

[106] *Ius Matrimoniale*, n. 632, note 68, p. 824.

[107] n. 435, in fine, quoted in Payen, *De Matrimonio*, II, n. 2353, footnote, p. 678.

[108] *De Matrimonio*, II, n. 2353, note 4, p. 679.

[109] Woeber, *The Interpellations*, p. 61, note 93.

The Sacred Congregations, both in their statement of general principles and in their solution of particular cases have either explicitly or implicitly taught that the omission of the interpellations without any concomitant dispensation renders a second marriage invalid, since the bond of the marriage contracted in infidelity still perseveres, and is, therefore, an obstacle to the validity of any further marriage.[110] An illustration of these instructions is had in a response of the Holy Office; to the question: "An defectus interpellationis aut Pontificiae dispensationis, praeter illiceitatem, etiam nullitatem matrimonii dein contracti, secum ferat?" This Sacred Congregation answered briefly: "Affirmative."[111]

In yet another case the Holy See stated the general and accepted principle that good faith "is never sufficient to make valid a marriage that was entered into with a diriment impediment," and then it applied this principle to a case wherein a marriage had been contracted without the previous making of the interpellations: "Thus, if anyone goes to some other country and, after having been instructed and baptized, marries a Christian without having interpellated his first and legitimate consort, he is bound to do so, unless there is sufficient cause for allowing a dispensation, as has been provided for in the Synod of Suchow."[112]

From this it is certain that the Holy Office demands the making of the interpellation as a necessary means for the removal of the obstacle of the first marriage bond; in other words, the interpellation is needed as a necessary preparation for the validity of the second marriage.[113]

[110] S.C.S. Off., instr. (ad Superior. Mission. Peguan.), 11 iun. 1760—*Fontes*, n. 811; S.C.S. Off. (Chen-si et Chan-si), 23 nov. 1769—*Fontes*, n. 825, *Coll. S.C.P.F.*, n. 475; S.C.S. Off., instr. (Ad Archiep. Quebecen.), 16 sept. 1824—*Fontes*, n. 866, *Coll. S.C.P.F.*, n. 784; S.C.S. Off. (Coreae), 11 sept. 1878—*Fontes*, n. 1057, *Coll. S.C.P.F.*, n. 1499; S.C. Prop. de Fide, (Sutchuen.), 17 ian, 1836—*Coll. S.C.P.F.*, n. 845.

[111] S.C.S. Off., 10 sept. 1856, quoted in Payen, *De Matrimonio*, II, n. 2354, page 680, 1°.

[112] S.C.S. Off. (Siam), 4 iul. 1855—*Fontes*, n. 931.

[113] Payen, *De Matrimonio*, II, n. 2354, p. 681.

In its handling of particular cases the Holy See has obviously invoked distinctions. In three cases wherein the interpellations had been omitted and in which no proof of the *discessus* of the infidel had been derived from any other sources, the Holy See answered that the second marriages were invalid.[114]

However, in a case where the departure was known and proven the interpellation was omitted since the will and intent of the infidel was considered to have been sufficiently evident. In this case the Sacred Congregation for the Propagation of the Faith answered that the parties to the second marriage were not to be disquieted, thus attesting to the validity of this second marriage.[115]

A Rota decision in 1925 upholds the opinion that the interpellations are required for the validity of the second marriage at least where the departure of the unbaptized consort is not proved from some other source. For after the marriage of two Christians the wife learned that the man, before his baptism, had been married to a pagan woman who was still alive at the time of the second marriage. Nullity of the second marriage was declared on proof of these facts, and of the fact that neither had the interpellations been made nor had a dispensation from them been obtained.[116]

It is to be noted, further, that the Holy See has refused to grant *sanationes in radice* for marriages contracted without either the interpellations or a dispensation from them,

[114] S.C. de Prop. Fide (C.P. Pro Sin. Tunk. Occid.), 5 mart. 1816—*Coll. S.C.P.F.*, n. 704; S.C.S. Off. (Pondichery), 20 iun. 1858—*Fontes*, n. 947; S.C.S. Off., 8 mart. 1816, cited in Payen, *De Matrimonio*, II, n. 2353 (not in *Fontes*).

[115] S.C. de Prop. Fide (C.P. pro Sin-Sutchuen.), 5 mart. 1787—*Coll. S.C.P.F.*, n. 589.

[116] S. Romana Rota, *Vicariatus Apostolici de Wonsan*, nullitatis matrimonii, coram R.P.D. Maximo Massimi, Pro-Decano, 5 dec. 1925—*S. Romanae Rotae Decisiones seu Sententiae ab anno 1909* (Romae: Typis Polyglottis Vaticanis), XVII (1925), 396-399 (hereafter cited *Decisiones Rotae*). Quoted in Bouscaren, *The Canon Law Digest*, II, p. 341.

and has demanded a renewal of consent between the parties.[117]

A *sanatio* was granted, however, in a case wherein the interpellations were not entirely omitted, though in themselves they were judged insufficient.[118]

The text of the Code seems to be just as clear in demanding the making of the interpellations for the valid use of the privilege. Canon 1121 states:

> §1. Antequam coniux conversus et baptizatus novum matrimonium valide contrahat, debet, salvo praescripto canon 1125, partem non baptizatam interpellare:
>
> 1°. An velit et ipsa converti ac baptismum suscipere;
>
> 2°. An saltem velit secum cohabitare pacifice sine contumelia Creatoris.
>
> §2. Hae interpellationes fieri semper debent, nisi Sedes Apostolica aliud declaraverit.

Canon 1123 adds:

> Si interpellationes ex declaratione Sedis Apostolicae omissae fuerint, aut si infidelis eisdem negative responderit expresse vel tacite, pars baptizata ius habet novas nuptias cum person Catholica contrahendi...

The wording of these canons seems to indicate that, without a doubt, the Church not only considers the objective fact of the infidel's desertion as a condition for the valid application of the Pauline privilege but also requires proof of that desertion through the making of the interpellations. The right to enter a second marriage would depend then on the making of the interpellations or the obtaining of a legitimate dispensation from them.[119]

[117] S.C.S. Off. (Coreae), 11 sept. 1878, ad 1—*Fontes*, n. 1057; *Coll. S.C.P.F.*, n. 1499.

[118] S.C. de Prop. Fide (Sutchuen.), 17 ian. 1836—*Fontes*, n. 4760; *Coll. S.C.P.F.*, n. 845.

[119] Gasparri, *De Matrimonio*, II, n. 1140: "Ab exposita doctrina Apostoli et Innocentii III ... manifeste sequitur privilegium fidei se-

The intent and import of the text seem at first glance to be so clearly evident that they have led some recent authors to state simply and unconditionally that the interpellations are always required by ecclesiastical law for the valid use of the Pauline privilege.[120] This attitude, in fact, seems hardly defensible. Notwithstanding the decrees and responses of the Holy See and the wording of the canons, not all the authors feel sure that the precise text of the canons is so explicit as to remove all doubt that all marriages contracted in violation of the canons are thereby rendered certainly invalid.[121]

These authors are not merely assuming their position but offer solid arguments to support their contention. In the first place, one cannot give the force of definition to the In-

cumferre disciplina interpellationum praemittendarum." Cf. Bouscaren, "An inquiry into the Practical Application of Canon 1125," *Miscellanea-Vermeersch,* I, 279-302, and especially p. 289.

[120] Doheny, *Informal Procedure,* p. 520, "From the point of view of the ecclesiastical law there is unanimity of opinion that the provisions of canon 1121 must be conscientiously observed ... This is a strict obligation which always binds *sub gravi.*" The writer feels certain that Doheny is here contemplating the factor of licitness, not of validity, though this statement occurs under a heading that points to the consideration of validity. If not, he would find it most difficult to defend his statement; he offers no authorities to substantiate his claim to the "unanimity of opinion." Romani, *De Matrimonio,* n. 1147; Gregory, *The Pauline Privilege,* p. 69; De Becker, "Criticism of Charles Augustine's *Rights and Duties of the Ordinaries According to the Code and Apostolic Faculties*" (St. Louis: B. Herder Book Company, 1924)—*ETL,* II (1925), 444, "The interpellations are required by the ecclesiastical law, and that as a condition for the validity of the second marriage." Cf. Petrovits, *The New Church Law on Matrimony,* n. 560.

[121] Coronata, *De Matrimonio,* n. 631, pp. 884-885; Payen, *De Matrimonio,* II, n. 2355; Vermeersch, *Theologia Moralis,* III, n. 755, p. 691; Cappello, *De Matrimonio,* n. 777, p. 767; Wernz-Vidal, *Ius Matrimoniale,* n. 632, note 68, p. 825; Chelodi, *Ius Matrimoniale,* n. 158; De Smet, *De Sponsalibus et Matrimonio,* n. 352; Vlaming, *Praelectiones,* II, n. 722, p. 322, note 1; Vermeersch-Creusen, *Epitome,* II, n. 430, p. 298; Bouscaren-Ellis, *Canon Law: A Text and Commentary,* n. 551; Burton, *A Commentary on Canon 1125,* p. 97; Woeber, *The Interpellations,* p. 62.

structions of the Holy See referred to above.[122] Thus Cappello states that one cannot gather a decisive, certain and undisputed argument from the responses of the Holy See, since they spoke only in generalities concerning the necessity of the interpellations or were given as answers in individual and particular cases, and did not refer specifically to the cases in which the interpellations are useless or impossible or where the departure of the infidel is already determined.[123] Wernz-Vidal state simply that the quoted text in no way prove the absolute nullity of the second marriage.[124] Burton agrees that "these together do not give incontrovertible proof."[125]

Coronata holds that these decrees of the Holy See can best be interpreted as demanding the necessity of the interpellations for the *licit* use of the privilege, or even for the *valid* use of the privilege if in this latter instance the interpretation be restricted to the cases where the interpellations are *de facto* necessary, not only as a means of verifying the departure of the infidel party, but also as a means of determining from that party the reason for his departure, which knowledge could not otherwise be had, at least not with certainty. No decisive argument can be drawn from the decree of the Holy Office under date of the 17th of January 1900, for this decree merely stated that the particular marriage in question, which had been contracted in infidelity, continued in existence inasmuch as the new marriage had been contracted by the convert party apart from any previous interpellations, and upon later investigation it appeared that the deserted infidel wife was unwilling to adopt the Faith or to make any response to interpellations. All are ready to grant that there cannot be any valid use of the privilege when there is no willful and malicious desertion of the convert by his unbaptized consort. In other words, the

[122] Cf. *supra*, pp. 94, 99, 114.

[123] *De Matrimonio*, n. 777, p. 767.

[124] *Ius Matrimoniale*, n. 632, note 68, p. 824: "... neque ex textibus allegatis efficaci modo [auctores] probant absolutam *nullitatem actus*."

[125] *A Commentary on Canon 1125*, p. 96.

decree under consideration in no way proves that the ecclesiastical law demands the making of the interpellations in every instance for the valid use of the Pauline privilege.[126]

Bouscaren-Ellis see in the cited decision of the Rota a proof that the Church does not require the interpellation of the infidel for the valid use of the privilege as long as the departure and evil intent of that infidel are known from other sources.[127]

Similar authority and argument is offered for affirming that even when subjected to close scrutiny the text of the canons is not so definite and explicit as not to admit of exceptions. Thus Payen stated that at first glance the words of canons 1121, 1122, and 1123 seem to favor the interpretation which always demands the interpellations for the valid use of the privilege, but that if they be examined carefully, it becomes evident that these words were purposely chosen as a means to urge the making of the interpellations without, however, clearly demanding them in every case.[128]

Woeber indicates that according to this interpretation the words of these canons are to be understood in the sense that they require the interpellations unless the fact of desertion be known and proved in some other way, and that, "though canon 1121 says: 'Hae interpellationes semper fieri debent . . . ', it does not add an annulling clause, and finally that it seems that the legislator purposely omitted such a clause."[129]

Coronata staunchly defends the opinion that for licitness of procedure the law of the Code demands the interpellations in all cases, but that for validity it requires them only

[126] Coronata, *De Matrimonio,* n. 631, p. 885.

[127] *Canon Law: A Text and Commentary,* p. 551.

[128] "Sed, re penitus inspecta, videntur haec eadem verba caute electa ad consequendum hoc duplex propositum: urgere interpellationem et simul motam controversiam non dirimere,"—*De Matrimonio,* II, n. 2355.

[129] *The Interpellations,* p. 62; Cf. also Burton, *A Commentary on Canon 1125,* p. 97.

in cases wherein it would be impossible otherwise to verify objectively the physical or moral departure of the infidel party. It hardly seems possible that the Holy See should restrict the use of the Pauline privilege by adding to it an invalidating clause not demanded even by the author of the privilege. Rather, the Church has not only always shown itself solicitous to grant the favor of the law in doubtful cases,[130] but has actually in its universal law granted an extension of the favor in cases wherein the necessary condition of departure cannot in any way be verified.[131]

In consideration of all of this Coronata affirms that the words of the Code, "antequam . . . valide contrahat," general as they are, are to be understood only in the cases where the interpellations are necessary for determining the departure of the infidel.[132]

The text of the canon still has validity of application, since there are cases in which the ill will and intent of the infidel can be established only by means of the interpellations. However, the Code does not explicitly state that the interpellations are always required for the subsequent valid use of the Pauline privilege,[133] and consequently no other interpretation can possibly be read into the text without a destroying of the obvious and common meaning of the words.

As Vermeersch pointed out, if the legislator had wished to make the obligation so extensively and so exclusively binding, he could well have chosen other expressions that would have rendered the meaning free of all doubt.[134]

[130] Canon 1127; cf. Wernz-Vidal, *Ius Matrimoniale,* n. 632, p. 825, note 68 in fine.

[131] Can. 1125.

[132] *De Matrimonio,* n. 631, in fine p. 885.

[133] Coronata, *loc. cit.*

[134] "Textus tamen explicantur eo quod interpellationes ad ipsum valorem sunt necessariae si non constet de discessu. Potuit igitur legislator dicere: ut valeat, certo et in omni hypothesi, matrimonium, interpellationes debent praecessisse. Sed ipse in c. 1121 § 2 consulto omisisse videtur voces: *ad valorem,* dum interpellationes semper faciendas esse declarat." *Theologia Moralis,* III, n. 755, p. 691.

Notwithstanding the occasional interpretation of canon 1123 to the contrary, it is to be added that the Code itself in canon 1124 obviously recognizes that the right to use the Pauline privilege is fundamentally based not upon the making of the interpellations but upon the objective and real fact of the infidel's departure or upon his intent to cohabit only in disrespect to and blasphemy toward the Creator. This is said in so many words in the canon, in which the right to enter a second marriage is expressly recognized without any reference to the necesstiy of making the interpellations, for here the departure or ill will of the infidel is known immediately and at first hand.

Thus the Code attests that even the ecclesiastical law does not demand that the interpellations be made in *every* case for the *valid* application of the Pauline privilege.[135]

In view of the tenableness of both opinions, defended by eminent authors and supported by responses of the Holy See, the Church without issuing any decisive definition in favor of either opinion,[136] does require in practice that the interpellations be made invariably. Thus, in practice, before entering a second marriage the convert must either make the interpellations or obtain a legitimate dispensation from them, even if it seems, or actually is certain, that the interpellations will be useless, or impossible of completion, or certainly and gravely dangerous.[137]

If, however, the interpellations were illegitimately omitted insofar as there was no official declaration that authorized their omission, the case must be referred to the Holy Office, which alone is competent to make any final decision in regard to the Pauline privilege.[138]

[135] Coronata, *De Matrimonio,* n. 631, p. 884, note 4; Wernz-Vidal, *Ius Matrimoniale,* n. 632, p. 825, n. 68 in extremo fine.

[136] Coronata, *De Matrimonio,* n. 681, p. 884, note 4 in fine, states that the Holy See has shown itself unwilling to make any such definition except by way of answer to some particular petition.

[137] Wernz-Vidal, *Ius Matrimoniale,* n. 632, p. 824, note 68; Payen, *De Matrimonio,* II, n. 2356, p. 686; Winslow, *The Pauline Privilege,* p. 16.

[138] Canon 247, § 3.

In the meantime the second marriage of the convert is to be presumed valid in virtue of canons 1014 and 1127.[189]

[189] Cappello, *De Matrimonio*, n. 777, p. 767; Woeber, *The Interpellations*, p. 62; Chelodi, *Ius Matrimoniale*, n. 158; Vermeersch-Creusen, *Epitome*, II, n. 340, p. 298; for refutation of this stand cf. Gregory, *The Pauline Privilege*, p. 70.

CHAPTER II

CHOICE OF TERMINOLOGY

Although the interpellations are ordinarily demanded by the law of the Church, if not for the valid, then at least for the licit, use of the Pauline privilege, the same universal law[1] recognizes cases in which the interpellations may be legitimately dispensed with under the Supreme Authority of the Church.

The dispensation may be granted by the Holy Father himself or by others acting as his delegate. These latter may have their power by grants of special faculties and indults[2] or in virtue of grants conceded by the universal law.[3] The dispensation may cover one or the other or even both of the interpellations.

Although the Holy See has and does still use the expression "dispensation from the interpellations," the Code speaks of a "declaration" in which the omission of the interpellations is authorized by legitimate authority.

Prior to the Code the Holy See consistently spoke of "dispensing from the interpellations" and faculties to "dispense" were granted to subordinate authorities. In the famous Constitution *Populis,* now a part of the universal law of the Church,[4] Pope Gregory granted the *facultas dispensandi* to bishops, pastors and Jesuit confessors. This

[1] Canon 1121, §2; 1123.

[2] *Formula Facultatum S.C. de Prop. Fide, Formula III* (*Maior*), nn. 25, 26, 27; *Formula III* (*Minor*), nn. 24, 25, 26; S.C.S. Off., 8 iun. 1836—*Fontes,* n. 874; *Coll. S.C.P.F.*, n. 848; S.C.S. Off. (Siam), 22 nov. 1871—*Fontes,* n. 1019; S.C.S. Off. (Mongoliae), 29 nov. 1882—*Fontes,* n. 1075; S.C.S. Off. (Siouxormen.), 18 maii, 1892—*Fontes,* n. 1155; S.C.S. Off. (ad Ep. Deverien.), 15 nov. 1934—Private, Protoc, Num. 2619/34—Bouscaren, *Canon Law Digest, Supplement through 1948,* p. 169; S.C.S. Off. (ad Archiep. Detroiten.), 22 maii. 1947, Private Protoc. Num. 1026/47—Bouscaren, *Canon Law Digest, Supplement through 1948,* pp. 170-171.

[3] Canon 1125.

[4] Canon 1125; cf. Appendix C, *infra,* p. 244.

expression was used regularly in responses of the Sacred Congregations,[5] and is still so used today.[6] The same words were employed in the granting of pre-Code faculties,[7] and likewise in those granted after the promulgation of the Code.[8]

The Apostolic Delegation today speaks of its faculty to "dispense from the interpellations,"[9] and uses the words in the formula of application for a dispensation from the interpellations.[10]

In view of this constant use of the word *"dispensare"* by the Holy See in its practical procedure, it is not out of order to investigate the various reasons why the codifiers of the law so studiously avoided to use the word *"dispensare"* and substituted in its place the word *"declarare."* Thus in canon 1121, § 2, the text reads, "... nisi Sedes Apostolica aliud declaraverit," and in canon 1123, "Si interpellationes ex declaratione Sedis Apostolicae omissae fuerint."

[5] S.C.S. Off. (Chen-si et Chan-si), 23 nov. 1796—*Fontes*, n. 825; S.C.S. Off. (Mongoliae), 29 nov. 1882—*Fontes*, n. 1075; *Coll. S.C.P.F.*, n. 1581.

[6] S.C.S. Off. (ad Ep. Denverien.), 15 nov. 1934—Protoc. Num. 2619/34; S.C.S. Off. (ad Archiep. Detroiten.), 22 maii, 1947—Protoc. num. 1026/47; both quoted in Bouscaren, *Canon Law Digest, Supplement through 1948*, pp. 169-170.

[7] Facultates Apostolicae, Formula I, C. D, E,—Joseph Putzer, *Commentarium in Facultates Apostolicas* (3. ed., Ilchester College, Maryland: Typis Congr. Sanctissimi Redemptoris, 1893), n. 97.

[8] Vermeersch, "Commentaria de Formulis Facultatum Quas S. Congr. de Prop. Fide Concedere Solet," *Periodica*, XI (1922), n. 29, p. 70. Vermeersch here referred to a letter of the Sacred Congregation for the Propagation of the Faith under date of July 1, 1919, and Protoc. Num. 1522/19. Cf. Also index of faculties granted after the Code in Vermeersch-Creusen, *Epitome*, I, n. 872, pp. 658 ff.

[9] Letter of the Apostolic Delegate to the Ordinaries of the United States, 17 July, 1935, No. 116/35, reporting faculty received from the Holy See. Letter quoted in Bouscaren, *Canon Law Digest, Supplement through 1948*, pp. 169-170.

[10] Copies of this formula are available from the Apostolic Delegation, 3339 Massachusetts Avenue, Washington 8, D.C. Formula quoted in Bouscaren, *op. cit.*, p. 171.

Though various reasons are offered for this choice of words, it is agreed that the final choice was made deliberately and designedly.[11] This is evidenced primarily by the fact that, in the various stages of the codification of the Code, the legislators wavered back and forth between the two phrases before deciding definitely to use the various forms of *"declarare"* in preference to *"dispensare."*

In the 1913 Schema of the Code canon 398, § 2, read, "Ab his interpellationibus una Sedes Apostolica per se vel per delegatum *dispensare* potest." And canon 400 stated, "Se *dispensatum* fuerit ab interpellationibus . . . ". In the Schema of 1915, however, canon 1124, § 1, which corresponded to canon 398, § 2, of the 1913 Schema, and to canon 1121, § 1, of the present Code, was changed to read, "Hae interpellationes fieri semper debent, nisi Sedes Apostolica aliud *declaraverit.*" But at the same time canon 1126, which corresponded to canon 400 of the 1913 Schema, and to canon 1123 of the present Code, still read, "Si *dispensatum* fuerit ab interpellationibus . . . ," and thus remained unchanged from the earlier reading. In the final codification the latter was altered so that it now reads, "Si interpellationes ex *declaratione* Sedis Apostolicae omissae fuerint," and the former canon 1126 was placed in the Code as canon 1121, § 1, just as it had read in the 1915 Schema.[12]

The final choice seems to have been dictated in consequence of the disagreement up to the time of the Code, and even yet among a few authorities, as to the precise nature of the pontifical power involved in these cases. This is gathered from the words of Cardinals Billot and Lorenzelli who opposed the use of the word *"dispensare,"* on the grounds that properly the Holy See could not dispense from the interpellations, but merely made other suitable provi-

[11] Woeber, *The Interpellations*, p. 105; Doheny, *Informal Procedure*, p. 530; Capello, *De Matrimonio*, n. 781, p. 770; Payen, *De Matrimonio*, II, n. 2403.

[12] Cappello, *op. cit.*, p. 770, note 53; Coronata, *De Matrimonio*, n. 638, p. 892, note 4.

sion for the cases in which the interpellations could not be made.[13]

The Sacred Congregations, however, have no scruple in using the phrase. Doheny[14] insists that it is incorrect to refer to the dispensation from the interpellations. He, therefore, insists on and consistently uses the words, "declaration authorizing the omission of the interpellations." With this one exception, authors commonly use the variations of the word *"dispensare."*[15]

The present writer will continue to use the expression, "dispensation from the interpellations," for in this he is in the company of the majority of the authors and reflects the traditional practice of the Holy See.

In the adoption of these terms it is necessary to distinguish three quite different senses in which they may be used. In the first place, "dispensation" may mean simply a declaration by the Holy See, which alone has the right to

[13] Card. Billot: "Non videtur quod Sedes Apostolica possit dispensare ab interpellationibus, proprie loquendo. Potest enim dispensationes dare praeter privilegium Paulinum, sed si de ipso privilegio Paulina sermo sit, non valet mutare conditiones eius, aut aliquid demere de iis quae ad ipsum requiruntur." And Card. Lorenzelli, "Quia Sedes Apostolica proprie non dispensat ab interpellationibus quando hae possibiles sunt, idcirco non dicerem absolute quod ab eis dispensare, sed quod Ipsa, cum interpellationes fieri nequeant, providere potest."—*Riassunto delle Osservazione* ... ad libr. III del Cod., ad can. 398, p. 173 quoted by Rayanna, "De Constitutione S. Pii Papae V, *Romani Pontificis,*" *Periodica,* XXVIII (1939), pp. 123-124, note 133.

[14] *Informal Procedure,* p. 530ff.

[15] Payen, *De Matrimonio,* II, n. 2403, p. 733; Gregory, *The Pauline Privilege,* p. 77; Vermeersch-Creusen, *Epitome,* II, n. 434ff; Wernz-Vidal, *Ius Matrimoniale,* n. 633; Gasparri, *De Matrimonio,* II, nn. 1148-1155; Coronata, *De Matrimonio,* nn. 638ff; Chelodi, *Ius Matrimoniale,* n. 160, p. 175; Cappello, *De Matrimonio,* nn. 781ff; Burton, *A Commentary on Canon 1125,* pp. 93ff; Buscaren-Ellis, *Canon Law: A Text and Commentary,* p. 551; Vromant, *De Matrimonio,* p. 278; Ayrinhac-Lydon, *Marriage Legislation,* p. 312; Vlaming, *Praelectiones,* II, n. 709, p. 312; Romani, *De Matrimonio,* n. 1149, p. 781; Bouscaren, "An Inquiry into the Practical Application of Canon 1125," *Miscellanea-Vermeersch,* I, 290; V. Heylen, *Tractatus de Matrimonio* (Mechliniae: H. Dessain, 1945), p. 347; Léry, *Le Privilège de la Foi,* n. 23, p. 99.

declare that the interpellations are no longer required in those cases wherein the departure and evil intent of the infidel party are already certain, for in such cases the interpellations are, of their very nature, useless and superfluous,[16] and the dispensation is granted merely *ad cautelam* for the removal of all doubt as to the valid use of the privilege and the validity of the subsequent marriage.[17]

In this particular case the two are not mutually exclusive, for actually there is a combination of them. It does in fact involve a mere declarative interpretation to the effect that the essential condition for the valid use of the Pauline privilege has been verified in the objective certainty of the infidel's departure. It also involves a dispensation, properly so called, relaxing the ecclesiastical law which requires the making of the interpellations in every case for the licit use of the Pauline privilege.[18]

In the second place, if the departure of the infidel is not known or not proved with certainty, a dispensation from the interpellations in view of the factors of impossibility, or of danger, or of uselessness would be a dispensation in the true and strict sense of the word, a relaxation of the ecclesiastical law which requires the making of the interpellations.[19]

Those who hold that the interpellations are required by the divine law will acquiesce in this and call it a strict dispensation from the binding force of that divine law,[20] or a

[16] Woeber, *The Interpellations*, p. 106; Cappello, *De Matrimonio*, n. 781; Payen, *De Matrimonio*, II, n. 2403; Chelodi, *Ius Matrimoniale*, n. 160, p. 175.

[17] Gregory, *The Pauline Privilege*, p. 77; Doheny, *Informal Procedure*, p. 530; Bouscaren, "An Inquiry into the Practical Application of Canon 1125," *Miscellanea-Vermeersch*, I, 290.

[18] Coronata, *De Matrimonio*, n. 638, p. 893.

[19] Gregory, *The Pauline Privilege*, p. 77; Doheny, *Informal Procedure*, p. 530; Bouscaren, "An Inquiry into the Practical Application of Canon 1125," *Miscellanea-Vermeersch*, I, 290.

[20] Coronata, *De Matrimonio*, n. 638, p. 892; Wernz-Vidal, *Ius Matrimoniale*, n. 632, note 68, p. 823.

declaration that in the circumstances of the case at hand the requirements of the divine law no longer oblige.[21]

Finally—in the third possibility—the dispensation assumes added force and uniqueness in that it goes beyond the limits of the Pauline privilege and, in effect, leads to the emergence of an entirely different privilege. For when the infidel partner of the convert has in fact also received baptism before the second marriage is contracted after a legitimate dispensation from the interpellations, that dispensation carries with it the extraordinary effect which constitutes the second marriage within the estate of a valid and indissoluble union. And, therefore, that which started out simply to be a normal dispensation from the interpellations is recognized by the Church in practice[22] and in law,[23] and cannot possibly be restricted within the limits of the Pauline privilege as a mere exemption from the formality of making the interpellations.

[21] Romani, *De Matrimonio,* n. 1149, p. 781; Vlaming, *Praelectiones,* II, n. 717, p. 319.

[22] Gregorius XIII, const. *Populis,* 25 ian. 1585—*Codex Iuris Canonici,* Documentum VIII; Benedictus XIV, ep. *In suprema,* 16 ian. 1745, ad 2—*Fontes,* n. 353.

[23] Can. 1125.

CHAPTER III

NATURE OF THE DISPENSATION

Article I: Mere Extension of the Pauline Privilege

The development of the canonical thought in the years following the 16th century grants of privileges split itself into two major opinions. The first, led mainly by Pope Benedict XIV and Pontius, held that the Constitutions of Popes Paul III, Pius V and Gregory XIII were merely an extension of the scope of the Pauline privilege. In the cases envisioned in the Constitutions the Holy See was merely providing for the omission of the interpellations where the fulfillment of this formality was impossible or useless. Gradually this theory lost ground, however, as the more tenable doctrine, so that only a scattered few authors could be found in its support in the years proximately preceding the Code.[1]

Subsequent to the promulgation of the Code this explanation of the nature of the power of these Constitutions found even less support, so that today it is acknowledged as insufficient and unacceptable.

To complete the study of the nature of this power and as an example of the reasoning of those who tried to force the favors of these constitutions within the limits of the Pauline privilege is the explanation of Augustine.

Many of the early commentators, unaware of the power of the popes to dissolve marriages *in favorem fidei,* as exemplified in the Helena case,[2] could find a doctrinal or canonical basis for these favors only in the Pauline privilege. They sought, therefore, to interpret them in the light of and according to the specific conditions and requirements of the Pauline privilege.

Augustine summarized the conditions and privileges of the constitutions and placed the three side by side in an

[1] Cf. Part One, Chapter Three, Art. 2, section 1, pp. 23-26.

[2] Private, Holy Office, 5 nov. 1924, quoted in Bouscaren, *Canon Law Digest,* I, 553-554.

attempt to compare them according to the norms of the Pauline privilege. His comment betrays a conscious suspicion of the validity of his stand, for he was aware of and disturbed by the total disregard for the necessity of the interpellations on the part of Popes Paul III and Pius V. For that reason he felt that a purer notion of the Pauline privilege was manifested by Pope Gregory XIII, while actually, his constitution least of all, can be interpreted within the limits of the Pauline privilege in the cases where both parties to the marriage contracted in infidelity have actually been baptized at the time of the second marriage.[3]

He explained the omission of any demand of the interpellations in the first two Constitutions as a formal declaration on the part of the Holy See that in the particular cases for which the constitutions were granted the law demanding the making of the interpellations ceased to bind.

In commenting on the Constitution *Populis,* he did not advert to the words of Pope Gregory XIII to the effect that the second marriage of the convert was nevertheless to be held as valid and indissoluble when his former spouse had also been converted, even if this conversion took place before the celebration of the second marriage, as long as the knowledge of this conversion had not come to the attention of the first convert.

In discussing the papal power to dissolve marriage Burton clearly concludes that the effort to bring under the Pauline privilege the cases considered in the constitutions "seems forced and without justification. A comparison of the grants with the fundamental requirements of the Paul-

[3] "From this iuxtaposition it will easily be perceived that the most favorable interpretation is that of St. Pius. But at the same time it is the least canonical, stretching the privilege to its very limit, because it pays regard neither to the former marriage nor to the interpellations. Paul III's constitution attempts to preserve a semblance of legitimate marriage, since it requires that the first wife must be retained, if remembered, and the consent renewed. A purer notion of the Pauline privilege is manifested by the Constitution of Gregory XIII."—*A Commentary,* V, 363.

ine privilege shows irreconcilable differences."[4] He states further, in reference to the Constitution *Romani Pontificis,* that the privileges granted in the constitution are applicable even when the *discessus* of the Pauline privilege was not verified in the cases where the first wife was willing to cohabit peacefully with her convert husband. Then, referring to the text of this same constitution and that of Pope Gregory XIII, he concludes further, "it can scarcely be presumed that the Popes, when using such terms, were only legislating that when it was impossible to make the interpellations they need not be made. The objective was one of greater significance."[5] All in all it is here agreed that the privileges of these papal constitutions extend far beyond the normal use of the Pauline privilege, so that they involve the use of a more extensive power of the Holy See. And yet, when faced with a "possible restriction" of the Constitution *Romani Pontificis,* he reverts to the Pauline privilege as the juridical basis for the grants, and tries to comprise the privileges of Pope Pius V within the restrictions of the Pauline privilege.[6]

The impossibility of reconciling these constitutions with the fundamental and prescribed conditions for the application of the Pauline privilege together with the practically unanimous agreement of the authors to the contrary argues incontestably for the rejection of this opinion which attempts to explain the constitutions as a mere extension of the Pauline privilege.

Article II: Actual Dissolution of the Marriage by Papal Power

Shortly after the issuance of the papal constitutions it became evident from a careful analysis of their grants that they were not, as it was first thought, a variation or exten-

[4] *A Commentary on Canon 1125,* p. 80.

[5] *Op. cit.,* p. 81; cf. also pp. 153-155.

[6] *Op. cit.,* p. 159, "The juridical background of the concession was the Pauline privilege which requires that even a pagan spouse is to be retained who will live peacefully and without insult to the Creator."

sion of the Pauline privilege, but actually an application of a far wider power which effected, in favor of the Faith, a dissolution of a marriage which had been contracted and consummated in infidelity, and even in a given case a dissolution of a sacramental marriage bond.

Today the arguments in favor of this interpretation of the nature of the power granted by the constitutions are recognized as valid and conclusive.

Section 1: Argument from Interpretation

In the first place, if the constitutions contained merely an authentic declaratory interpretation of the Pauline privilege, they would involve an act of the Church's *magisterium* in that they would officially interpret that privilege. As such they would be valid everywhere and oblige everyone, for the interpretation would be as extensive as the privilege itself.[7] Actually, however, the constitutions were originally directed exclusively to certain and definite places and peoples, which could not have been done if it was meant that they simply were to interpret the applicable use of the Pauline privilege.[8]

And at the same time, if the constitutions had contained an extensive interpretation of the Pauline privilege, they would likewise have involved a use of the same apostolic authority that was used by St. Paul, for in effect a new law would have been issued. But the newly extended privilege was no longer one with the Pauline privilege, but transcended the privilege granted by St. Paul and became applicable in cases not comprehended by that original privilege.[9]

[7] Canon 17; cf. John Rogg Schmidt, *The Principles of Authentic Interpretation in Canon 17 in the Code of Canon Law,* The Catholic University of America Canon Law Studies, n. 141 (Washington, D.C.: The Catholic University of America Press, 1941) for general principles regulating the interpretation of law.

[8] Wernz-Vidal, *Ius Matrimoniale*, n. 635, p. 834; Cappello, *De Matrimonio,* n. 787, p. 779; Burton, *A Commentary on Canon 1125*, p. 82.

[9] Cappello, *op. cit.*, p. 82; Burton, *loc. cit.*

Section 2: Constitutions do not Fulfill the Conditions for Pauline Privilege

If the text of the constitutions and the privileges which they grant are studied carefully, it is obvious that they fail to fulfill all of the conditions specifically required for the normal use of the Pauline privilege. Such a comparison uncovers fundamental and irreconcilable differences patently proving that these constitutions imply the use of a power different from a mere declaration of the Pauline privilege.[10]

In abstraction from the fact that the constitutions make no mention of the Epistle of St. Paul to the Corinthians or of the privilege itself, the marked difference between the grants of the constitutions and the normal requirements for the use of the Pauline privilege is clearly evident in an investigation of each constitution separately.

It is clear that Paul III granted a privilege openly different from that of the Pauline privilege, for he permitted

[10] G. Arendt, S.J., "De Clausula Restrictiva Canon 1123," *ETL*, III (1926), 336, "Huius principii allegatio significat Congregationem voluisse providere solutioni matrimonii in casu, recurrendo ad plenitudinem potestatis Primae Sedis, quemadmodum iam tunc constabat, fecisse et Gregorium XIII et Paulum III et Pium V, si unquam revera non sufficeret privilegium Paulinum." Cappello, *De Matrimonio*, n. 787, p. 799, 4°: "In memoratis Constitutionibus deficiunt omnino conditiones privilegii Paulini." De Smet, *De Sponsalibus et Matrimonio*, n. 354, p. 303: "... cum autem non censeatur dissolutum vi privilegii Paulini, ob omnimodam absentiam essentialium conditionum, sponte recurrimus ad exercitium potestatis pontificiae, ... dissolvendi ipsum vinculum matrimonii legitimi consummati, supposito alterutrius partis baptismo." Rayanna, "De Constitutione S. Pii Papae V *Romani Pontificis*," *Periodica*, XXVIII (1939), 204: "Quod privilegium etiam respicit et dependet a voluntate primae coniugis; inde necessitas eam interrogandi num velit converti. Sed Paulus III et Gregorius XIII ulterius procedunt et dant facultatem dimittendi primam coniugem si nota non sit, vel difficillimum sit eam reperire vel adire ... Facultas vero a S. Pio V concessa toto coelo differt, cum non respiciat discessum infidelis nec ignorantiam quae sit prima uxor nec ubi sit, nec difficultatem eam adeundi, sed duritiem separandi neophytum ab uxore cum qua habitat." Ayrinhac-Lydon, *Marriage Legislation*, p. 320; Matthew Ramstein, *The Pastor and Marriage Cases* (New York: Benziger Brothers, 1945), pp. 198-199.

the infidel who had many wives and could not remember which one of the many was the first and legitimate one, upon his conversion, to choose any one he pleased, even though she was not the first one. Then, having dismissed all of the others, he was permitted to contract marriage with this one. If the one chosen was not a Christian, the constitution itself granted a dispensation from the impediment of disparity of cult.[11] A few authors have demanded the obtaining of this dispensation if the one chosen is not a Christian,[12] but actually the constitution is silent on the obligation, and the dispensation is to be considered a part of the privilege granted by Pope Paul III; however the *cautiones* prescribed now by canons 1061 and 1071 must be made. This has been recently confirmed by a reply of the Holy Office.[13]

No interpellation of the first wife or of any of the others was required nor was it necessary to obtain a dispensation from making the interpellations. But this second marriage could not have been allowed if the one chosen was not the first consort, unless that first marriage had been dissolved. The conditions of this privilege do not fulfill the requirements of the Pauline privilege, which would allow the second marriage only if the first wife had had the opportunity and failed to reply or had actually responded negatively to the interpellations. The solution of the first mar-

[11] Woods, *The Constitutions of Canon 1125*, p. 44; Vermeersch-Creusen, *Epitome*, II, n. 436, p. 302; Winslow, *The Pauline Privilege*, p. 60; Vromant, *De Matrimonio*, n. 343; Doheny, *Informal Procedure*, n. 552; Burton, *A Commentary on Canon 1125*, p. 148; Coronata, *De Matrimonio*, n. 647, p. 904.

[12] De Smet, *De Sponsalibus et Matrimonio*, n. 353, p. 300, note 2: "Si uxor, vi privilegii electa, est infidelis, opus est dispensatione, super disparitate cultus." Payen, *De Matrimonio*, II, n. 2405 bis, p. 736: "Exigendae sunt solitae cautiones et danda est, super disparitate cultus, dispensatio, quae videtur posse concedi vi Facultatis Tertiae Minoris."

[13] 30 June 1937, Private, Bouscaren, *Canon Law Digest Supplement through 1948*, p. 175; cf. also Winslow, *The Pauline Privilege*, p. 60; Burton, *A Commentary on Canon 1125*, p. 148; Doheny, *Informal Procedure*, p. 552; Vermeersch-Creusen, *Epitome*, II, n. 436, p. 267.

riage, therefore, can only be attributed to the authority of the Roman Pontiff, who dissolved the first marriage in permitting the second.[14]

Likewise the Constitution *Romani Pontificis* does not fulfill the requirements of the Pauline privilege, for in it Pope St. Pius V granted a favor to infidels who had been living in polygamy, so that upon their conversion they were permitted to remain with the wife who received baptism with them, on the ground that it would be most difficult to force them to separate a man from the wife with whom he was living and who had already been baptized or would do so. Again the convert was not obliged to determine the will of any of his other wives regarding baptism or cohabitation, even if the first wife was certainly known and could easily be interpellated.[15]

There are some who say that this privilege cannot be used if the first spouse is known or is willing to be baptized. These would make the absence of the infidel partner a necessary condition for the use of the privilege, thus admittedly confusing it with the requirements for the use of the Pauline privilege.[16] To these Cappello answers that, if one considers the conditions of the constitution objectively and independently, it is evident that it has validity even when the former spouse is known and wishes to be baptized, as long as the one necessary condition required by the privilege is

[14] Gasparri, *De Matrimonio*, II, n. 1157; Vlaming, *Praelectiones*, II, n. 730, p. 326; Cappello, *De Matrimonio*, n. 787, p. 778; Payen, *De Matrimonio*, II, n. 2404-2405; Doheny, *op. cit.*, p. 551; Léry, *Le Privilège le la Foi*, nn. 74-77, pp. 100-102.

[15] Winslow, *op. cit.*, p. 71: "The Interpellations of the true spouse are *ipso iure* omitted, and no further dispensation is necessary." Woods, *The Constitutions of Canon 1125*, p. 55; Rayanna, "De Constitutione S. Pii V *Romani Pontificis*," *Periodica*, XXVIII (1939), 295ff; Vermeersch-Creusen, *op. cit.*, II, n. 436, p. 303: "Vi Constitutionis Pii V non videtur interpellanda uxor legitima, etiamsi cognoscatur." Doheny, *Informal Procedure*, p. 553: "The privileges of this Constitution were granted to the Indians even when the first wife was certainly known and could have been interpellated."

[16] Cf. Chapter I, Art I, pp. 88-93; Cf. also Payen, *De Matrimonio*, II n. 2407 bis, p. 449; Burton, *A Commentary on Canon 1125*, p. 160.

verified, namely that it would be unreasonably difficult for the convert to give up the woman with whom he is now cohabiting, and who had become a convert with him.[17]

Rayanna points out that the true sense of the phrase can only mean that the one and only required condition for the use of the privilege is the hardship that would be occasioned, for any one of a number of reasons, by the forced separation of the consorts.[18]

Once more, only by an unjustifiable forcing of the obvious meaning of the words could the favor be interpreted as an application of the Pauline privilege even in its widest extension,[19] for there is not postulated either the making of the interpellations[20] or the departure of the first and legitimate spouse.[21]

[17] *De Matrimonio,* n. 787, p. 776.

[18] "De Constitutione S. Pii Papae V, *Romani Pontificis,*" *Periodica,* XXVIII (1939), 201: "Quae omnia his paucis verbis resumi possunt: Ad validum usum Privilegii Piani, quod polygamis per Constitutionem *Romani Pontificis* c. 1125 conceditur, requiruntur et sufficiunt conditiones vel adiuncta casus, quae sequuntur: 1) Durissimum sit separare polygamum ab uxore cum qua vivit; 2) Haec uxor sit parata ad baptismum simul cum marita recipiendum."

[19] Gasparri, *De Matrimonio,* II, n. 1158, p. 233: "... ut patet ... S Pii V nullum vestigium de privilegio Paulino; nam S Pontifex viro, qui in infidelitate plures uxores duxerat, permittit illam retinere, quae cum ipso conversa est, etiamsi non si prima; hoc autem fieri nequit, nisi soluto matrimonio cum prima."

[20] Doheny, *Informal Procedure,* p. 554: "The Constitution exempted from the interpellations." Woeber, *The Interpellations,* p. 109; Payen, *De Matrimonio,* II, n. 2406, in fine; Vermeersch-Creusen, *Epitome,* II, n. 436, p. 303; Léry, *Le Privilège de la Foi,* n. 82, p. 107; Vlaming, *Praelectiones,* II, n. 730, p. 326; Vermeersch, "Commentaria de Formulis Facultatum," *Periodica,* XI (1922), 139: "Iam vero a *Romani Pontificis* permittit ut polygamus maneat cum uxore quae cum ipso baptizetur sine ulla distinctione primae vel alterius et sine interpellatione primae."

[21] Cappello, *De Matrimonio,* n. 787, pp. 779-780: "Iam vero hic nulla fit mentio de discessu partis infidelis, qui est *conditio sine qua non* pro applicatione privilegii Paulini." Burton, *A Commentary on Canon 1125,* p. 81: "It could happen that the first wife would be willing to cohabit peacefully with her convert husband and thus eliminate the *discessus* required for the use of the Pauline privilege, yet St. Pius V allowed the convert to marry another."

Pope Gregory XIII clearly went beyond the possibilities of the Pauline privilege in his Constitution *Populis*. Exercising his apostolic power, he granted a privilege totally distinct in its ultimate application from that comprehended by that privilege. For he granted to all converts from paganism the right, by Apostolic dispensation, to validly enter a second marriage without any interpellation of the convert's first spouse. This second marriage he declared valid and absolutely indissoluble even if the infidel was legitimately impeded from manifesting his intention, and even though at the time when the second marriage was contracted the other spouse had also received baptism.

In virtue of this latter grant it is absolutely impossible in any way to restrict this favor within the more limited scope of the Pauline privilege. It is definitely determined that the Pauline privilege ceases to be applicable upon the conversion of both parties, to such an extent that a second marriage contracted in virtue of the Pauline privilege is invalid if the other party of the marriage that was contracted in infidelity had also actually received baptism. Thus, "Gasparri recognized that the constitution of Gregory XIII meant that even if the absent wife had been converted *before* the second marriage of her husband, this latter marriage would be valid, and that this result did not follow from an application of the Pauline privilege but rather from the use of the papal power."[22]

In virtue of the Constitution *Populis*, however, the second marriage is not only valid under such circumstances but also absolutely indissoluble.[23]

[22] Burton, *op. cit.*, p. 66; Gasparri, *De Matrimonio*, II, n. 1159, p. 235: "... haec autem supponunt primum matrimonium non privilegio Paulino, sed Pontificia potestate solutum fuisse." Coronata, *De Matrimonio*, n. 644, p. 900, a.

[23] Text of the Constitution: "Quae quidem matrimonia etiamsi postea innotuerit coniuges priores infideles suam voluntatem iuste impeditos declarare non potuisse, et ad fidem etiam tempore transacti secundi matrimonii conversos fuisse, nihilominus rescindi numquam debere, sed valido et firma, prolemque inde suscipiendam legitimam

Cappello states that these words of Pope Gregory are so clear and manifest that they are said to have decisive value in this question; at any rate, even a casual comparison of the text of St. Paul with those of the constitutions indicates that these are two entirely distinct uses of the vicarious power granted by God to His Church.[24]

Section 3: Practice of the Holy See

This positive view that the constitutions in general and the dispensation from the interpellations granted by Pope Gregory XIII in particular effect the actual dissolution of a legitimate marriage is quite definitely the majority opinion of late pre-Code and post-Code authors. They argue primarily from the actual practice of the Church, which is, of course, not only a valid but also a most cogent argument. In other words, throughout the centuries the Popes have used this power and are using it today. Their right to use the power is based in the ultimate analysis upon the fact that they have used it. If the fact therefore is certain, then also is the right. But the fact is now historically undisputed and canonically recognized, for there have been certain dispensations granted by the Holy See which are not mere declarations nor simply comprehensive interpretations of the Pauline privilege,[25] but are actually extensive interpre-

fore decernimus." Cf. Appendix C; also Bouscaren-Ellis, *Canon Law: A Text and Commentary*, p. 559.

[24] *De Matrimonio*, n. 787, in extremo fine, p. 780; Cf. Cappello, *Summa Iuris Canonici* (3 Vols., Vol. II, 4. ed., Romae: Apud Aedes Universitatis Gregorianae, 1945), n. 407, p. 375: "In istis Constitutionibus non habetur declaratio et applicatio privilegii Paulini, quia facultas in iisdem Constitutionibus manifeste extenditur ultra privilegium Paulinum, sed usus potestatis vicariae ex parte Romani Pontificis." Vermeersch-Creusen, *Epitome*, II, n. 436, p. 303: "Ex his facile perspicitur RR. Pontifices privilegia concessisse quae ambitum privilegii Paulini, quale e Scriptura et Traditione cognoscitur, superant."

[25] For a thorough and able treatment of this question confer further, Francis J. Kieda, "Direct Dissolution of a Legitimate Marriage," *The Jurist*, II (1942), 134-144.

tations of the same privilege or implicit dissolutions of marriages contracted in infidelity.[26]

But any extensive interpretation is to be considered as a new law covering the cases not comprehended in the original grants. The dissolution of any marriage demands a true power of dispensing or relaxing the bond. The fact that legitimate marriages have been pronounced dissolved by the Holy See, and new marriages permitted in cases in which the first marriage could not come under the conditions of the Pauline privilege, postulates that they were dissolved by a declaration of this same Supreme Authority.[27] In such a way the constitutions of 1125 effect the dissolution of legitimate marriage bonds.[28]

This was in a special way stated by two of the Popes themselves, who in their constitutions were expressly aware of the nature of their grants and the source of the power by which they were acting. Pope St. Pius V explicitly declared that he was acting in virtue of his Supreme Apostolic Authority: "Nos ... motu proprio et ex certa scientia Nos-

[26] Cappello, *De Matrimonio*, n. 791, p. 785; Chelodi, *Ius Matrimoniale*, n. 160, p. 175: "At in aliis casibus, ubi conditiones Casus Apostoli ex toto deficiunt, dispensatio naturam induit iuridicam implicitae solutionis coniugii ex plenitudine potestatis."

[27] Chelodi, *loc. cit.;* Wernz-Vidal, *Ius Matrimoniale*, n. 635, pp. 833-834: "Qua in Constitutione Gregorius XIII *decrevit* nova matrimonia sine ulla interpellatione ex apostolica *dispensatione valide* iniri posse, etiamsi tempore contracti matrimonii secundi *utraque pars* iam suscepisset baptismum. Qui casus in privilegio Paulino non continetur, vi cuius novae nuptiae coniugii *fideli* solummodo permittuntur, si pars infidelis discedat. Quare non est recurrendum ad privilegium Paulinum a Gregorio XIII non allegatum, sed ad *plenitudinem potestatis* pontificiae *iustasque causas* et *minorem firmitatem* vinculi istorum matrimoniorum, quibus R. Pontifex insistit." Cappello, *De Matrimonio*, n. 791, p. 785.

[28] Vlaming, *Praelectiones*, II, n. 730, p. 325; Vermeersch-Creusen, *Epitome*, II, n. 434, p. 300; Heylen, *Tractatus de Matrimonio*, p. 320; De Smet, *De Sponsalibus et Matrimonio*, n. 354, p. 303; P. Chrétien, *De Matrimonio* (2. ed., Metis: Typis Imprimerie du Journal "Le Lorrain," 1937), n. 262, pp. 436-437; Bouscaren-Ellis, *Canon Law: A Text and Commentary*, p. 559; Burton, *A Commentary on Canon 1125*, p. 80.

tra ac apostolicae potestatis plenitudine ... apostolica auctoritate, tenore praesentium declaramus matrimoniumque huismodi inter eos legitime consistere ... "

Pope Gregory XIII is nonetheless explicit in the same affirmation: " ... plena auctoritate apostolica, tenore presentium, concedimus facultatem dispensandi ... "

In the light of these forceful and explicit declarations it becomes further evident that these Popes, aware that the conditions necessary for the application of the Pauline privilege could not be verified in the cases envisioned in their constitutions, intended to use and did, in fact, use their supreme power to dissolve legitimate marriages. Thus Kieda concludes:

> "And consequently there is no other alternative but to admit that the Papal constitutions just discussed are no application of the Pauline privilege but rather that they imply the employment of a special power, the vicarious power of the Pope, contained in the Apostolic power of the keys. Because interpellations are not resorted to, especially when there is question of unbaptized persons whose intentions are unknown, it appears very clearly that the Pontiff exercises special power."[29]

Though the power of the Holy See to dissolve the natural bond of legitimate marriages was once disputed, to insist on that power today is to belabor an accepted issue.[30]

This power is recognized in canon 1127, which leaves room for the dissolution of a legitimate union, even though consummated, in favor of the Faith when there is a doubt of fact or of law concerning its validity.

Clearly, therefore, these Pontiffs, in granting such dispensations, expressly appealed to the plenitude of their

[29] Kieda, "The Direct Dissolution of a Legitimate Marriage," *The Jurist*, II (1942), 140; Cf. Cappello, *Summa Iuris Canonici*, II, n. 407, p. 375.

[30] Cappello, *De Matrimonio*, n. 790, p. 784 says that this doctrine reflects not only a probable opinion but also a certainty. He lists over 50 authors who support this certainty.

Apostolic power and to the fact that such natural bonds are not absolutely indissoluble.[31]

In these cases the Popes are merely applying the supreme authority given to them by God. The power used in dissolving these legitimate marriages is contained in the general power of the "keys" given to St. Peter and his successors. It is a power which is to be used vicariously by them. St. Paul used this Apostolic power in the institution of the Pauline privilege; Popes Paul III, St. Pius V and Gregory XIII used it in the granting of the wider privileges listed in their constitutions; it is used today by the Holy See for the dissolving of legitimate marriages in favor of the Faith.[32]

This same power is exercised in the dispensation from the interpellations as granted in virtue of the Constitution *Populis,* and now in consequence of the provision contained in the universal law, and this dispensation truly effects the dissolution of the first marriage contracted in infidelity in the cases wherein the departure of the unbaptized party is actually not verified, or wherein that party has also received baptism at the time of the second marriage.[33] The same far-reaching effect is attained no matter who has granted the dispensation, provided that it was granted validly according to the law.[34]

It is to be stressed again that in the use of this power

[31] Ioannes Chelodi-Pius Ciprotti, *Ius Canonicum: De Matrimonio* (Vicenza: Societa Anonima Tipografica Editrice, 1947), n. 160 bis, p. 203 (hereafter cited *De Matrimonio*); Bouscaren-Ellis, *op. cit.*, p. 559; Coronata, *De Matrimonio,* n. 645, p. 900; Gasparri, *De Matrimonio,* II, n. 1165; Cappello, *De Matrimonio,* nn. 789-792, pp. 783-790; Vermeersch-Creusen, *Epitome,* II, n. 437, p. 303; Wernz-Vidal, *Ius Matrimoniale,* n. 636, p. 836; Woeber, *The Interpellations,* pp. 108-109; Burton, *A Commentary on Canon 1125,* pp. 80-82; Woods, *The Constitutions of Canon 1125,* pp. 21-28.

[32] Vlaming, *Praelectiones,* II, nn. 731-732, pp. 327-328; Cappello, *Summa, Iuris Canonici,* II, n. 407, p. 375; Chrétien, *De Matrimonio,* n. 262, p. 436.

[33] De Smet, *De Sponsalibus et Matrimonio,* n. 354, p. 303; Coronata, *De Matrimonio,* n. 644, p. 900.

[34] Bouscaren-Ellis, *Canon Law: A Text and Commentary,* p. 559.

to dissolve the purely natural bond of marriage, whether through the Pauline privilege, whether through the Constitutions mentioned in Canon 1125, or whether through the privilege of the Faith, the Holy See has always been prompted exclusively by an ardent desire to aid converts, whether in preparing the way for their conversion or by making it easier for them to live their Faith after their baptism.

Cappello speaks of a double motive prompting this benign attitude of the Holy See: the good of the Faith and the salvation of souls. The first occurs whenever a marriage is dissolved in favor of the Faith, so that a convert to the Catholic Church can contract a new marriage. The other occurs as often as the spiritual good of one or the other spouse demands the dissolution of an earlier marriage without any reference, at least immediately and directly, to any future marriage.[35] Gasparri also noted that "hanc potestatem eidem misericors Deus concessit in fidei favorem et salutem animarum."[36]

Article III: Still Referred to as Pauline Privilege

It is universally recognized today that the privileges granted in the three Papal Constitutions are wider than the Pauline privilege in that they include cases which cannot in any way be said to fulfill the conditions prescribed as necessary for the valid use of the Pauline privilege. Yet, in practice, the cases mentioned are dealt with as though they were actually only applications of the more restricted Pauline privilege. This is usually prompted by convenience, and many times with a view to the avoidance of the possible scandal that might arise among those who do not recognize or are not acquainted with the Papal power to dissolve marriage.[37]

[35] *De Matrimonio,* n. 792, p. 790; Cf. also Wernz-Vidal, *Ius Matrimoniale,* n. 637, p. 838.

[36] *De Matrimonio,* II, n. 1165, p. 238.

[37] Bouscaren, "An Inquiry into the Practical Application of Canon 1125," *Miscellanea-Vermeersch,* I, 291-292.

The Holy See itself, speaking of the dispensation from the interpellations and of the far-reaching effect flowing from that dispensation, refers to it as though it were a special use of the Pauline privilege. In an answer to the Vicar Apostolic of Japan the Holy Office, without a specific reference to the Constitution, nevertheless quoted its conditions and declared that under these conditions the interpellations could validly be dispensed with. The heading, however, refers to the entire case as though it were really a legitimate use of the Pauline privilege.[38]

Then, too, authors and commentators treat the subject of the dispensation under the heading of the Pauline privilege though they recognize that the validity of the second marriage after the omission of the interpellations as also the non-verification of the departure of the infidel cannot be admitted as an effect of the Pauline privilege.[39] The same is true when they discuss the dissolution of the marriage after the baptism of both parties in virtue of the extraordinary effect of the dispensation granted by the Constitution *Populis*, and they then explain the dissolution of the marriage as a "peculiar effect of the dispensation from the interpellations."[40]

Not every dispensation from the interpellations carries with it this extraordinary effect of dissolving the bond of a sacramental marriage, but in fact merely prepares the way for the normal use of the privilege.[41] Coronata[42] and Wernz-Vidal,[43] however, consider this particular effect of

[38] S.C.S.Off. (ad Vic. Ap. Iaponiae Merid.), 4 febr. 1891—*Fontes*, n. 1130; *Coll. S.C.P.F.*, n. 1746.

[39] Cappello, *De Matrimonio*, n. 782, p. 772; De Smet, *De Sponsalibus et Matrimonio*, n. 354, p. 303; Wernz-Vidal, *Ius Matrimoniale*, n. 633, p. 826; Vermeersch-Creusen, *Epitome*, II, n. 434, p. 300; Doheny, *Informal Procedure*, p. 530; Gasparri, *De Matrimonio*, II, n. 1148.

[40] Bouscaren, "An Inquiry into the Practical Application of Canon 1125," *Miscellanea-Vermeersch*, I, 291-292; cf. also, Bouscaren-Ellis, *Canon Law: A Text and Commentary*, p. 559.

[41] Cf. Chapter II, in fine, pp. 123-129.

[42] *De Matrimonio*, n. 644, p. 900.

[43] *Ius Matrimoniale*, n. 634, p. 829.

the dispensation from the interpellations in its own right independently of the Pauline privilege. And Payen under the general heading of the dispensation from the interpellations lists all the various sources of faculties by which such a dispensation is validly granted, whether that be by ordinary power, or by power conceded by the universal law or by special faculty.[44]

[44] *De Matrimonio,* II, nn. 2403-2415, pp. 732-758.

CHAPTER IV

SCOPE OF THE DISPENSATION

Article I: From Both Interpellations

The juridical act of interpellation involves the asking of a twofold question of the infidel spouse after his partner has become a Christian: 1) whether he is willing to be converted and to receive baptism, and 2) whether he is willing to continue peaceful conjugal life without offering offense to God or to the Faith of the Christian.

The obligation of making the interpellations as a condition for the use of the Pauline privilege arises purely from ecclesiastical law. In line with the general norms of the Code such an obligation, therefore, can be relaxed entirely or in part by the Supreme Authority of the Church or by others to whom the faculty of dispensing has been conceded by means of a particular grant of power or through the universal law.[1]

The Roman Pontiff as the supreme legislator of the Church has frequently dispensed from the obligation of making the interpellations, so that, without any warning at all, the convert is allowed to validly enter a new marriage, thus totally disregarding the desires and legitimate intentions of the former consort.[2]

The same power, namely, of granting a dispensation, has been given in the Formula of Faculties issued by the Sacred Congregation for the Propagation of the Faith to Ordi-

[1] Canon 80.

[2] Benedictus XIV, *In suprema*, 16 ian, 1745, ad 2—*Fontes*, n. 353; Const. *Apostoli ministerii*, 16 sept. 1747, ad 2—*Fontes*, n. 381; S.C. de Prop. Fide (ad C.P. pro Sin.), 3 ian. 1777—*Coll. S.C.P.F.*, n. 517; S.C.S. Off. (ad Archiep. Quebecen.), 8 iun. 1836—*Fontes*, n. 874; *Coll. S.C.P.F.*, n. 848; S.C.S. Off., instr. (pro Vic. Ap. ad Gallos), 20 iun. 1866—*Fontes*, n. 994; *Coll. S.C.P.F.*, n. 1293; Cappello, *De Matrimonio*, n. 781, p. 770; Gregory, *The Pauline Privilege*, p. 77; De Smet, *De Sponsalibus et Matrimonio*, n. 353, p. 299; Gougnard, *Tractatus de Matrimonio*, p. 296; Kearney, *The Principles of Canon 1127*, p. 125.

naries in mission countries under the direction of that Sacred Congregation. The two faculties to be considered here grant the power of dispensing from the interpellation of the spouse who yet remains unbaptized. The first was granted for the covering of the ordinary cases, namely when the making of the interpellations is not possible or will be evidently futile.[3] The second of the two faculties was expressly conceded for the covering of the cases in which the interpellations could not be made without the occasioning of evident serious harm to the convert, even though he has not yet been actually received into the Church, or when an attempt to make the interpellations would cause danger to the entire Christian community or simply to other Christians in general.[4]

Both of these faculties grant the power of dispensing from both interpellations under the condition that their fulfillment would be impossible, useless or dangerous.[5]

The power of relaxing the obligation to make the interpellations is also granted in the Papal Constitutions, now a part of the universal law in canon 1125. The first two, *Altitudo* and *Romani Pontificis,* precisely do not consider the question of dispensing from this obligation, but provide simply and automatically for the total omission of the interpellations.

There is no doubt concerning the Constitution *Altitudo,* but occasionally there arises an erroneous interpretation of the Constitution *Romani Pontificis,*[6] an interpretation which demands the interpellation of the first spouse if he or she is known and available. It would require the convert to resume cohabitation with this first spouse under these con-

[3] Facultates a S.C. de Prop. Fide concessae, Facultas XXV.

[4] Facultates a S.C. de Prop. Fide concessae, Facultas XXVI.

[5] Payen, *De Matrimonio,* II, nn. 2412-2414; Putzer, *Commentarium in Facultates Apostolicas,* n. 130; Winslow, *The Pauline Privilege,* pp. 34-40; Blat, *De Sacramentis,* n. 532, explicite.

[6] Cf. Coronata, *De Matrimonio,* n. 648, pp. 904-905, for a thorough and highly competent answer to this interpretation of the Constitution and the conditions for its use.

ditions. Actually, the Constitution nowhere speaks of such an exception to its privilege that the convert is allowed to choose any one of his former wives as long as that one is willing or has already been baptized with him. Those who subscribe to this interpretation are trying to interpret the Constitution in line with the requirements of the Pauline privilege, which requirements are in no way applicable here, for this is a privilege granted specifically for the covering of cases that lie beyond the limits of the Pauline privilege.[7]

Actually, no interpellations are required in the Constitution. The Holy See has recognized this in a affirmative answer to the First Council of China in 1924. The Ordinaries of China were aware of the general principle that a convert from polygamy could not retain as his proper wife the woman who was baptized with him, unless the interpellations were previously made in order to learn whether or not the first wife wished to be converted. On the other hand, they were equally aware that in the Constitution *Romani Pontificis* Pius V seemed to state absolutely that in case of successive polygamy the convert could retain as his wife the woman who was baptized with him, without any questions being raised about any previous interpellation of his first or any of the former wives.

In the face of this dilemma the Ordinaries of China asked the Holy See whether, according to the mind of the above cited Constitution, they could baptize such catechumens together with the wife that was willing to be baptized with him absolutely and without any interpellation of the first wife even if she could easily be found and questioned. To this inquiry the Holy See answered in the affirmative.[8] Many

[7] Winslow, *The Pauline Privilege*, p. 70; Doheny, *Informal Procedure*, p. 553.

[8] Votum XII, Primum Concilium Sinense, Vota et Postulata, Bouscaren, *Canon Law Digest, Supplement through 1948*, pp. 173-174; Cf. Payen, *De Matrimonio*, II, n. 2407 bis; Woods, *The Constitutions of Canon 1125*, p. 58; Burton, *A Commentary on Canon 1125*, pp. 156-157.

authors also affirm that no interpellations are required for the valid use of the Constitution *Romani Pontificis.*[9]

The Constitution *Populis* of Gregory XIII expressly grants the faculty of dispensing from the interpellations, and this general faculty covers both of the interpellations to such an extent that, when the necessary conditions of impossibility or inutility are verified, those to whom the faculty is given by the universal law can both validly and licitly dispense from both interpellations.[10]

Article II: From One or the Other Interpellation

No one today would contest the power of the Pope to dispense from the ecclesiastical law obligation of making the interpellations; it is evident, therefore, that the Supreme Pontiff can, *a fortiori,* dispense or grant the faculty of dispensing from either one of the two interpellations.[11]

The faculties of the Sacred Congregation for the Propagation of the Faith were made available for the granting of a dispensation from both interpellations, but they may also be used for the granting of a dispensation from just one or the other of the interpellations. Thus, if the infidel has answered negatively to the question whether he wishes to be converted, a dispensation from the question whether or not the infidel wishes to continue peaceful cohabitation with

[9] Burton, *op. cit.,* p. 154; Cappello, *De Matrimonio,* n. 787, p. 776; Vermeersch-Creusen, *Epitome,* II, n. 436, p. 303; Woeber, *The Interpellations,* p. 123; Coronata, *De Matrimonio,* n. 648: "Verificata conditione quod mulier, quam retinere ut uxorem intendit vir conversus, baptizata est, nihil aliud requiritur ut cum ea matrimonium contrahatur nec ulla interpellatio aliarum uxorum, ne primae quidem est necessaria." Cf. Doheny, *Informal Procedure,* p. 554.

[10] Burton, *A Commentary on Canon 1125,* p. 81; Woeber, *The Interpellations,* pp. 123-125; Vermeersch-Creusen, *op. cit.,* n. 436, p. 303; Cappello, *De Matrimonio,* n. 787, p. 777; Coronata, *op. cit.,* n. 649, p. 907; Doheny, *op. cit.,* p. 558.

[11] S.C.S. Off. (Cochinchin.) 1 Aug. 1759, ad 2—*Fontes,* n. 810; S.C.S. Off. (Siam) 4 iul. 1855—*Fontes,* n. 931; *Coll. S.C.P.F.* n. 1114; S.C. de Prop. Fide (C.P. pro Sin-Sutchuen.), 3 ian. 1777—*Coll. S.C. P.F.,* n. 517; Synodus Vicariatus Sutchuensis, cap. IX, n. VIII in fine; Cappello, *De Matrimonio,* n. 781.

his convert spouse can be given in favor of the convert.[12]

The same faculty is granted in the Constitution *Populis*. While no interpellation at all is required in the use of the privileges of Popes Paul III and Pius V, Ayrinhac-Lydon and Payen speak of the Constitution *Altitudo* as granting the dispensation in certain cases of impossibility, and in reference to the use of the Constitution *Romani Pontificis* postulate the difficulty of finding the first wife as a factor which serves as the very condition for the use of the privilege. If she is located, they say, she is to be interpellated about whether she wishes to be baptized, and they state that *ipso iure* there is granted a dispensation from the second interpellation concerning the continuance or the resumption of cohabitation.[13]

Payen states that the constitution certainly grants the faculty of interpellating the first wife about one point only, namely concerning her intention about receiving baptism. After having received a negative answer to this question the convert was allowed to marry whichever of his wives was willing to be baptized with him. He is forced to admit, however, that the constitution *probably* grants the faculty of omitting both interpellations, and even concedes that this "is the obvious sense of the words."[14]

Actually such a condition of finding the first spouse and interpellating her is not required by the Constitution; though there is mention of the difficulty of finding the first wife merely as an impelling cause for the use of the privilege. In other words, if the first spouse cannot be found, there is all the more reason for the use of the privilege, which nevertheless is applicable without any respect to the presence or absence of the infidel.[15]

[12] Wernz-Vidal, *Ius Matrimoniale*, n. 633, p. 827; Gregory, *The Pauline Privilege*, p. 77.

[13] *Marriage Legislation*, pp. 318-319; *De Matrimonio*, II, n. 2406, p. 737.

[14] *De Matrimonio*, II, 2406, p. 738.

[15] Winslow, *The Pauline Privilege*, pp. 62-74; Coronata, *De Matrimonio*, n. 648, p. 905; Burton, *A Commentary on Canon 1125*, p. 81;

Woods concludes that the convert must retain the first spouse if it is certain that she is his valid spouse, and if she spontaneously and voluntarily offers to be baptized with him.[16] But Cappello states that, even if the first spouse volunteers the information that she wishes to be baptized, the convert can still use the privilege of St. Pius V if it would be difficult for him to separate from the wife who was baptized with him and with whom he is now cohabiting, for this was the prime motive cause for the granting of the privilege.[17]

No interpellation at all is required by the Constitution, and accordingly no question of any needed dispensation is involved.[18] This is approved by the Holy See.[19]

Article III: To Make the Interpellations before Baptism

The universal law of the Church[20] requires that the interpellation of the party remaining in infidelity is to be made by the convert only after the latter's baptism. This has always been the prescribed policy of the Church,[21] and it flows from the very nature of the privilege. For the convert

---

Woods (*The Constitutions of Canon 1125*, pp. 50-55) covers the question in all its interpretations. Vermeersch-Creusen (*Epitome*, II, n. 436, p. 303) state that this interpretation arises from the practice of the Holy See, which forbids the use of the privilege under these conditions.

[16] *The Constitutions of Canon 1125*, p. 55.

[17] *De Matrimonio*, n. 787, p. 777, note 68 also.

[18] Vermeersch-Creusen, *op. cit.*, n. 436, p. 303: "Vi constitutionis Pii V non videtur interpellanda uxor legitima, etiamsi cognoscatur." Woods, *op. cit.*, p. 55: "From the context of the Brief it appears that no interpellation to the first wife need be made." Winslow, *The Pauline Privilege*, p. 71: "The interpellations of the true spouse are *ipso iure* omitted and no further dispensation is necessary." Wernz-Vidal, *Ius Matrimoniale*, n. 633, p. 829: "... habemus ... in duplici casu Const. Pauli III et S. Pii V sublatam necessitatem interpellationis..." Burton, *A Commentary on Canon 1125*, p. 80.

[19] Cf. *supra*, footnote 8, p. 147.

[20] Canon 1121, § 1.

[21] S.C.S. Off. (Techely Orient.), 13 apr. 1859—*Fontes*, n. 951; *Coll. S.C.P.F.*, n. 1175.

has the right to apply the privilege only when the departure of the unbaptized party or his evil intent has become manifest *after* the conversion of the other party. In every normal use of the Pauline privilege, therefore, the prospective convert must of necessity wait until after his baptism before attempting to determine the will of his unbaptized consort.[22]

Since both the obligation of making the interpellations and the postulated presence of the conditions under which that obligation are to be fulfilled are of ecclesiastical law origin and are controlled by that law, it follows that the supreme legislator can change these conditions when the circumstances of certain cases warrant such a variation. It is admitted that the Holy See can dispense from the obligation in its entirety; it can, therefore, and *a fortiori*, dispense from the ordinary conditions regulating the fulfillment of the obligation.

The Holy See, in practice, has shown itself ready to grant exceptions to the general and common rule, thus permitting the prospective convert to interpellate his unbaptized spouse before his own baptism.[23] The Holy See has not only granted the dispensation, but has given the faculty to individual bishops and vicars apostolic for a varying, but a definite, number of cases.[24]

[22] Vromant, *De Matrimonio*, n. 323, p. 250.

[23] S.C.S. Off., instr. (ad Vic. Ap. Sutchuen. Orient.), 3 iun. 1874—*Fontes*, n. 1030, *Coll. S.C.P.F.*, n. 1415; S.C.S. Off. (Bengal), 21 nov. 1883 ad 3—*Coll. S.C.P.F.*, n. 1607; Cf. Gregory, *The Pauline Privilege*, p. 72; De Smet, *De Sponsalibus et De Matrimonio*, n. 349. De Becker ("Criticism of Augustine's *Rights and Duties of Ordinaries According to the Code and Apostolic Faculties*," *ETL*, II [1925], 446) records that Archbishop Hanna of San Francisco obtained an indult to allow the *neoconversus* to make the interpellations before baptism. Vermeersch ("Apostolicae Facultates", *Periodica*, XXI [1922], 141), stated: "Haec facultas subdelegabilis sicut tres praecedentes ante Codicem rarissime concedebatur." Romani, *De Matrimonio*, n. 1153, p. 785.

[24] S.C.S. Off., instr. (ad Vic. Ap. Sutchuen, Orient.), 3 iun. 1874—*Fontes*, n. 1030; Coll. *S.C.P.F.*, n. 1415.

Likewise, through the Sacred Congregation for the Propagation of the Faith general faculties have been granted to all territories operating under the direction of the same Sacred Congregation.[25]

For a grave reason this faculty gives mission ordinaries the power to permit the making of the interpellations before the actual baptism of the one party, still a catechumen. The faculty also allows these ordinaries to dispense the convert before his baptism from the obligation of making the interpellations as long as a summary and extrajudicial investigation has proved that the fulfilling of the obligation will be impossible, or certainly useless. Ordinarily a dispensation is not granted in favor of a non-Catholic, even the while he actually contemplates joining the Church.

Earlier the Holy See had stated that it was prompted to grant such a dispensation in a particular case as an effective means of bringing about the conversion of the infidel. This is a further indication of the benign interest of the Church in its converts and in their salvation.[26]

In regard to the first grant, which allows the making of the interpellations before baptism, there is postulated a grave cause for the use of the faculty. Such a dispensation, for example, was granted by the Holy See, in order that the convert could enter a valid and licit marriage immediately after baptism without any further delay. Thus the dispensation would remove the necessity of requiring a temporary separation until the interpellations could be made and the prescribed negative answers received.[27]

In recognizing this as a sufficient cause, Vromant pointed to the practical case of a catechumen, who after having left

[25] Formula Facultatum, Formula Tertia Maior, n. 27; Coronata, *Institutiones Iuris Canonici* (5 vols., Vol. V, Taurini: Marietti, 1936), V, 321.

[26] Vromant, *Facultates Apostolicae,* p. 84; S.C.S. Off., instr. (ad Vic. Ap. Sutchuen. Orient.), 3 iun. 1874—*Fontes,* n. 1030; *Coll. S.C.P.F.,* n. 1415.

[27] S.C.S. Off., instr. (ad Vic. Ap. Sutchuen. Orient.), 3 iun. 1874—*Fontes,* n. 1030; *Coll. S.C.P.F.,* n. 1415.

his first spouse, has contracted an invalid marriage, perhaps wholly without fault on his part, and then continued living in good faith with this second person. By being allowed to make the interpellations before his baptism such a prospective convert could derive much encouragement for his adoption of the Faith.[28] Other authors list this case along with the following.[29]

The Holy See has even allowed the use of the faculty when it was feared that the unbaptized spouse, if interpellated in the ordinary way and time, might answer maliciously in the affirmative.[30]

The faculty can likewise be used when the anticipated interpellations will prove helpful to a catechumen who otherwise will only reluctantly fulfill some of the conditions necessary for the reception of baptism, for example, when the convert has a well founded fear that the restoration of conjugal life with his former spouse will actually prove a serious spiritual danger. The same is true if the convert has a good reason for believing that his former consort will not be faithful to the promise of living peacefully and respectfully in the marital union.[31]

In general, any danger of a great spiritual harm is to be considered a grave cause, for this seems to be the spirit of the faculty. Accordingly, although the foregoing are the most common causes, they do not constitute an exhaustive list.[32]

[28] *Facultates Apostolicae*, n. 85, p. 83.

[29] Payen, *De Matrimonio*, II, n. 2415; Vermeersch, "Facultates Apostolicae," *Periodica*, XI (1922), 141; Coronata, *De Matrimonio*, n. 640, p. 896; Winslow, *The Pauline Privilege*, p. 41; Winslow, *Commentary on the Apostolic Faculties*, p. 159.

[30] S.C.S. Off. (Bengal), 21 nov. 1883, ad 3—*Coll. S.C.P.F.*, n. 1607; Payen, *De Matrimonio*, II, n. 2415; Winslow, *The Pauline Privilege*, p. 41.

[31] Vermeersch, "Facultates Apostolicae," *Periodica*, XI (1922), n. 122, pp. 140-141; Winslow, *The Pauline Privilege*, p. 41; Winslow, *A Commentary on the Apostolic Faculties*, p. 159; Vromant, *Facultates Apostolicae*, n. 85, p. 83; Payen, *De Matrimonio*, II, n. 2415.

[32] Payen, *loc. cit.*

For the use of the faculty to dispense the prospective convert from the obligation of making the interpellations, there is explicitly postulated as a necessary condition the presence of proof with certainty derived from a summary investigation, namely that the making of the interpellations would, in fact, be impossible or wholly useless.[33] This moral certainty is required for the valid granting of the dispensation. The use of summary and extrajudicial investigation is postulated for the licitness of the procedure.[34]

To these cases other authors add the cases in which the interpellating of the infidel would occasion the danger of harm to the convert or to other Christians.[35] They point out that besides the general conditions of impossibility, inutility or harm, the faculty requires further some other grave reason if there is to be granted this dispensation before baptism, otherwise there would be nothing to distinguish this grant from that of number XXV of the Faculties. The causes required here are the same as those listed above, the factors that prepare the way for the ultimate baptism of the convert.[36]

A dispensation from the interpellations granted in virtue of this faculty guarantees the absolute validity of the second marriage, and in this regard Vromant states that it partakes of the same extraordinary effect as that which is produced by means of the dispensation which is granted

[33] Formula Facultatum, Formula Tertia Maior, n. 27; Payen, *loc. cit.;* Winslow, *The Pauline Privilege*, p. 42; Winslow, *A Commentary on the Apostolic Faculties*, p. 160; Léry, *Le Privilège de la Foi*, n. 95, p. 122; Blat, *De Sacramentis*, n. 532, p. 678.

[34] Vromant, *Facultates Apostolicae*, p. 85.

[35] Payen, *De Matrimonio*, II, n. 2415, p. 755.

[36] Payen, *loc. cit.*, "Sed, ut ab utraque interpellatione *ante* baptismum dispensetur, videtur exigi, praeter certam impossibilitatem aut certam inutilitatem, gravis causa." Vermeersch-Creusen, *Epitome*, II, n. 435, p. 302: "Notetur necessitas processus saltem sumarii et extraiudicalis praeter gravem causam ut ab omni interpellatione dispensetur; dum gravis causa sufficit ad illam ante baptismum faciendam." Blat, *De Sacramentis*, n. 532, p. 678; Vermeersch, "Facultates Apostolicae," *Periodica*, XI (1922), 141; Winslow, *The Pauline Privilege*, p. 42; Winslow, *A Commentary on the Apostolic Faculties*, p. 160.

through a use of the privilege bestowed in the Constitution *Populis.*[37]

It is to be noted, however, that the dispensation from the interpellations that are to be made before baptism cannot be granted in virtue of canon 1125, but only in consequence of a special faculty obtained from the Holy See.

[37] Vromant, *Facultates Apostolicae,* p. 86; cf. S.C.S. Off. (ad Vic. Ap. Iaponiae Merid.), 4 febr. 1891—*Fontes,* n. 1130; *Coll. S.C.P.F.,* n. 1746.

CHAPTER V

CAUSES RECOGNIZED AS VALID BY POST-CODE AUTHORS

Any requirement of ecclesiastical law origin admits of exceptions and relaxations in particular cases. Such a dispensation in general can always be granted by the authority who promulgated the law, by his successor or superior, as well as by those to whom a special faculty for dispensing has been conceded.[1]

However, none of these, not even the Supreme Pontiff, can rightfully grant such a dispensation from the universal law of the Church apart from a sufficiently impelling cause. In general such a cause must be both just and reasonable.[2]

The notion of justice in this regard looks to the existence of the cause, while that of reasonableness relates to the proportion between the gravity of the law and the sufficiency of the cause allowing a dispensation from it. The reasonableness of the cause will be determined in the light of the gravity and the binding force of the law from which a dispensation is sought. A just and reasonable cause is, therefore, required before a dispensation from the interpellations can be granted in any case regardless of the one who actually grants the dispensation.[3]

Coronata here makes a distinction. If the departure of the unbaptized party is certain, a just cause is no longer required, and the Holy See can authorize the omission of the interpellations without any further consideration. He notes, though, that generally this is not done, and that those who dispense in virtue of delegated power must have a just

[1] Canon 80.

[2] Canon 84 § 1.

[3] Cappello, *De Matrimonio*, n. 781, p. 770; Coronata, *De Matrimonio*, n. 641, p. 896; cf. Edward Roelker, "The Meaning of the term '*Rationabilis*' in the Code of Canon Law," *The Jurist*, IX (1949), 163-166.

reason for doing so even when the actual departure or evil intent of the infidel is both known and proved.[4]

Since the interpellations are required by the divine law for the licit use of the Pauline privilege,[5] when the *discessus* of the heathen is not known or certain, even the Holy See would depend on the existence of a just cause for the validity of a granted dispensation. All others, whether acting under power granted by the universal law or through special faculties, would *a fortiori* need a sufficiently grave reason for using their power to dispense from the interpellations.[6]

Here the Pope is not dispensing from his own law, but is using his ministerial vicarious power to dispense from a divine law requirement, and hence a cause is always required, not only for the licit, but also for the valid use of the power, and for the validity of the subsequent marriage.[7]

Since this same instrumental vicarious power is used in granting the privileges of the Constitutions of Popes Paul III and St. Pius V and particularly that of Gregory XIII, the validity of any dispensation granted in virtue of canon 1125 is, therefore, conditioned upon the actual existence of a sufficiently grave cause.[8]

Article I: Causes Sufficient for Allowing the Holy See to Dispense

The Holy See in determining causes sufficiently grave for granting a dispensation from the interpellations has listed them under the general headings of impossibility, inutility or danger.[9]

[4] *De Matrimonio,* n. 641, p. 897; cf. Cappello, *De Matrimonio,* n. 781, p. 772.

[5] Cf. *supra,* Part III, Chapter I, Art. 3, sect. 1, p. 101.

[6] Coronata, *De Matrimonio,* n. 641, p. 897.

[7] Woods, *The Constitutions of Canon 1125,* p. 28; Chelodi, *Ius Matrimoniale,* n. 160, p. 175; Cappello, *op. cit.,* n. 762, p. 749; Coronata, *op. cit.,* n. 641, p. 897.

[8] Burton, *A Commentary on Canon 1125,* p. 90.

[9] S.C.S. Off., (ad Vic. Ap. Iaponiae Merid.), 4 febr. 1891—*Fontes,* n. 1130; *Coll. S.C.P.F.,* n. 1746. If just and reasonable causes are

Impossibility and inutility have been identified as the *ordinary causes,* while those in which the making of the interpellations would occasion some harm, physical or spiritual, to the convert, to Christians in general, or to the one making the interpellations are listed as *extraordinary causes.*[10]

Post-Code authors take their clue from the pre-Code responses and practice of the Church in grouping the causes sufficient for allowing the Holy See to dispense from the interpellations under these headings,[11] as well as in recognizing the causes already approved by the Holy See.[12]

Not all of these causes are of equal application today. Years of material progress as well as changing social standards and customs can certainly affect even these in some varying degree or form; yet all are valid and of some use today.

Section 1: Impossibility

1) The most commonly recognized cause for dispensing and one that would actually be most frequently applicable in practice is had when the present whereabouts of the infidel party is entirely unknown.[13] Such a situation could

---

present then a dispensation from these interpellations will be granted. Such just causes will be present when upon at least a summary and extrajudicial procedure of investigation it has become morally certain that the infidel party cannot be interpellated, or that interpellation will be useless or harmful. Thus a just cause would exist 1) when it would be absolutely impossible to question the unbaptized person; 2) when this would bring great danger to the one making the interpellations or to the converted partner, or 3) when the interpellations would be patently useless. Cf. Wernz-Vidal, *Ius Matrimoniale,* n. 633, note 80, p. 827; Coronata, *De Matrimonio,* n. 641, p. 897.

[10] S.C.S. Off. (Mongoliae), 29 nov. 1882—*Fontes,* n. 1075; *Coll. S.C.P.F.,* n. 1581; Formula Facultatum, Formula Tertia Minor, nn. 25-26.

[11] Doheny, *Informal Procedure,* pp. 531-532; Woeber, *The Interpellations,* p. 112; Winslow, *The Pauline Privilege,* pp. 35-37.

[12] Cf. Part One, Chapter IV, Art. 4, pp. 42-48, for enumeration of and references to these causes.

[13] Cappello, *De Matrimonio,* n. 781, p. 771; Coronata, *De Matrimonio,*

arise easily even today, notwithstanding the vastly improved methods of travel and correspondence in this country or in the world at large. It may well be that the convert has long ago been divorced by his former spouse, so that neither has made any attempt in the ensuing time to keep in contact with the other. As a part of our typically floating population they could, even after a brief space of time, lose all knowledge of the other's residence. Such a condition could likewise be verified even though the infidel actually is living within the same city or nearby. It is not uncommon in our larger communities for people to be totally unknown even to their nearest neighbor.

It is not sufficient to presume this absence; the one concerned must make a diligent attempt to locate the party through the use of all possible avenues of contact, such as the newspapers, radio spot announcements, police records, etc.[14]

The increasing arrival in this country of persons displaced from home and relatives by the fortunes of war will certainly occasion many complications in regard to marriage that can be solved only through the granting of a dispensation.

2) A cause for dispensing can also exist when the convert no longer remembers who was his first and legitimate spouse among the many wives with whom he had lived while he was still a heathen.[15]

Even the most prolific of polygamists today could scarcely

n. 641, p. 897; Wernz-Vidal, *Ius Matrimoniale*, n. 633, note 80, p. 827; Doheny, *op. cit.*, p. 532; Gregory, *The Pauline Privilege*, p. 79; Woeber, *op. cit.*, p. 112; Petrovits, *The New Church Law on Matrimony*, p. 567; Vermeersch-Creusen, *Epitome*, II, n. 434, p. 300; Vromant, *De Matrimonio*, n. 362, p. 287; Gougnard, *Tractatus de Matrimonio*, p. 296; Kearney, *The Principles of Canon 1127*, p. 126; Farrugia, *De Matrimonio et Causis Matrimonialibus*, n. 322, p. 473; Heylen, *Tractatus de Matrimonio*, p. 347.

[14] Cf. *infra*, art. III, notes 94 and 95, p. 181.

[15] Woeber, *op. cit.*, p. 112; Coronata, *loc. cit.;* Wernz-Vidal, *loc. cit.;* Cappello, *loc. cit.;* Kearney, *loc. cit.*

fall under this heading, for the cases would indeed be rare when such circumstances could be verified. The cause does have force and possible application if and when considered in conjunction with the following approved cause.

3) A cause for dispensing can also be present when the convert is uncertain whether he ever gave true matrimonial consent to any of the women with whom he lived, so that he can seriously and with reason doubt that he was validly married to any of them.[16] This possibility was often verified among polygamous people, many of whom married simply to determine the qualities of their prospective wives, and then promptly dismissed those who did not come up to expectations.[17]

On the other hand, it may be that the frequency of divorce may in a particular case give reason for doubt as to the actual identity of the true partner. Doheny indicates that if a thorough investigation does not reveal the first in a series of polyandrous or polygynous spouses, the privilege of the Faith may be invoked for solving the doubt and thus preparing the way for the application of the Pauline privilege.[18]

Such a notion is not at all excluded today in the light of an ever increasing popular and conventional approval of trial marriage and free love. Since the essential notion of marriage consists in an exchange of consent, and that matrimonial consent consists in an act of the will by which each party gives and accepts a *perpetual* and *exclusive* right over the other for the exercise of acts suitable of themselves for the procreation of children,[19] it becomes increasingly evident that many marriages today are contracted under conditions contrary to this essential notion and with intentions con-

[16] Doheny, *loc. cit.;* Woeber, *op. cit.*, p. 113; Coronata, *loc. cit.*, Wernz-Vidal, *loc. cit.;* Cappello, *loc . cit.;* Heylen, *loc. cit.;* Petrovits, *op. cit.*, n. 567, p. 409.

[17] S.C.S. Off. (Siouxormen.), 18 maii 1892—*Fontes*, n. 1155; *Coll. S.C.P.F.*, n. 1796; *ASS*, XXIX (1896-1897), 641.

[18] *Informal Procedure*, p. 575.

[19] Canon 1081, §§ 1-2.

trary to and exclusive of the essential characteristics of unity and indissolubility. In many such cases a thorough and careful investigation of the facts will throw considerable doubt on the validity of the matrimonial contract.

Actually in such a case it may not be necessary to seek or grant a dispensation from the interpellations, for the law, under these circumstances, as Woeber pointedly indicates, favors the conversion of the infidel with the privilege of a new marriage rather than the validity of the former but doutful marriage.[20]

4) Listed separately is the case wherein the impossibility of locating the former spouse arises immediately from a total lack of knowledge concerning the spouse. It differs from the foregoing case, in which the convert indeed knew all his wives but was unable to remember who was the first.[21] This cause would include any case in which there is a real doubt about the validity of the first marriage.[22]

5) There is cause also for a dispensation when the distance to the residence of the infidel is so great as to render the journey an excessive hardship for the making of the interpellations, or even to render the fulfillment of this obligation a moral impossibility.[23]

The difficulty envisioned in this cause could arise, exclusive of the mere fact of distance, also from the great financial expense involved or simply because of the tremendous inconvenience that would necessarily be incurred,[24] for any great inconvenience suffices.[25]

[20] *The Interpellations*, p. 113, cf. canon 1127.

[21] Woeber, *op. cit.*, p. 112; Coronata, *op. cit.*, n. 641, p. 897; Cappello, *op. cit.*, n. 781, p. 771; Wernz-Vidal, *loc. cit.*, Doheny, *op. cit.*, p. 532; Petrovits, *op. cit.*, n. 567, p. 409.

[22] Ayrinhac-Lydon, *Marriage Legislation*, p. 312.

[23] Vermeersch-Creusen, *Epitome*, II, n. 434, p. 300; n. 435, p. 301; Payen, *De Matrimonio*, II, n. 2426; Vromant, *De Matrimonio*, n. 362, p. 287; Blat, *De Sacramentis*, n. 536, p. 682; Farrugia, *De Matrimonio et Causis Matrimonialibus*, n. 322, p. 473.

[24] Woeber, *The Interpellations*, p. 112; Doheny, *Informal Procedure*, p. 532.

[25] Gougnard, *Tractatus de Matrimonio*, p. 296.

Over a century ago the Holy See recognized that a journey which involved seven or eight days for a round trip was sufficient to make the obligation of interpellating the unbaptized consort morally impossible. It has been the consistent practice of the Holy See to decline to determine any definite time limit as applicable in all cases, and no commentators will attempt to suggest anything definite. For the distance is not the sole factor in the determination of the sufficiency of the cause, but it is to be judged in the light of the persons involved, the exact residence of the infidel, the cost of the trip, the available means of travel, or any other concomitant circumstance that may render communication with the infidel morally impossible.[26] These circumstances must be considered in relation to the convert in question, and not in relation to the inconvenience that would be caused the ordinary or his delegate in the making of the interpellations.[27]

Ordinarily today all parts of the nation can be reached through the postal service of the Federal government, which service is accordingly to be used if through personal contact it remains impossible to reach the party.

6) Closely allied are the cases in which the infidel is residing in a locality which can, under normal circumstances, be reached without any grave inconvenience, but which, at the moment, is cut off from normal access by a state of terrorism or warfare.[28]

It does not seem necessary to restrict the application of this cause to the cases wherein the infidel is subject to or a member of the enemy's forces. Actually, however, the experience of the recent war revealed the reliability and com-

[26] S.C.S. Off. (Mongoliae), 29 nov. 1882—*Fontes*, n. 1075; *Coll. S.C. P.F.*, n. 1581; Gougnard, *loc. cit.;* Farrugia, *op. cit.*, n. 322, p. 473.

[27] Woods, *The Constitutions of Canon 1125*, p. 67.

[28] Woeber, *op. cit.*, p. 112; Coronata, *op. cit.*, n. 641, p. 897; Wernz-Vidal, *op. cit.*, n. 633, note 80, p. 827; Vermeersch-Creusen, *op. cit.*, II, n. 435, p. 301; Cappello, *op. cit.*, n. 781, p. 770; Kearney, *op. cit.*, p. 126; Farrugia, *op. cit.*, n. 322, p. 473; Vromant, *De Matrimonio*, n. 362, p. 287; Blat, *De Sacramentis*, n. 536, p. 682.

parative promptness of mail delivery to and from members of the armed forces of this country, even in the face of the far flung and rapidly changing theaters of military operations. Even under such circumstances and conditions the interpellations can often be made without an unduly long and inconvenient delay.

One can easily imagine circumstances of upheaval or confusion resulting from a state of catastrophe or pestilence which all but renders hopeless any attempt to contact the infidel party. Coronata lists also in this regard the case of the infidel party's confinement in a prison to which access is denied.[29]

It is this kind of impossible communication that gives validity to the cause regardless of the circumstances from which the impossibility arises,[30] and the dispensation can be granted when it is reasonably certain that it will be impossible to get the interpellations to the infidel consort.[31]

7) A cause for dispensing can furthermore be present when the interpellations have been made according to the normal formalities required by the practice of the Church, but no answer has been received from the interpellated within the time limit attached as a condition to the interpellation itself.[32]

Normally this time limit should be stated explicitly in the form of the interpellations, so that proper provision will be made for this particular eventuality, namely when the infidel proves himself deliberately obstinate and uncooperative. Under usual circumstances a full month is considered a sufficient duration of time that will allow the one interpellated to consider the consequences and the nature of his answers.[33]

[29] *De Matrimonio*, n. 649, p. 907.

[30] Vermeersch-Creusen, *op. cit.*, II, n. 435, p. 301.

[31] Gougnard, *op. cit.*, p. 296.

[32] Woeber, *op. cit.*, p. 112; Coronata, *op. cit.*, n. 641, p. 397; Wernz-Vidal, *loc. cit.*, Doheny, *op. cit.*, p. 532; Cappello, *op. cit.*, n. 781, p. 771; Petrovits, *The New Church Law on Matrimony*, n. 567, p. 409.

[33] Doheny, *loc. cit.*, Burton, *A Commentary on Canon 1125*, p. 171.

However, individual cases are to be considered carefully by the competent authority for the determining of the time limit. In any event the time is to be reckoned according to the rules applying for the computation of available time (*tempus utile*) which stipulate that the duration of the period does not lapse as long as one is ignorant of the fact in question or is legitimately impeded from acting.[34]

Actually this cause resolves itself into a negative answer to the interpellations, in which case no dispensation is required and the Pauline privilege is applied according to its natural and ordinary procedure. For a negative answer is considered as a proof of the essential departure of the infidel party.[35]

8) A cause is present also when there is a well-founded basis for suspecting the sincerity of the veracity of the infidel in his answers to the interpellations. For it may well happen that the affirmative answers of the unbaptized party are openly contradicted by his actions and attitude in general toward the convert, or with reference to the Christian Faith.[36]

If it is proved by the prescribed summary investigation that the answers of the infidel are clearly not sincere, they are again to be considered as negative, and the Pauline privilege is applicable in its normal procedure. Such is equally true if the infidel party "resorted to deceptive evasions and exasperating subterfuges."[37] If the evidence against the sincerity is not sufficiently proved, then a dispensation should be sought or granted *"ad cautelam."* Any such doubt about the conversion and intention of the unbaptized consort

[34] Canon 35; Winslow, *The Pauline Privilege*, p. 30, note 80; p. 78; Doheny, *loc. cit.*

[35] Vermeersch-Creusen, *op. cit.* II, n. 433, p. 299; Cappello, *De Matrimonio*, n. 780, p. 770; Coronata, *op. cit.*, n. 637, p. 891.

[36] Cappello, *op. cit.*, n. 770, p. 762; also n. 780, p. 769; Petrovits, *op. cit.*, n. 567, p. 409; Ayrinhac-Lydon, *Marriage Legislation*, p. 317; Doheny, *op. cit.*, p. 575; Woeber, *op. cit.*, p. 117; Vermeersch-Creusen, *op. cit.*, II, n. 437, p. 304; Coronata, *op. cit.*, n. 652, p. 911.

[37] Doheny, *Informal Procedure*, p. 575; cf. *Infra*, art. III; Const. *Populis*, Gregory, XIII, 25 ian. 1585.

can be solved through an application of the prescripts of canon 1127, so that in favor of the Faith the first marriage may be dissolved.[38]

9) Finally, the presence of a cause for dispensing from the interpellations may be occasioned when the infidel, upon becoming acquainted with the plan of his converted spouse and the purpose of the interpellations, deliberately and purposively goes into hiding in order to deprive the convert or his agent of any and every opportunity to make the interpellations.[39]

To these causes some authors add another, namely the need or the demand of a dispensation because of some grave necessity. In this matter they consider as sufficient anything that parallels the kind of necessity postulated for the granting of a dispensation from the ecclesiastical impediments when a person is in danger of death, or when everything is prepared for the marriage before the impediment is discovered.[40]

It will be noted that all of these causes in some way resolve themselves into an impossibility—physical or moral—of making the interpellations, and that is all that is necessary, regardless of the source of the impossibility, for the granting of a dispensation from the interpellations by the Holy See, or for the requesting of a faculty to dispense on the part of any subordinate authority.[41]

A moral impossibility suffices as a postulate for the dispensation. It is not essential that the circumstances be such

[38] Wernz-Vidal, *op. cit.*, n. 637, p. 838; Woeber, *op. cit.*, p. 75; Coronata, *op. cit.*, n. 652, p. 911; Vermeersch-Creusen, *op. cit.*, II, n. 437; Doheny, *loc. cit.*

[39] Winslow, *The Pauline Privilege*, p. 36; Coronata, *op. cit.*, n. 637, p. 891; Cappello, *op. cit.*, n. 780, p. 770.

[40] Cans. 1043-1045; Vermeersch-Creusen, *op. cit.*, II, n. 435, p. 300; Woeber, *The Interpellations*, p. 113. This question will be considered in its own right more thoroughly. Cf. *infra*, Chapter VII, art. II.

[41] Bouscaren, "An Inquiry into the Practical Application of Canon 1125," *Miscellanea-Vermeersch*, I, 294; Winslow, *op. cit.*, p. 37; Doheny, *op. cit.*, p. 560, n. 8.

that they render physically impossible the making of the interpellations.[42]

Section 2: Futility

Beyond the factors which connate the presence of some physical or moral condition of impossibility it is further acknowledged that the Holy See can readily dispense from the obligation of making the interpellations in all cases wherein the fulfilling of that formality would be futile or useless, and therefore unnecessary. In many cases the purpose of the interpellations is clearly ascertained by some other and often more effective means, so that this requirement can be dispensed with.[43]

It is possible to distinguish two separate causes under this heading, for futility and uselessness need not be identified, although the terms are usually used interchangeably.

The interpellations are *futile* whenever the infidel is impeded in some way from answering. A specific example is the case wherein he is incapable of performing a human act in consequence of insanity. The Holy See has expressly recognized this case,[44] and it is approved as valid today.[45]

[42] Doheny, *op. cit.*, p. 560; Payen, *De Matrimonio*, II, n. 2409, p. 728; Bouscaren, "An Inquiry into the Practical Application of Canon 1125," *Miscellanea-Vermeersch*, I, 294.

[43] Gregory, *op. cit.*, p. 78; Kearney, *op. cit.*, p. 126; Woeber, *op. cit.*, pp. 112-113; Farrugia, *op. cit.*, n. 322, p. 473; Ayrinhac-Lydon, *loc. cit.*; Cappello, *op. cit.*, n. 781, p. 770; Romani, *De Matrimonio*, n. 153, p. 784; Coronata, *op. cit.*, n. 641, p. 897; Vermeersch-Creusen, *op. cit.*, II, n. 435, p. 301; Chelodi, *Ius Matrimoniale*, n. 160, p. 175; Chelodi-Ciprotti, *De Matrimonio*, n. 160, p. 202; Gougnard, *op. cit.*, p. 298; Vromant, *De Matrimonio*, n. 373, p. 287; Blat, *De Sacramentis*, n. 532, p. 679; Vlaming, *Praelectiones*, II, n. 724, p. 323; De Smet, *De Sponsalibus et Matrimonio*, n. 353, p. 301; Doheny, *op. cit.*, p. 531, among others.

[44] S.C. de Prop. Fide (pro Sin. Sutchuen.), 5 mart. 1787—*Coll. S.C.P.F.*, n. 589.

[45] Winslow, *The Pauline Privilege*, p. 37; Payen, *De Matrimonio*, II, n. 2413; Woeber, *The Interpellations*, pp. 34 and 114; Paventi, *Brevis Commentarius*, p. 44; Vromant, *De Matrimonio*, n. 363, p. 287; Vromant, *Facultates Apostolicae*, p. 80.

Under this heading Vromant lists in general the cases wherein it is known ahead of time that the infidel will not be able to signify his answer within the usual time limit for any reasonably grave cause.[46]

The interpellations are to be considered *useless* whenever the circumstances of the particular case prove without a doubt that the infidel has clearly indicated that he will not resume or continue the normal conjugal life. This refusal can be ascertained from earlier statements or deeds of the infidel party, as long as one can be certain that this attitude still perseveres. A practical and valid example of the uselessness of the interpellations is found in the case of an unbaptized man who obtained a civil divorce from his former wife, also unbaptized, but who has subsequently been converted and baptized. In the meantime this husband has entered a second civil union. The testimony of the divorce proceedings and the fact of the present cohabitation of the former husband stand as a clear indication of the man's *"discessus"* from the convert. This would be further established ordinarily if he has fathered children by his second wife.

Woeber, it seems, erroneously interpreted this latter cause as not being sufficiently grave to warrant the granting of a dispensation.[47] He sought to borrow substantiation for his statement from a response of the Holy Office.[48] Actually this response merely stated that a civil divorce and a remarriage were not to be considered as sufficient for the omission of the interpellations entirely, and it explicitly stated that the bishop was to use his faculty to dispense in the event that he enjoyed the faculty; if he did not, he was to obtain the faculty from the Holy See.[49] In another and

[46] *De Matrimonio*, n. 363, p. 287; *Facultates Apostolicae*, p. 80; cf. also *Privilège de la Foi*, n. 95, p. 122.

[47] *The Interpellations*, p. 34.

[48] S.C.S. Off. (Portland), 18 iun. 1884—*Fontes*, n. 1088; *Coll. S.C. P.F.*, n. 1620.

[49] "La mente è che nè il divorzio, nè il secondo matrimonio civile sane sufficienti per esimere dall'obbligo dell'interpellazione.—Quatenus

earlier case the Sacred Congregation for the Propagation of the Faith was asked whether the solemn expulsion of a wife, made by the husband before the civil leader of the community and according to the law of the land, could be considered as a sufficient substitute for the interpellations, since from this it was evident that the husband had absolutely no intention to have her as his wife. The answer stated briefly that the interpellations were to be made or a dispensation from them was to be granted.[50] The cause seems valid today in a particular application.[51]

Section 3: Danger of Grave Spiritual or Physical Harm

Besides the cases in which the interpellating of the infidel is impossible or useless, the Holy See can also dispense or grant the faculty of dispensing from the interpellations when the fulfillment of this obligation would occasion spiritual or temporal harm to the convert or to other Christians, as well as when it might arouse general persecution and strife.[52]

Not every danger in which these people find themselves, no matter how grave, is sufficient to allow a dispensation from the interpellations, but the danger must arise directly from the making of the interpellations; it must be manifest and unavoidable.

The danger must arise actually from the fact of the making of the interpellations, and proceed from the evil

---

vero saltem summarie et extraiudicialiter constet interpellationem impossibilem vel inutilem fore, utetur (Episcopus) facultatem dispensandi, si ea polleat; sin minus supplicandum SSmo pro facultate pro decem casibus. SSmus approbavit et facultatem concessit."

[50] S.C. de Prop. Fide (pro Sin. Tunk. Occident), 5 mart. 1816—*Coll. S.C.P.F.*, n. 704.

[51] Winslow, *The Pauline Privilege*, pp. 15-16; Burton, *A Commentary on Canon 1125*, p. 170.

[52] Cappello, *op. cit.*, n. 781, p. 771; Winslow, *op. cit.*, p. 39; Coronata, *op. cit.*, n. 641, p. 897; Woeber, *op. cit.*, p. 33: Vermeersch-Creusen, *op. cit.*, II, n. 434, p. 300; Heylen, *Tractatus de Matrimonio*, p. 347; De Smet, *op. cit.*, n. 353, p. 301; Petrovits, *The New Church Law on Matrimony*, n. 567, p. 408.

will of the one interpellated or from that of the other pagans with whom he is living. Ordinarily this danger will find expression through some form of physical force.

The threatening danger which warrants the granting of a dispensation from the interpellations frequently is one that imperils life, but a danger that threatens one's personal liberty or endangers one's personal fortune can likewise constitute a basis for the warranted granting of the dispensation.[53]

Woeber states that the Holy See does not accept as sufficiently grave the fact that the unbelieving woman might possibly suffer in reputation.[54] The Holy See did recognize a case in which the infidel after having obtained a civil divorce considered the interpellations as being injurious to him.[55]

The danger of some physical harm will differ from the danger of a spiritual harm in that the latter as often as not is deducible from an affirmative answer to the interpellations. By answering affirmatively the infidel will seek either to prevent the convert from applying the favor of the Pauline privilege, or he may actually intend to resume conjugal relationship with the convert, and then use this cohabitation as an occasion to do harm to the Christian's Faith or morals.[56]

Though this spiritual danger most often is in the form of a temptation to the convert or an abuse directed toward his conscience or Faith, it may be that in localities of more bitter bigotry the making of the interpellations would run the risk of prompting a general outbreak of persecution against the Christians of that community.[57]

[53] Doheny, *Informal Procedure*, p. 532; Winslow, *op. cit.*, p. 39.

[54] *The Interpellations*, p. 34.

[55] S.C.S. Off. (Portland), 18 iun. 1884—*Fontes*, n. 1088; *Coll. S.C. P.F.*, n. 1620.

[56] Payen, *De Matrimonio*, II, n. 2414; Vermeersch-Creusen, *Epitome*, II, n. 434, p. 300; Cappello, *De Matrimonio*, n. 781, p. 771.

[57] Ayrinhac-Lydon, *op. cit.*, p. 312; De Smet, *op. cit.*, n. 353, p. 301; Heylen, *op. cit.*, p. 347; Petrovits, *op. cit.*, n. 567, p. 408, Farrugia, *De Matrimonio et Causis Matrimonialibus*, n. 322, p. 473.

In every case the danger must be manifest and evident. It is not required that the injury itself be certain, but the danger that such an injury will be inflicted must be morally certain. One may not, therefore, act on a mere presumption or upon an unfounded fear.[58]

This danger may actually be realized even when the response of the infidel could be or actually was affirmative.[59] At the same time the danger must be such that under the present circumstances, at least, it is so inevitable that nothing can be done to escape from it.[60]

It is sufficient that the danger be directed toward the convert himself,[61] or toward other Christians, whether this be toward a particular person or toward Christians in general, in other words toward the Faith itself.[62]

In this regard Woeber excludes the one making the interpellations, so that any threat or abuse directed toward him is not to be considered as a cause that suffices for the granting of a dispensation.[63]

There seems to be no valid reason for explicitly excepting this one individual.[64] This particular danger may in many cases be obviated with the appointing of a different interpellator or through an executing of the obligation by means of registered mail.

[58] Payen, *De Matrimonio*, II, n. 2414; Winslow, *The Pauline Privilege*, p. 39.

[59] Kearney, *The Principles of Canon 1127*, p. 126.

[60] Payen, *op. cit.*, II, n. 2414, p. 753; Winslow, *loc. cit.*

[61] Heylen, *op. cit.*, p. 347; Vermeersch-Creusen, *op. cit.*, II, n. 434, p. 301; Woeber, *op. cit.*, p. 33; Cappello, *op. cit.*, n. 781, p. 771; Ayrinhac-Lydon, *op. cit.*, p. 312.

[62] Doheny, *Informal Procedure*, p. 532; Petrovits, *op. cit.*, n. 567, p. 408; Coronata, *op. cit.*, n. 641, p. 897; De Smet, *op. cit.*, n. 353, p. 301; Woeber, *op. cit.*, p. 33.

[63] *Op. cit.*, p. 33. Woeber here refers again to the response of the Holy Office to the Bishop of Portland. Actually in this response, as has been indicated earlier, the Holy See simply stated that among other causes this was not to be considered as sufficient for the omission of the interpellations.

[64] Winslow, *The Pauline Privilege*, p. 40; Payen, *De Matrimonio*, II, n. 2414, p. 753.

Vermeersch-Creusen include also the case in which harm would come to either of the parties to the prospective marriage.[65]

These then are the causes recognized and approved as sufficiently impelling to urge the Holy See to grant a dispensation from the interpellations. They are also valid for requesting a faculty to dispense whether that faculty is sought for a single case or for multiple instances.

All ordinaries and the clergy who have the faculty of dispensing from the interpellations should not hesitate to use this power when any of these conditions are verified, unless their delegation in this regard is expressly limited.[66]

It is clear from the law as it is also from the practice of the Church and the agreement of authors that the Pauline privilege can never be applied in favor of a convert who has given his infidel consort sufficient cause for separating.[67] For the same reason a dispensation from the interpellations must in every case be refused to a convert who after his baptism has given his partner sufficient reason for refusing to continue peaceful cohabitation, even though one or several of the causes that warrant the granting of a dispensation may truthfully be alleged.

Article II: Causes Sufficient for the Granting of a Dispensation in Virtue of Canon 1125

Since the privileges originally granted in the Papal Constitutions *Altitudo, Romani Pontificis* and *Populis* and now extended to the Church at large through its universal law, are but specifications of the supreme apostolic power of the popes, it follows that their application will be conditioned

[65] *Epitome*, II, n. 435, p. 301.

[66] Canons 49-50.

[67] Canon 1123; S.C. de Prop. Fide, instr., 30 iun. 1807—*Coll. S.C. P.F.*, n. 690; Cappello, *De Matrimonio*, n. 770, p. 761: "Si pars fidelis *iustam* causam praebuerit infideli discedendi, v.g. per adulterium *post* baptismum commissum, non potest uti privilegio Paulino." Vermeersch-Creusen, *op. cit.*, n. 433, p. 299; Coronata, *De Matrimonio*, n. 628; p. 878. Cf. also, Cerato, *Matrimonium*, n. 123, p. 212.

on specific requirements. Not all of the causes recognized as sufficient for the granting of a dispensation from the interpellations by the Pope, or in virtue of a special faculty conceded by him, will necessarily have validity for the granting of a similiar dispensation in virtue of the favor granted by Pope Gregory XIII in his Constitution *Populis*.

This constitution grants to all local ordinaries, pastors and Jesuit confessors the faculty of dispensing from the interpellations: "dummodo constet etiam summarie et extraiudicialiter coniugem, ut praefertur, absentem moneri legitime non posse, aut monitum intra tempus in eadem monitione praefixum suam voluntatem non significasse."[68]

The constitution expressly grants the faculty of dispensing from the interpellations under two separate conditions: 1) when it is impossible to make them, and 2) when the absent spouse has failed to manifest his or her intentions within the time limit specified in the form of the interpellations.

The first of these faculties covers the cases in which a careful investigation of the facts of the case reveals that the interpellations simply cannot be made in consequence of the specific circumstances relating to the absent infidel party.

The constitution itself suggests examples of the impossibility envisioned in the privilege, namely, when the parties are separated as a result of the fortunes of war or in consequence of the slave trade; when distance separating the two constitutes an exceptionally great inconvenience; when communication is impossible for the reason that the infidel lives in a hostile and barbarous part of the country; or when the convert does not know in fact where the infidel now lives.[69]

When Pope Gregory listed these specific examples, he did not intend to present an all-inclusive list; he intended simp-

[68] Gregorius XIII, const. *Populis*, 25 ian. 1585,—*Codex Iuris Canonici*, Documentum VIII.

[69] Burton, *A Commentary on Canon 1125*, p. 168; Winslow, *The Pauline Privilege*, p. 76.

ly to let the listed examples stand as representative of the cases in which the constitution became applicable.[70] In this regard again one is not to confuse the causes which were merely impelling and those which were actually the fundamental motives for the granting of the favor.[71]

Any cause, therefore, which under careful analysis is judged as rendering the making of the interpellations impossible is to be considered as sufficient for the granting of a dispensation under the provisions of the grant of Pope Gregory XIII.[72] Therefore, any of the cases mentioned in Section 1 of the previous article may find verification in present day circumstances, so that individually or conjunctively they will give cause for the conceding of a valid dispensation from the making of the interpellations. In a particular case there may arise a cause entirely different from any mentioned here. The important and only essential thing is that the parties be separated in some way, and that now it is impossible to interpellate the infidel spouse.

In general terms the Holy See has defined that any great difficulty, though physically not an impossibility, may morally be considered as one, and as such also suffices as a sufficient cause.[73]

[70] Cf. *supra*, pp. 13-15.

[71] Burton, *op. cit.*, p. 166; Woeber (*The Interpellations*, p. 124) confuses this distinction and demands a forceable separation for the use of the privilege. The essential *dummodo* clause of the Constitution does not require this condition.

[72] Woods, *The Constitutions of Canon 1125*, p. 66: "Gregory XIII also mentions that the interpellations may be omitted if they cannot be made without great difficulty due to the distance that separates husband and wife. In this case, however, it is necessary that the infidel be in a distant place the exact location of which is not known or to which access is difficult. The difficulty of interpellation must arise from the distance and the place and not from some other cause." The text of the constitution does not demand that these causes be combined in the same case.

[73] Woeber, *op. cit.*, p. 121; Léry, *Le Privilège de la Foi*, n. 89; Cappello, *De Matrimonio*, n. 787, p. 777; Payen, *De Matrimonio*, II, n. 2409, p. 746; Burton, *op. cit.*, p. 168; Vromant, "De Dispensatione ab Interpellationibus," *Periodica*, XX (1931), 116*; Bouscaren, "An In-

The Constitution grants a second faculty, namely of dispensing from the interpellations when it has become evident that the infidel party has failed to acknowledge or to answer the interpellations within a definite period of time clearly specified in the form of the interpellations.

No limit of time is specified in the constitution; therefore, the ordinary, or whoever is to grant the dispensation, is to be guided by circumstances of time and place in determining how much time should be allowed the unbaptized party for considering the consequences of the warning and for subsequently signifying his intentions. Normally charity, if not also justice, demands that he be allowed a full month as available time.[74]

This faculty is to be interpreted in the light of canon 1122, § 1; the infidel is to be warned that his failure to answer will be considered as a negative answer, which thus allows his former spouse the full right to enter a second marriage with a Catholic. Cappello indicates that for the verification of the latter condition it is sufficient that the absent spouse be warned; hence it matters not whether the failure to answer was culpable or not.[75] One may therefore ask whether the faculty has any value today in the light of the purpose and effect attaching to canon 1122, as was noted above. It does with certainty insofar as it operates as a safeguard which establishes beyond all doubt the validity of the second marriage.

That the dispensation can be granted under the two general classifications of impossibility and failure of the infidel to answer is evident from the explicit wording of the

---

quiry into the Practical Application of Canon 1125," *Miscellanea-Vermeersch*, I, 294; Doheny, *Informal Procedure*, p. 560; Winslow, *The Pauline Privilege*, p. 76. But Woods (*The Constitutions of Canon 1125*, p. 66) states that a moral impossibility does not suffice; he concludes this from a strict reading of the text of the Constitution.

[74] Canon 35; Doheny, *op. cit.*, p. 561; Woeber, *op. cit.*, p. 125; Winslow, *op. cit.*, p. 78; Gregory, *The Pauline Privilege*, p. 93; Burton, *op. cit.*, p. 171.

[75] *De Matrimonio*, n. 787, p. 777.

constitution. The dispensation can be granted further in virtue of the same Constitution of Pope Gregory XIII when the summary investigation of the circumstances affords moral certainty that the making of the interpellations would manifestly be absolutely futile or useless.

This has been recognized expressly by the Holy See in reference to a case that clearly came under the provisions of the papal grant. The wording of the response was clearly a paraphrase of the text of the Constitution *Populis,* so much so that evidently the Holy See was consciously identifying the case with one that for a solution could look to the favor granted in the Constitution. It spoke of the necessity of a summary extrajudicial investigation, and referred to the sweeping effect of the dispensation, which, like that granted in virtue of the papal constitution, was to be valid, and the second marriage likewise valid and indissoluble, even in the cases wherein the former spouse had also been converted and baptized at the time of this second marriage. Even under these conditions the Holy See allowed the dispensation as long as the careful summary inquiry showed that the interpellating of the infidel spouse would be impossible, useless or dangerous.[76]

The validity of the adoption of the view that cases in which the interpellations were useless furnished a sufficient cause for the granting of a dispensation is warranted fur-

[76] S.C.S. Off. (ad Vic. Ap. Iaponiae Merid.), 4 febr. 1891- "A qua interpellatione, si iustae rationabiliesque causae adsint, dispensabitur. Iustae autem huiusmodi causae tunc aderunt cum ex processu saltem summario et extraiudiciali moraliter constet coniugem infidelem interpellari non posse, aut interpellationem vel *inutilem,* vel graviter periculosam futuram esse. Matrimonium vero eius cum quo dispensatum fuerit, etiamsi postea innotuerit coniugem infidelem suam voluntatem iuste impeditam declarare non potuisse, et ad fidem etiam tempore initi matrimonii conversum fuisse, nihilominus numquam rescindi, sed validum esse debebit."—*Fontes,* n. 1130; *Coll. S.C.P.F.*, n. 1746; *ASS,* XXVI (1893-1894), 62-64; Doheny (*Informal Procedure,* p. 560, footnote 38), lists also: S.C.S. Off., 11 aug. 1859—*Fontes,* n. 954; *Coll. S.C.P.F.*, n. 1180, and S.C.S. Off. (Portland) 18 iun. 1884—*Fontes,* n. 1088; *Coll. S.C.P.F.*, n. 1620.

ther in the identification of the conditions as postulated by the Constitution *Populis* with the approved "ordinary cases" recognized by the pre-Code canonists and acknowledged by the Holy See in its post-Code practice.[77]

The wording of Faculty XXV of the Sacred Congregation for the Propagation of the Faith is so explicitly identical with that of the constitution that one cannot pass off the similiarity with the simple commentary that the Holy See was merely reminding the missionaries of the power that was theirs by the extant law. Although some authors seem ready to reduce the faculty to that interpretation, a far more reasonable explanation is offered by approved authors who have made careful and thorough studies of the Pauline privilege, of its relation to the Papal Constitutions, and of the practical application of both to modern circumstances.[78]

This faculty, which identified the ordinary cases with the conditions for the use of the favor granted in the Constitution *Populis*, recognized inutility on a par with impossibility as a factor that furnished an approved cause for the granting of a dispensation from the interpellations in virtue of the grant of Gregory XIII. The dispensation carried with it the far-reaching effect of that privilege.[79]

The two most common examples of futility or uselessness in the making of the interpellations are the following very practical cases:

1) when the infidel party of the former legitimate marriage is now permanently and hopelessly insane, and

[77] Cf. *supra*, pp. 42-43.

[78] Vermeersch, "Commentaria de Formulis Facultatum Quas S. Congr. de Propaganda Fide Concedere Solet," *Periodica*, XI (1922), 139; Léry, *Le Privilège de la Foi*, n. 94, p. 121; n. 95, p. 122; Winslow, *The Pauline Privilege*, pp. 35, 76-77; Payen, *De Matrimonio*, II, nn. 2413-2414; Vermeersch-Creusen, *Epitome*, II, n. 435, p. 301; Doheny, *Informal Procedure*, p. 560; Winslow, *Commentary on Apostolic Faculties*, p. 151; Vromant, *De Matrimonio*, n. 354, p. 279; Vromant, *Facultates Apostolicae*, p. 79; Paventi, *Brevis Commentarius*, p. 44.

[79] Léry, *op. cit.*, n. 95, p. 122: "De Plus, les derniers mots *dummodo ... constet ... coniugem monitum ... suam voluntatem non significasse* donnent un exemple d'interpellation inutile."

2) when the same party has upon a civil divorce entered a second civil marriage and in doing so has completely alienated himself from his former spouse who is now a Christian.

Both of these cases, the one involving the infidel party's insanity,[80] and the other, his divorce and subsequent remarriage,[81] were recognized by the Holy See as furnishing a sufficient cause for the granting of a dispensation from the interpellations.[82]

Although the authors indicate that some may prefer to list these two causes under the title of moral impossibility rather than under the title of futility,[83] as causes they prove sufficient and serve as a reason for the granting of a dispensation from the interpellations, whether by use of a particular faculty, or in virtue of the common concession made by the law in canon 1125.[84]

It seems particularly unreasonable that there should be insistence on the formalities of the interpellations when it

[80] Winslow, *The Pauline Privilege*, p. 77; Payen, *De Matrimonio*, II, n. 2413, p. 751; Vromant, *De Matrimonio*, n. 373.

[81] Arturus Vermeersch, *De Matrimoniali Casu Quem Apostoli Vocant seu de Privilegio Fidei* (Brugis: Typis Houdmont Fratrum, 1911), n. 87, p. 35; Winslow, *op. cit.*, p. 77, note 49: "A response of the Holy Office, June 18, 1884, which does not admit divorce as a cause for the complete omission of the interpellations, has sometimes been misunderstood and interpreted to mean that a divorce is never a cause to justify the canonical omission—i.e., dispensation from the interpellations." Burton, *A Commentary on Canon 1125*, p. 170; Woeber (*The Interpellations*, p. 34), citing the response mentioned by Winslow, claims that the cause is not sufficient, while actually quoting the final paragraph of the response where the Holy See explicitly states that it is so accepted as sufficient cause for a dispensation. On pages 48 and 59 he admits that the cause is sufficient.

[82] S.C. de Prop. Fide (C.P. pro Sin.), 5 mart. 1787—*Coll. S.C.P.F.*, n. 589; S.C.S. Off. (Portland.), 18 iun. 1884—*Fontes*, n. 1088; *Coll. S.C.P.F.*, n. 1620; Holy Office to the Archbishop of Detroit, Private, 22 May, 1947, Protoc, Num. 1026/47, quoted in Bouscaren, *Canon Law Digest, Supplement through 1948*, pp. 170-171.

[83] Burton, *op. cit.*, pp. 169-170; Winslow, *op. cit.*, pp. 37, 77; Payen, *op. cit.*, II, n. 2413, p. 751.

[84] Ayrinhac-Lydon, *Marriage Legislation*, p. 312.

is known beforehand and with certainty, either that there can be no response, as in the case of the insane person, or that the answer will be definitely negative. If, in the case of the man legally divorced and remarried, the answer should happen to be affirmative, any continued cohabitation at all would belie the sincerity of his intentions, which lack of sincerity in itself constitutes an approved reason for the granting of the dispensation.[85]

In either case the future achievement of the purpose of the interpellations is frustrated from the very beginning; actually that purpose has already been attained by means of a more effective and immediate knowledge than the interpellations themselves could bring as their result.

Article III: Causes Proved by Means of a Summary and Extrajudicial Investigation

The Holy See has continually warned bishops, vicars apostolic and others who have the faculty of dispensing from the interpellations, whether by special grant or in consequence of the universal law, that they may not act upon an assumption no matter how well it may be founded,[86] and has consequently required that a summary and extrajudicial,

[85] Cappello, *De Matrimonio,* n. 770, p. 762; Coronata, *De Matrimonio,* n. 652, p. 911; Vermeersch-Creusen, *op. cit.,* II, n. 437, p. 304; Woeber, *op. cit.,* p. 117; Ayrinhac-Lydon, *op. cit.,* p. 317.

[86] S.C.S. Off. (Chen-si et Chan-si), 23 nov. 1796—*Fontes,* n. 825; *Coll. S.C.P.F.,* n. 425; S.C. Off., instr. (ad Superior. Mission. Peguan.), 11 iun. 1760—*Fontes,* n. 811; S.C. Off., resp. (Vicar. Apostol. N.), 24 sept. 1896, ad 2: "Non sufficere ut Vicarius Apost. vel Missionarii omnino sint persuasi de impossibilitate aut difficultate interpellationem exsequendi; sed omnino faciendum esse in singulis casibus, et in scriptis, processum saltem summarium et extraiudicialem, in Formulis facultatum praescriptum."—*Coll. Hong.,* n. 1490, as quoted in Burton, *A Commentary on Canon 1125,* p. 171, note 26. Cf. De Smet, *De Sponsalibus et Matrimonio,* n. 353, p. 301; Gasparri, *De Matrimonio,* II, 224, footnote: "Sed animadvertat diligenter et cum omni cautela P. Superior Missionis, quod in uno quoque horum casuum, in quibus ab interpellatione dispensandum esse censebit, satis non erit ut hoc sibi persuasum habeat, sed conficiendus erit processus compendarius ex quo pro quovis futuro tempore huiusmodi necessitas apparet..."

but nevertheless careful, investigation be made concerning the sufficiency of the cause which warrants the granting of the dispensation.

Pope Gregory XIII in his Constitution *Populis* decreed that the interpellations could be dispensed with: "dummodo constet etiam summarie et extraiudicialiter, coniugem, ut praefertur, absentem moneri legitime non posse, aut monitum intra tempus in eadem monitione praefixum suam voluntatem non significasse."[87] This condition thenceforth became a standard and accepted prerequisite for the use of the power to dispense from the interpellations. It has shaped the practical policy of the Holy See in the granting of particular faculties.[88] It is also listed in the decrees of the Synod of Suchow, a Chinese Council which has formed much of the background for the canonical legislation of the Code.[89] And it has been included verbatim in the general Formula of Faculties issued by the Sacred Congregation for the Propagation of the Faith for all localities under the direction of the same Sacred Congregation.[90]

The condition is recognized by all post-Code commentators as essential, and is adopted ordinarily and almost exclusively in the words of Pope Gregory XIII.[91]

Most of the authors are satisfied in this matter to indicate the necessary condition of making the careful investi-

[87] Const. *Populis,* 25 ian. 1585—*Codex Iuris Canonici,* Documentum VIII.

[88] S.C.S. Off. (ad Vic. Ap. Iaponiae Merid.), 4 febr. 1891—*Fontes,* n. 1130; *Coll. S.C.P.F.*, n. 1746.

[89] Cap. IX, n. VIII, *Coll. Lac.*, VI, 623.

[90] *Facultates Prop. Fide,* Facultates Formulae III Minoris, Facultates nn. XXV et XXVI.

[91] Woeber, *op. cit.*, pp. 33, 111, Doheny, *op. cit.*, pp. 531, 534, 559; Cappello, *op. cit.*, n. 781, p. 770; Coronata, *op. cit.*, n. 641, p. 897; Payen, *op. cit.*, II, n. 2408, p. 744; n. 2363, p. 692; Vermeersch-Creusen, *op. cit.*, II, n. 435, p. 301; Wernz-Vidal, *op. cit.*, n. 633, note 80, p. 827; Winslow, *The Pauline Privilege,* p. 38; Heylen, *Tractatus de Matrimonio,* p. 347; Kearney, *The Principles of Canon 1127,* p. 126; Chelodi, *Ius Matrimoniale,* n. 160, p. 175; Gougnard, *Tractatus de Matrimonio,* p. 299; Woods, *The Constitutions of Canon 1125,* p. 67; Burton, *op. cit.*, p. 171.

gation of the existence and the gravity of the causes. In order to determine, therefore, precisely what is entailed in a summary and extrajudicial investigation, one can find a parallel in canon 1122, § 1, where it is stated that ordinarily the obligation of making the interpellations is fulfilled in a summary extrajudicial way.

Even when the bishop or the priest is convinced of the impossibility or futility of making the interpellations, he must nevertheless establish the existence of this hindrance in this summary manner.[92] The ordinary can act on his own information, or he can delegate any priest to make the investigation. In particular cases it may happen also that this investigation can most effectively and immediately be made by some lay person, who can, then, be appointed for the task. Ordinarily if a lay person is so delegated, another person should accompany him as a witness. A priest may fulfill the position alone, since he is considered a *"testis qualificatus."*[93]

Although all strictly judicial formalities are omitted, every precaution and care must be exercised for the ascertaining of the facts of the case with all truthfulness, and then upon a careful analysis of these circumstances a judgment is to be made regarding the gravity and sufficiency of the cause. This final judgment pertains to the bishop or to the priest who has made the investigation, unless the latter acted merely as a delegate of the bishop. If, however, the priest is to grant the dispensation in his own right, it belongs to him to determine whether or not the cause is sufficient. The judgment obviously is never left to the lay persons making the investigation; to them is assigned only the task of gathering the information. The final judgment in such cases will pertain to him who appointed them as investigators.

Every available means of modern communication must be

[92] Gasparri, *De Matrimonio*, II, n. 244, note 1.

[93] Canons 373, §§ 2-3; 1791; Doheny, *op. cit.*, p. 527; Woeber, *op. cit.*, p. 78.

utilized in an effort to contact the infidel or to learn the particular circumstances of the case.[94] One may suggest here the prudent use of the personal column in newspapers, of spot announcements on the radio where such service is available, and of the careful sifting of the civic and police records of missing persons.[95]

All the facts known or gathered in the investigation together with the judgment of the ordinary or the investigating priest should be committed to writing, and there should be listed briefly all the reasons that warrant the granting of the dispensation.[96] The ordinary should require this written process for the chancery files then, also when the investigation was made and the dispensation granted by a pastor or a confessor, even when he belongs to an exempt institute.[97]

Coronata points out that this summary process seems to be necessary for validity when there is question of a dispensation which involves the dissolving of a legitimate marriage as could well happen in a use of the favor granted by Pope Gregory XIII.[98] He indicates, however, that the written process is not always necessary, and it is agreed that this is not required for the validity of the dispensation "when the impossibility of making the interpellations is evident or when it is certain that no answer was received within the time set.[99]

[94] S.C.S.Off. (Mongoliae), 29 nov. 1882: "Etenim haec exigit, ut ante dispensationem in interpellatione omnia adhibeantur media et diligentiae ut pars in infidelitate relicta reperiatur et interpellari possit." —*Fontes*, n. 1075; *Coll. S.C.P.F.*, n. 1581.

[95] Vermeersch-Creusen, *Epitome*, II, n. 435, pp. 301-302; Woods, *op. cit.*, p. 67.

[96] S.C.S. Off. (Vic. Apostol. N.), 24 sept. 1896, ad 2—*Coll. Hong.*, n. 1490; Burton, *op. cit.*, p. 171, note 26; Blat, *De Sacramentis*, n. 679, p. 532; Vromant, *De Matrimonio*, n. 364, p. 287; Winslow, *op. cit.*, p. 38; Coronata, *op. cit.*, n. 649, p. 907; Woeber, *op. cit.*, p. 111; Payen, *op. cit.*, II, n. 2409, p. 746.

[97] Woeber, *op. cit.*, p. 125.

[98] *Op. cit.*, n. 649, p. 907.

[99] Burton, *A Commentary on Canon 1125*, pp. 171-172; Cf. also

The greatest advantage of having the process preserved in writing is that it stands as a record of the cause. This record should therefore be kept in the archives of the chancery of the residence of the convert to whose advantage the dispensation was granted.[100] This record of the existence and the sufficiency of the cause would naturally prove a help in the solving of any doubt concerning the validity of the marriage contracted in virtue of the dispensation.[101] Woeber indicates further that these important records should be preserved as a safeguard against any legal charges or law suits brought against the convert, the ordinary or the pastor by the infidel in any alleged charge of the alienation of affection.[102]

Particular prudence and tact must be exercised in this regard, as also in the actual making of the interpellations, if the infidel has already or is about to enter a second civil marriage. Any attempt to investigate his present association or intentions in the light of his former union could quite readily be interpreted as an attempt to alienate the affection of his present consort, and would therefore constitute sufficient grounds for a civil lawsuit.[103]

Vermeersch, "Commentaria de Formulis Facultatum," *Periodica,* XI (1922), 140*; Payen, *op. cit.*, II, n. 2409, p. 747; Vromant, *op. cit.*, n. 364, p. 287; Winslow, *op. cit.*, p. 78; Woeber, *op. cit.*, p. 125.

100 Vromant, *op. cit.*, n. 364, p. 287; Payen, *loc. cit.*, Burton, *op. cit.*, p. 171; Coronata, *op. cit.*, n. 649, p. 901; Vromant, *Facultates Apostolicae,* n. 80.

101 Coronata, *De Matrimonio,* n. 649, p. 901.

102 *The Interpellations,* p. 111.

103 William E. Vaughan, *Constitutions for Diocesan Courts,* The Catholic University of America Canon Law Studies, n. 210 (Washington, D.C.: The Catholic University of America Press, 1944), p. 175, art. 131; Doheny, *Informal Procedure,* p. 228. The civil law statute reads: "A husband (wife) generally has the right of action for damages for the enticing away or alienation of affection of his wife (husband) except where it has been abolished by statute. This right of action for alienation of affection is subject to legislative control, and in some states the right has been abolished by statutes, which have been upheld. When so abolished, the filing or serving of a pleading or process seeking a recovery for alienation of affection is unlaw-

If the dispensation is to be restricted to the internal sacramental forum, as could happen when it is to be granted by a confessor in virtue of the Constitution of Gregory XIII, the written process is not necessary and need not be executed.[104]

Vermeersch-Creusen note also that there may be causes other than those commonly recognized as sufficient for the granting of a dispensation, but in any case this summary and extrajudicial process is constituted as the mode of determining their validity.[105] The investigation in a particular case may indicate that, although there is not sufficient reason to allow a dispensation from the interpellations, the circumstances may warrant the execution of the interpellations according to the private form.[106]

---

ful." *Corpus Iuris Secundum, A Complete Restatement of the Entire American Law,* Donald E. Kiser, Editor, Vol. XLII (Brooklyn New York: The American Law Book Company, 1944), Husband and Wife: n. 660, Husband's Right of Action Generally; n. 661, Wife's Right of Action Generally. The statute reads further that an improper motive, malice and intention on the part of the defendant to effect an alienation generally are essential to his liability, although an actual intent is not necessary if the defendant's acts are inherently wrong. N. 662, Motive and Intent.

The laws of each state will, therefore, vary. In Indiana the statute has been abolished, and this action of the state legislature has been upheld by the Supreme Court of the State. On October 25, 1937, in the case entitled Pennington vs. Stewart et Ux., the court rendered this decision: "In our judgement the act in question, in so far as it abolishes an action for alienation of affections is not in violation of art. 1, section 12, of the Indiana Constitution, and that said section does not prohibit the legislator from legislating upon a subject growing out of the marital relation. Such legislation is not prohibited by any provision of the Constitution." *North Eastern Reporter,* 10, N.E., (2nd), p. 619.

[104] Coronata, *De Matrimonio,* n. 649, p. 901; Woeber, *op. cit.,* p. 126.

[105] *Epitome,* II, n. 435, pp. 301-302.

[106] Woods, *The Constitutions of Canon 1125,* p. 67.

CHAPTER VI

JURIDICAL EFFECT OF THE DISPENSATION

Article I: Allows Entrance into Second, Catholic Marriage

Canon 1123 equates a dispensation from the interpellations with a negative answer to the interpellations in regard to the effect produced by both. Thus, if the interpellations are legitimately omitted in consequence of a dispensation, the convert has the right to contract a second marriage, but solely with a Catholic party.[1]

Since no distinction is made in the law, this effect is verified independently of the proximate source of the power used in the granting of the dispensation. It is immaterial whether the dispensation was granted by the Holy See immediately, or by someone else through delegated power received in a particular case, or, finally, in virtue of the concession contained in the Church's universal law as expressed in canon 1125. In ordinary cases the dispensation is granted from the ecclesiastical law obligation that requires the formalities of the interpellations. In these cases the dispensation simply readies the case for the normal procedure of applying the Pauline privilege.[2]

[1] Canon 1123. Si interpellationes ex declaratione Sedis Apostolicae omissae fuerint, aut si infidelis eisdem negative responderit expresse vel tacite, pars baptizata ius habet novas nuptias cum persona catholica contrahendi, nisi ipsa post baptismum dederit parti non baptizatae iustam discendendi causam.

[2] S.C.S. Off. (Siam), 22 nov. 1871—*Fontes*, n. 1019: "An liceat dare dispensationem disparitatis cultus quando data fuit antea dispensatio de interpellatione, vel quando interpellatio facta fuit in vanum? Resp. Negative, et detur decretum feriae IV, 29 aug. 1866 (*Coll. S.C. de Prop Fide.*, I, n. 1297), tenoris sequentis: In casibus de quibus agitur R.P.D. Vicarius Apostolicus, adeoque missionarii ab eo deputati non possunt dispensare super disparitate cultus v. facultatis III Formulae 6. Et quoad matrimonia, si quae contracta iam sint cum huiusmodi dispensatione, sileant, et coniuges relinquantur in bona fide. Quoad futurum vero ipse Vicarius Apostolicus recurrat in casibus particularibus, expositis omnibus cuiusque casus adiunctis." Coronata, *De Matri-*

This second marriage must, of course, be contracted according to the canonical form in all its prescriptions,[3] and the former marriage which the convert had contracted in infidelity is dissolved at the moment this second and valid marriage is ratified.[4]

Although this principle has always been applied to the use of the Pauline privilege, it is valid also in the cases accompanied with a dispensation from the interpellations. Gasparri indicated this as evident from the general tone of canon 1126, particularly, however, from its position in the Code as immediately following canon 1125.[5]

In speaking of the effect of the dispensation from the interpellations Coronata makes a distinction. In addition to the normal and usual effect mentioned immediately above he adds that, if a dispensation is granted in cases wherein the departure of the infidel party is doutful, or when the interpellations are impossible of achievement, the dispensation is, in a way, a true privilege of the Faith, and is equivalent to a dispensation from the divine law. In all such cases wherein the essential departure is not objectively verified the dispensation effects the dissolution of the prior marriage bond.[6]

---

monio, n. 642, p. 897; Vermeersch-Creusen, *Epitome*, II, n. 435, p. 302; Cappello, *De Matrimonio*, n. 782, p. 773; Doheny, *Informal Procedure*, pp. 532, 561; Wernz-Vidal, *Ius Matrimoniale*, n. 634, p. 829; De Smet, *De Sponsalibus et Matrimonio*, n. 353, p. 302; Ayrinhac-Lydon, *Marriage Legislation*, p. 318; Petrovits, *The New Church Law on Matrimony*, n. 568, p. 409; Chrétien, *De Matrimonio*, n. 259, p. 434; Bouscaren-Ellis, *Canon Law: A Text and Commentary*, p. 553.

[3] Canons 1094-1103; Coronata, *op. cit.*, n. 649, p. 908; Gregorius XIII, const. *Populis*, 25 ian. 1585, "... in facie ecclesiae solemnizare." —*Codex Iuris Canonici*, Documentum VIII.

[4] Canon 1126—Vinculum prioris coniugii, in infidelitate contracti, tunc tantum solvitur, cum pars fidelis reapse novas nuptias valide iniverit. Wernz-Vidal, *op. cit.*, n. 631, note 62, p. 820; Coronata, *op. cit.*, n. 626, p. 875; Doheny, *op. cit.*, p. 561; Gasparri, *De Matrimonio*, II, n. 1153, p. 226; n. 1155, p. 230; Vermeersch-Creusen, *op. cit.*, II, n. 427, p. 295.

[5] *Op. cit.*, n. 1167, p. 239.

[6] *De Matrimonio*, n. 642, p. 898.

It is to be noted here that the convert does not lose his right to use these privileges in consequence of a continued cohabitation with his infidel consort after his baptism, even in such cases in which the conjugal status was observed for a long time.[7]

Thus if the infidel upon a change of mind separates from the convert and refuses to resume peaceful cohabitation, the Pauline privilege can then be invoked. Further, if the unbaptized consort would disappear and all efforts to locate him would fail, then a dispensation from the interpellations could be granted, even though for a time the convert had cohabited with the infidel. Actually the convert is bound in conscience to remain with his infidel spouse as long as that partner is willing to live peacefully and does so.

Gasparri seems to confuse the issue in his study of the import of canon 1124. He states that, if the convert does not or cannot use the privilege immediately after his conversion, and then has lived with his unbaptized consort for a time, only two avenues are open to him: 1) if the marriage with the infidel has remained unconsummated after the baptism, then the marriage can be dissolved in virtue of canon 1119, which provides for the possibility of a papal dispensation over a non-consummated marriage, or, 2) if the marriage was consummated after the baptism, then the Holy See could be approached with the request to dissolve the marriage *in favorem fidei.* In the first instance, no marriage in which an infidel is a party can ever be a ratified marriage, and thus cannot come under the provisions of canon 1119; in the second, Gasparri's argument clearly abstracts from the concession in which canon 1124 grants the continued application of the Pauline privilege.[8]

The second union, the marriage namely that is rendered

[7] Canon 1124; S.C.S. Off. (Oceaniae Occident.), 27 sept. 1848—*Fontes*, n. 907; *Coll. S.C.P.F.*, n. 1032; S.C.S. Off. (Natal), 11 iul. 1866—*Fontes*, n. 996; *Coll. S.C.P.F.*, n. 1295; cf. Vromant, *De Matrimonio*, n. 345, p. 273; Cappello, *op. cit.*, n. 771, p. 763; Wernz-Vidal, *op. cit.*, n. 631, II, p. 817.

[8] *De Matrimonio*, II, n. 1155, 2°, p. 231.

possible in virtue of a dispensation from the interpellations, must be a union with a Catholic party. This requirement follows the normal conditions for the use of the Pauline privilege,[9] as well as from the nature of the dispensation which is granted "ut eorum quilibet, superstite coniuge infideli, et eius consensu minime requisito, aut responso non expectato, matrimonia cum quovis fideli alterius etiam ritus contrahere . . . valeant."[10] The dispensation, therefore, expressly provides for and allows interritual marriages in virtue of its concession.[11] By the same token a marriage with another infidel would be invalid, and one with a heretic illicit, if additional dispensations were not obtained to cover these contingencies.[12]

Although the granted dispensation and the use of the Pauline privilege look to a subsequent sacramental marriage, there is not excluded absolutely the contracting of a marriage with a non-Catholic, baptized or not.[13]

In either case, however, an impediment, the one diriment, the other merely impedient, stands in the way of the contracting of the union. In either case, then, a dispensation must be sought and obtained, the one a dispensation from the impediment of disparity of cult, the other, from that of mixed religion.

One cannot object here on the grounds that the granting of such a dispensation to allow the convert to contract marriage with an infidel or a heretic destroys the notion of "privilege of the Faith" inherent both in the Pauline pri-

[9] Canon 1123.

[10] Gregorius XII, const. *Populis*, 25 ian. 1585, *infra*, p. 244, Appendix C.

[11] Blat, *De Sacramentis*, n. 536, p. 684.

[21] Canons 1060, 1070; De Smet, *op. cit.*, n. 353, p. 302; Payen, *De Matrimonio*, II, n. 2220, p. 543.

[13] "Adn. Privilegium dicitur contrahendi novas nuptias cum persona Catholica, sed non per hoc excluditur, quod matrimonium possit contrahi etiam cum persona *acatholica* aut *non baptizata* ex dispensatione super impedimento mixtae religionis aut disparitatis cultus . . ." Cerato, *op. cit.*, n. 123, p. 212; Chrétien, *op. cit.*, n. 259, p. 434; Vlaming, *Praelectiones*, II, n. 727, p. 324.

vilege and in the constitutions of canon 1125. For the notion of the *"privilegium fidei"* does not look primarily or necessarily to the good of the Faith in general, but rather to the spiritual welfare of the individual who is to benefit by the privilege.[14]

Such a dispensation must be granted, therefore, to prepare the way for the use of the Pauline privilege if the convert in the use of that privilege intends to contract marriage with a non-Catholic. Likewise a dispensation from the impediments of disparity of cult or mixed religion in a similar case must accompany a dispensation from the interpellations when it is granted in virtue of canon 1125. It can, however, be granted only by the Holy See.[15]

Since, however, such a one intends to use one privilege in order to free himself from a natural union, the Holy See, naturally, is not going to be overly desirous to grant a request for a dispensation from the impediments of disparity of cult or mixed religion, and will consequently more readily allow a marriage with a baptized non-Catholic than with another infidel.[16]

Although Bouscaren-Ellis acknowledge in theory the power of the Pope to dispense in such a case from the im-

[14] This notion is certainly evident in the Pauline privilege, which was granted precisely for the good of the convert, whose infidel partner had deserted him or made it hard for him to live his Faith. St. Pius V granted the favor which is contained in the Constitution *Romani Pontificis* for the individual good of converts, who otherwise would have found it difficult to separate from the one with whom they were living. And in the Constitution *Altitudo*, Paul III allowed the convert to marry any one of his former spouses without requiring that the one chosen be even a Christian. Cf. Wernz-Vidal, *op. cit.*, n. 631, p. 817; Payen, *op. cit.*, II, n. 2403, p. 733.

[15] S.C.S. Off. (Natal), 29 aug, 1866—*Fontes*, n. 996; *Coll. S.C.P.F.*, n. 1297; S.C.S. Off. (Siam), 22 nov. 1871—*Fontes*, n. 1019, *Coll. S.C.P.F.*, n. 1377; Chrétien, *op. cit.*, n. 259, p. 434; De Smet, *op. cit.*, n. 353, p. 302; Winslow, *The Pauline Privilege*, p. 46.

[16] De Smet, *loc. cit.*: "Potest quidem Ecclesia dispensare, ac nonnumquam dispensat . . . sed difficiliorem ad id sese praebet in hoc casu quam aliter." Cf. Vlaming, *op. cit.*, n. 727, p. 324; Farrugia, *De Matrimonio, et Causis Matrimonialibus*, n. 323, p. 474.

pediment of disparity of cult, they claim that most probably a request for such a dispensation would be denied.[17] Actually, however, this kind of dispensation has been granted, and therefore if the merits of an individual case seem to warrant such a dispensation, the ordinary should not hesitate to apply for the faculty. In the application for such a dispensation express mention must be made of the fact if the person whom the Christian wishes to marry is a Jew or a Mohammedan. The mention of this condition in the petition is necessary for the validity of the granted dispensation, since special cautions are imposed by the Holy See in these cases.[18]

Although the diocesan quinquennial faculties for the granting of a dispensation from the impediments of disparity of cult and of mixed religion make no mention of any restriction or exception relative to their use for the unusual cases here considered,[19] it is to be noted that these faculties together with those granted to missionary countries by the Sacred Congregation for the Propagation of the Faith cannot be used in these cases.[20] Local ordinaries may not dispense, in virtue of their ordinary faculties as covering these impediments for the benefit of those who intend to use the Pauline privilege or have obtained a dispensation from the interpellations. This has been explicitly restricted by the Holy See.[21] In such circumstances the local ordinary is obliged to ask for a special indult in order to dispense the convert.[22]

Vromant lists a case in which a special faculty was granted to a certain vicar apostolic to dispense from the

[17] *Canon Law: A Text and Commentary*, p. 553.

[18] Winslow, *The Pauline Privilege*, p. 47.

[19] Eagleton, *The Diocesan Quinquennial Faculties*, pp. 50-61.

[20] S.C. de Prop Fide (Tunk. Occident) 5 mart. 1816—*Coll. S.C.P.F.*, n. 705; Winslow, *op. cit.*, p. 46; Woeber, *op. cit.*, p. 103.

[21] S.C. de Prop Fide. (Tunk. Occident) 5 mart. 1816—*Coll. S.C.P.F.*, n. 705; S.C.S. Off. (Kuitceu) 15 sept. 1858—*Coll. S.C.P.F.*, n. 1168; S.C.S. Off. (Siam), 17 iul. 1850—*Fontes*, n. 911; *Coll. S.C.P.F.*, n. 1045.

[22] Ayrinhac-Lydon, *op. cit.*, p. 318; Farrugia, *op. cit.*, n. 323, p. 474, Winslow, *op. cit.*, p. 46.

impediment of disparity of cult in conjunction with the Pauline privilege. Grave causes were demanded, viz., that there were only a few Catholics in the territory and that there was but little opportunity for a Catholic marriage, the *cautiones* of canon 1061 were to be demanded, and the dispensation was to be granted by the bishop himself.[23]

Cappello[24] introduces a disputed point relative to the cases wherein the dispensation is granted from the interpellations by the Holy See, and then asks whether the convert upon the reception of such a dispensation can validly enter marriage with an infidel or a schismatic without obtaining any further dispensation. He answers in the affirmative, giving as his reason *"quia non constet de clausula irritante."*

Payen[25] in answer to this opinion states simply that the contrary doctrine is clearly contained in canon 1123. This seems the more probably correct doctrine, for the dispensation from the interpellations does not carry with it a dispensation from the impediments of disparity of cult or mixed religion. That the latter opinion is more correct seems to be proven by a very recent response of the Holy Office in answer to a particular case. In this case a convert desired to marry a baptized non-Catholic in the use of the Pauline privilege to dissolve an earlier natural union. The Holy See answered that the ordinary could apply the Pauline privilege adding a dispensation from the interpellations and a dispensation from the impediments of mixed religion and *ad cautelam* from disparity of cult. Since the two dispensations were mentioned separately and disjunctively it is evident that neither is included in the other.[26] If one

[23] *De Matrimonio,* n. 343, p. 270; Some object that it is incorrect to refer to a use of the Pauline privilege in the cases where the convert contracts the second marriage with a non-Catholic, yet the Holy Office speaks of such as an application of the Pauline privilege—S.C. Off., 11 nov. 1949—Proc. Num. 1907/49 quoted *The Jurist,* X (1950), 215.

[24] *De Matrimonio,* n. 785, p. 774.

[25] *De Matrimonio,* II, n. 2403, p. 733.

[26] CLARA non baptizata matrimonium, anno 1932, contraxit cum RALPH non baptizato, a quo seiuncta est per civile divortium anno 1934. Anno 1936 coniuges reconciliati sunt ac denuo coram magistratu

who has not this specially needed faculty to dispense from these matrimonial impediments in conjunction with the Pauline privilege should invalidly dispense the convert, the marriage is invalid in view of the continuing presence of the diriment impediment of disparity of cult. If, however, the dispensation was invalidly granted from the impediment of mixed religion, the marriage is still valid, but gravely illicit, in the supposition, of course, that all the other requirements have been fulfilled.

In the first case, where the marriage is invalid because of the invalid dispensation, ordinary pastoral prudence will dictate whether the parties should be disturbed. It seems altogether better to leave them in good faith, and seek the necessary dispensation. In a particular case the Holy See has answered that the parties are not to be disquieted, and in the future all such causes are to be referred to the Holy Office with a sufficient explanation of the circumstances.[27]

A *sanatio* could be requested of the Holy See, since the validity of the marriage is obstructed by an impediment of the ecclesiastical law; it could not, however, be granted by

---

civili nuptias celebraverunt. Sed biennio post coniuges alterum divortium civile obtinuerunt.

Mulier nuptias attentavit novas, anno 1940, cum Edwardo, et mortua anno 1942 viro, ad alias nuptias convolavit cum acatholico baptizato Jacobo.

Mulier, anno 1948, fidem catholicam amplexata est.

Haec Suprema S. Congregatio, omnibus rite perpensis, hoc decrevit: Si res ita se habet, speciatim quoad certam carentiam baptismi in utroque coniuge CLARA-RALPH, Ordinarius poterit applicare Privilegium Paulinum, addita etiam dispensatione ab interpellationibus, et ab impedimento Mixtae Religionis et ad cautelam Disparitatis Cultus pro novo matrimonio; si vero exurgant difficultates, Ordinarius conficere poterit processum ut in casibus dissolutionis matrimonii in favorem fidei. S.C. Off., 11 nov. 1949—Proc. Num. 1907/49 quoted *The Jurist*, X (1950), 215.

[27] S.C.S. Off. (Kuitceun) 15 sept. 1858—*Coll. S.C.P.F.*, n. 1168; S.C.S. Off. (Natal), 29 aug. 1866—*Fontes*, n. 996; *Coll. S.C.P.F.*, n. 1297; Coronata, *op. cit.*, n. 626, in fine, p. 876; Farrugia, *op. cit.*, n. 323, p. 474; It is this case that Doheny (*op. cit.*, p. 533) by reference seems to confuse with the preceding.

the local ordinary since the validity of the marriage is obstructed by a diriment impediment from which the ordinary has no power to dispense.[28]

All marriages contracted in virtue of these dispensations are to be preceded by the ordinary precautions prescribed by the general law before mixed marriages are to be allowed.[29]

It is to be noted in conclusion that if a validly baptized non-Catholic wishes to avail himself of the Pauline privilege to free himself from an infidel union to which he was formerly an infidel party, any subsequent marriage with a non-Catholic is valid conditioned, of course, on the latter's freedom to marry, and the unwillingness of the first consort to cohabit. The baptized non-Catholic can satisfy himself of this necessary departure in any one of a number of ways; the summary and extrajudicial form of interpellating the unbaptized consort on the authority of the bishop (canon 1122 § 1) is an ecclesiastical law requirement and is not essential for the valid use of the Pauline privilege when the *discessus* of the first spouse is known from another source. The law of the Code itself (canon 1122 § 2) recognizes the validity of privately made interpellations, and conditions only their licitness.[30]

In the application of the privilege to baptized non-Catholics the procedure is the normal one; they are, however, in a less favorable position than Catholics, for a dispensation from the interpellations can never be granted in favor of a heretic.[31]

[28] Canon 1139, § 1. Quinquennial faculties from the Holy Office, Art. 4—Eagleton, *The Diocesan Quinquennial Faculties*, pp. 61-69; Woeber seems to indicate that a radical sanation cannot be granted in this case. Cf. *op. cit.*, p. 104.

[29] Canons 1061-1064, 1071.

[30] Vermeersch-Creusen, *Epitome*, II, n. 428, p. 296, note 1; Wernz-Vidal, *op. cit.*, n. 631, note 55b, p. 811; Coronata, *op. cit.*, n. 625c, pp. 872-3; Payen, *op. cit.*, II, n. 2220, p. 543; n. 2253, p. 571; Cf. Cappello, *op. cit.*, n. 785, *in fine*, p. 774, for a list of authorities.

[31] Wernz-Vidal, *op. cit.*, n. 631, note 55b *in fine*, p. 811; Gregory, *The Pauline Privilege*, p. 52.

No jurisdiction is involved in the application of the Pauline privilege. Actually it is self-operative; no sentence or declaration of any ecclesiastical authority is necessary. One can easily imagine a case wherein the entire application of the privilege could be validly effected without any mention of authority, on the suppostion, namely, that the interpellations had been made privately by the convert.[32] It is the convert who invokes the privilege, not the Church.

Article II: Particular Effect after Baptism of both Parties

Besides allowing the convert to enter a second marriage with a Catholic, a dispensation from the interpellations has also the effect of safeguarding the validity of the second marriage, even if later it becomes known through incontrovertible proof that the infidel party had been impeded from declaring his intentions regarding the resumption or continuance of cohabitation. This is true, further, even if the former infidel spouse had embraced the Faith and had been baptized at the very time the second marriage was contracted.

This extraordinary effect of the dispensation clearly distinguishes it from the normal use of the Pauline privilege, in which the regular procedure is followed and the usual conditions are fulfilled. For in these cases the normal application of the Pauline privilege becomes inoperative upon the conversion of the second party of the marriage that was contracted as a legitimate union, as it does also when the answers to the interpellations testify to the willingness of the infidel party to become a Christian and to continue peaceful cohabitation.[33]

[32] Canon 1122, § 2; Coronata, *De Matrimonio*, n. 635, p. 889; Cappello, *op. cit.*, n. 779, p. 769: "Forma privata sufficit ad valorem quolibet in casu, etiamsi possibilis sit forma iuridica, sed tunc est illicita."

[33] Canon 1123; Coronata, *De Matrimonio*, n. 627, *in fine*, p. 877; Cappello, *De Matrimonio*, 769, II, p. 759; Gasparri, *De Matrimonio*, II, n. 1132, p. 208; Vermeersch-Creusen, *Epitome*, II, n. 429, p. 297; De Smet, *De Sponsalibus et Matrimonio*, n. 253, p. 302.

Pope Gregory XIII was the first to give expression to the important effect produced through the granting of a dispensation from the interpellations. He stated explicitly: "... quae quidem matrimonia, etiamsi postea innotuerit coniuges priores infideles suam voluntatem iuste impeditos declarare non potuisse, et ad fidem etiam tempore transacti secundi matrimonii conversos fuisse, nihilominus rescindi numquam debere, sed valida et firma, prolemque inde suscipiendam legitimam fore decernimus."[34]

Benedict XIV, both as Pope and as private author, gave renewed authority to this teaching by reaffirming the juridic consequence of this dispensation as follows:

> "Praeterea matrimonia inter Neophytos huiusmodi et alios Fideles, et Catholicos alios rite contracta, etiamsi postmodum innotuerit priores coniuges Infideles, vel Turcas, vel Iudaeos, nonnullis legitimis impedimentis detentos, suam voluntatem significare minime potuisse, vel ad fidem etiam tempore secundi matrimonii conversos fuisse, ullo umquam tempore rescindi minime debere, sed illa semper firma, valida et inviolabilia existere."[35]

He later wrote that the first marriage of the convert is irrevocably dissolved at the moment the convert contracts marriage with a Catholic, and no objection can be alleged against the validity and stability of this second marriage even when the former consort could not answer the interpellations through no fault of his own, not even if he had shown his good will by also becoming a Christian and by receiving baptism.[36]

At the close of the last century the Holy See once more declared that the unique effect of this dispensation was still valid. At that time the Sacred Congregation of the Holy Office in the solution of a particular case answered in the words of Pope Gregory XIII, whose influence had also been marked in the writings of Pope Benedict XIV:

[34] Const. *Populis*, 25 ian. 1585—*infra*, p. 244. Appendix C.

[35] Ep. *In suprema*, 16 ian. 1745—*Fontes*, n. 353.

[36] *De Synodo Dioecesana*, lib. XIII, cap. XXI, n. 5.

"Matrimonium vero eius, cum quo dispensatum fuerit, etiamsi postea innotuerit coniugem infidelem suam voluntatem iuste impeditam declarare non potuisse, et ad fidem etiam tempore initi matrimonii conversum fuisse, nihilominus numquam rescindi, sed validum esse debebit."[37]

It is evident, therefore, that all dispensations granted by the local ordinary, by pastors or by Jesuit confessors in using the faculty granted them by law in canon 1125 produce this effect of upholding the validity of this second marriage when the fact of the former spouse's good will or conversion becomes apparent only after this second marriage has been contracted.

Some authors seem to restrict this particular effect of the dispensation to the cases in which it was granted precisely in virtue of the privilege originally promulgated by Gregory XIII. This conclusion is based on the fact that they speak of this effect only in the passages wherein they professedly deal with the papal constitutions.[38]

Others, however, attribute this far-reaching effect to all dispensations received from the Holy See, so that it is valid in all cases wherein the exceptional conditions are verified.[39]

Coronata and Woeber expressly equate the two possibili-

[37] S.C.S. Off., instr. (ad Vic. Ap. Iaponiae Merid.), 4 febr. 1891—*Fontes*, n. 1130; *Coll. S.C.P.F.*, n. 1746; Wernz-Vidal, *Ius Matrimoniale*, n. 634, p. 829; Woeber, *The Interpellations*, pp. 115-116.

[38] Vermeersch-Creusen, *op. cit.*, II, n. 436, p. 303; Payen, *op. cit.*, II, n. 2408, p. 744. Doheny (*Informal Procedure*, p. 561, also 558), notes that both of the second marriages would be valid if it were learned afterwards that the absent consort had previously received baptism and had likewise contracted marriage with a Catholic. Cf. Chelodi, *Ius Matrimoniale*, n. 160, p. 175; Vromant, *De Matrimonio*, n. 366, p. 289.

[39] Ayrinhac-Lydon, *Marriage Legislation*, p. 313; Wernz-Vidal, *op. cit.*, n. 634, p. 829; Winslow, *op. cit.*, pp. 43, 81; Woods, *The Constitutions of Canon 1125*, p. 98; Cappello, *De Matrimonio*, n. 782, p. 772, Farrugia, *De Matrimonio, et Causis Matrimonialibus*, n. 322, p. 474; De Smet, *De Sponsalibus et Matrimonio*, n. 353, p. 302; Ramstein, *Pastor and Marriage Cases*, p. 188.

ties, so that it matters not whether the dispensation is granted by the Holy See, either directly or by delegation, or through a use of the power conceded generally in the Church's universal law.[40]

This seems by far the more reasonable explanation; the source of power in either case is the same; a distinction in the effect produced seems wholly without warrant.[41] The references noted above from Pope Gregory XIII, Pope Benedict XIV and the response of the Holy Office are not to be understood as reflecting a solution merely in isolated cases, but rather as indications of the traditional practical policy of the Church. At the same time the silence of some commentators in this regard can scarcely be interpreted as contradicting this conclusion.

Evidently a convert cannot make use of a dispensation from the interpellations in order to enter a second marriage if he learns of the conversion of his former spouse prior to his contemplated contracting of the second union. Such a marriage would be invalid as well as gravely illicit, for upon receipt of such knowledge the dispensation, like the interpellations, becomes inoperative for the application of the Pauline privilege. A dispensation from the interpellations is intended primarily in all cases simply as a means that relieves the convert of the formality of the interpellations. The added juridical effect which vouches for the validity of the second marriage was granted by the Supreme Authority of the Church precisely to cover the specific contingency in

[40] Coronata, *op. cit.*, n. 649, *in fine*, p. 908; "Effectus dispensationis concessae vi Constitutionis Gregorianae est ius partis fidelis transeundi ad alias nuptias; effectus mediatus est solutio prioris matrimonii, quae locum habet momento quo pars conversa novum matrimonium contrahit; qui effectus in hoc casu sicut et in aliis casibus concessae dispensationis ab interpellationibus producitur quamvis eo momento quo celebratum matrimonium coniux infidelis in ea fuisset conditione ut respondere non potuisset et respondere affirmative interpellationibus forte factis paratus esset, immo quamvis postea innotuerit eo momento iam baptizatum eum fuisse." Cf. Woeber, *op. cit.*, p. 126.

[41] Coronata, (*op. cit.*, n. 649, note 4, p. 908) recognizes this as the more common teaching today.

which the knowledge of the former consort's willingness to cohabit peacefully, or of his conversion, becomes certainly known only subsequently to the second marriage.

This special characteristic of the dispensation serves to dispel all doubt as to the validity of this marriage and as to the marital status of the ones involved.[42] This same effect is achieved even in the cases wherein the convert validly contracts marriage with a heretic or an infidel after having received the necessary dispensation from the one or the other of these impediments.

In answer to the logical question how such an ample effect can be attributed to such a dispensation, or what is the nature of the power involved, the reader is referred to Chapter III where the various opinions and explanations have already been evaluated. At any rate, it is certain that, no matter what the explanation may be, the dispensation as given under these circumstances sustains the validity of the second marriage, thus evincing the absolute and irrevocable dissolution of the first.[43]

[42] Woeber, *op. cit.*, p. 119.

[43] Petrovits, *The New Church Law on Matrimony*, n. 570, p. 409.

CHAPTER VII

AUTHORITY COMPETENT TO GRANT THE DISPENSATION

Article I: The Holy See

The sole authority which possesses the power of dispensing from the required formalities of the interpellations is the Holy See. This is clearly indicated in the law itself. Canon 1121, § 2, expressly demands the fulfillment of the interpellations in all cases; it makes an exception for only those cases in which the Holy See has declared that the interpellations may be omitted. This exclusive right of the supreme authority of the Church to determine in which cases and under which circumstances the interpellations may be omitted is recognized further by canon 1123.[1]

This reservation flows immediately and naturally from the right of the Holy See as the Supreme Legislator in the Church to interpret and, if necessary, to dispense from the universally binding ecclesiastical laws.[2]

In accord with the various functions peculiar to the several Sacred Congregations, canon 247, § 3, assigns to the Holy Office whatever pertains directly or indirectly, in law or in fact, to the Pauline privilege. This Sacred Congregation likewise alone is competent to grant dispensations from the matrimonial impediments of disparity of cult and mixed religion. This competency is particularly exclusive when a convert, after having used the Pauline privilege or received a dispensation from the interpellations, wishes to contract a second marriage, but with a heretic or a schismatic.[3]

[1] Gasparri, *De Matrimonio*, II, n. 1150, p. 223; Bouscaren, "An Inquiry into the Practical Application of Canon 1125," *Miscellanea-Vermeersch*, I, 292.

[2] Canons 17, 80ff; Ayrinhac-Lydon, *Marriage Legislation*, p. 312.

[3] S.C.S. Off., instr. (ad Archiep. Quebecen.), 16 sept. 1824—*Fontes*, n. 866; *Coll. S.C.P.F.*, n. 784; S.C.de Prop. Fide (C.P. pro Sin.-Sutchuen.), 3 ian 1777: "Supplicandum SSmo pro concessione Indulti

The Sacred Congregation for the Propagation of the Faith, however, has the authority, as in all matters which relate to the countries under its jurisdiction, to dispense from the interpellations or to grant to missionaries the faculty that enables them to do so.[4] These faculties have been granted to the missionaries, as was indicated in Chapter I, Part II. They have continued in force after the Code and are still valid today.

Besides these general faculties the Holy See also grants particular faculties for individual cases. In these, very often, it is explicitly required that the one using the faculty make express mention of the delegation of the Holy See, thus attesting again to its supreme right in this regard.[5]

The reserved competency of the Holy Office in granting dispensations from the interpellations must be understood as modified not only by these special indults but also by the general authorization that derives from the law as expressed in canon 1125,[6] for this canon extends to the Church at large what had previously been granted to individual countries. This canon provides not only for the complete omission of the interpellations in the application of the privileges granted by Popes Paul III and St. Pius V, but also for the act of dispensing from the interpellations as outlined

---

iuxta decretum et Instructionem S. Officii anni 1760 quae transmittatur."—*Coll. S.C.P.F.*, n. 517. Cf. Heylen, *Tractatus de Matrimonio*, p. 347; Gougnard, *Tractatus de Matrimonio*, p. 298; Chrétien, *De Matrimonio*, n. 259, p. 432.

[4] Canon 252; Payen, *De Matrimonio*, II, n. 2403, p. 733; Doheny, *Informal Procedure*, p. 533.

[5] Canons 200, § 2; 1057, "Qui ex potestate a Sede Apostolica delegata dispensationem concedunt, in eadem expressam pontificii indulti mentionem faciant." S.C.S. Off. (Coreae), 11 sept. 1878—*Fontes*, n. 1057; *Coll. S.C.P.F.*, n. 1499; Holy Office, to the Bishop of Denver, 15 November 1934—Private, Protoc. Num. 2619/34, reported in Bouscaren, *Canon Law Digest, Supplement through 1948*, p. 169; cf. Woeber, *The Interpellations*, p. 126.

[6] Bouscaren, "An Inquiry into the Practical Application of Canon 1125," *Miscellanea-Vermeersch*, I, 293.

under the conditions of Pope Gregory XIII's Constitution *Populis.*[7]

Article II: Competency Arising from the Code

Section 1: In Virtue of the Universal Extension of Canon 1125

A. All Local Ordinaries

The most explicit delegation of power to dispense from the interpellations is granted to all local ordinaries by canon 1125, as it extends to the universal Church what initially had been a purely particular concession of power. The historico-canonical basis for the delegation is found in the Constitution *Populis,* where Pope Gregory XIII granted *"universis et singulis dictorum locorum Ordinariis . . . facultatem dispensandi."*[8]

As has been demonstrated earlier,[9] the only condition required for the use of the faculty is either the impossibility or the absolute futility of fulfilling the ordinary obligation of interpellating the former consort of the convert, inasmuch as it is presumed that that consort is still unbaptized. The faculty is granted to all local ordinaries, and thus includes all residential bishops, all abbots and prelates *nullius,* all administrators of vacant dioceses, together with all vicars and prefects apostolics.[10] Since the faculty is restricted to local ordinaries, all religious superiors are expressly excluded from the category of those who possess this faculty.[11]

As has been indicated, one contemporary writer, Ramstein, states quite definitely that ordinaries in the United States do not have the faculty by law to dispense from the

[7] Vermeersch-Creusen, *Epitome,* II, n. 434, p. 300; Coronata, *De* Matrimonio, n. 640, p. 894; Cappello, *De Matrimonio,* n. 781, p. 771.

[8] Const. *Populis,* 25 ian. 1585—*infra,* p. 244, Appendix C.

[9] Part Three, Chapter V, Article II.

[10] Canon 198, § 1; Vromant, *De Matrimonio,* n. 365, p. 288.

[11] Canon 198, § 2.

interpellations. Yet the faculty is so clearly given and determined that there is no longer any doubt that local ordinaries everywhere in the world have the faculty as long as they fulfill the required conditions.[12]

It is further evident that, since the power is attached by law to their office, it fulfills the requirement which according to the law of the Code serves to classify the power as denoting ordinary jurisdiction.[13] By the same token it can be delegated either totally or in part, either habitually or for particular cases,[14] and one who is delegated habitually can validly and licitly subdelegate this power of dispensing, but only in and for an individual case.[15]

In view of the fact that this power was granted for use in the external forum, it can moreover, and *a fortiori,* be used in the internal forum.[16] Such non-judicial jurisdiction can be exercised by all who have this power, so that they can dispense their own subjects not only within the limits of their own territorial jurisdiction but also when they are actually absent from the territory.[17] This faculty of dispensing from the interpellations can furthermore be utilized in favor of anyone who, although not a subject of the dis-

[12] Ramstein, *A Manual of Canon Law,* p. 504; Bouscaren, "An Inquiry into the Practical Application of Canon 1125," *Miscellanea-Vermeersch,* I, 295; Doheny, *Informal Procedure,* p. 561, n. 13; Winslow, *The Pauline Privilege,* p. 79; Cappello, *De Matrimonio,* n. 787, p. 778; Coronata, *De Matrimonio,* n. 649, p. 908; Ayrinhac-Lydon, *Marriage Legislation,* p. 312.

[13] Canon 197, § 1: Potestas iurisdictionis ordinaria ea est quae ipso iure adnexa est officio.

[14] Canon 199, § 1: Qui iurisdictionem habet ordinariam, potest eam alteri ex toto vel ex parte delegare, nisi aliud expresse iure caveatur. Cf. Cappello, *op. cit.,* n. 787, p. 778; Burton, *A Commentary on Canon 1125,* p. 173; Woeber, *The Interpellations,* p. 126.

[15] Canon 199, § 3; Burton, *op. cit.,* p. 174.

[16] Canon 202, § 1: Actus potestatis iurisdictionis sive ordinariae sive delegatae collatae pro foro externo, valet quoque pro interno, non autem e converso. Cf. Farrugia, *De Matrimonio et Causis Matrimonialibus,* n. 324, p. 476.

[17] Canon 201, § 3.

pensing power, is nevertheless actually residing within the territory.[18]

All of those who are canonically recognized as local ordinaries can make use of the power which canon 1125 asserts for them, namely of dispensing from the interpellations after they have assured themselves upon at least a summary and extrajudicial investigation that the required interpellations cannot be made, that they would prove absolutely futile, or that they would remain unanswered by the infidel party.

In any case they act with ordinary power. Not under any circumstances are they obliged to make any recourse to the Holy See for the rightful use of this power.[19]

B: All Pastors

The faculty that is granted to all local ordinaries by canon 1125 is granted also to all pastors in virtue of the same concession of the law. Not only to those who are pastors in the strict sense of the term, but to all who are regarded in the law as equivalent to pastors, is given the faculty of dispensing from the interpellations.

[18] Cappello, *op. cit.*, n. 787, p. 778; Farrugia, *loc. cit.*, Woods, *The Constitutions of Canon 1125*, p. 97; Doheny (*op. cit.*, p. 561, note 43) finds force for this in a parallel with canon 881, § 2, where it is stated that all priests approved for the hearing of confessions, whether with ordinary or delegated jurisdiction, can hear the confessions of all that come to them, even those from a different parish or diocese. Vermeersch-Creusen rather find another parallel in canon 1043 to support the contention that the dispensation from the interpellations can be granted to non-residents actually dwelling within the jurisdictional limits of the one granting the dispensation. This canon in providing for emergency power to dispense from the matrimonial impediments *urgente mortis periculo* expressly extends the jurisdiction to include not only the subjects whereever they are but also all others who are *de facto* within the territory of the grantor of the dispensation—*Epitome*, II, n. 435, p. 301; Winslow, *The Pauline Privilege*, p. 79; Woeber, *The Interpellations*, p. 126, note 101; Burton, *op. cit.*, p. 174, note 38. These latter all borrow from Vermeersch-Creusen.

[19] Cappello, *De Matrimonio*, n. 787, p. 776; Ayrinhac-Lydon, *Marriage Legislation*, p. 321.

Canon 451 defines the canonical pastor as a priest or a moral person to whom is entrusted a parish with the care of souls, which office is to be exercised under the direct jurisdiction of the bishop. With such a pastor the same canon equates the following:

a) quasi-pastors (can. 216, § 3), i.e., those who are assigned to parishes in a vicariate or prefecture apostolic;[20]
b) the actual vicar of a parish whose title is held by a moral person (can. 471);
c) the vicar econome (administrator) who is assigned to a vacant parish (can. 472, § 1, 473);
d) the substitute vicar approved by the ordinary, with the further approbation of the religious superior if the parish is in the care of a religious institute (can. 474, 465, §§ 4, 5);
e) the parish assistant who by law assumes the administration of a parish upon the death of the pastor until an administrator has been lawfully appointed (can. 472, § 2);
f) the adjutant vicar assigned to an incapacitated pastor with the commission from the bishop to fulfill the entire office of pastor (can. 475, § 2).

[20] The Commission for the Authentic Interpretation of the Code has cleared up all doubt that formerly concerned this class of pastors. The Secretary for the Sacred Congregation for the Propagation of the Faith presented the doubt to the Commission in the words: "On the other hand, it would seem that this faculty should be denied to quasi-pastors, because the faculty to dispense, granted by Pope Gregory XIII to pastors, is to be considered rather as a privilege than as a right, whereas canon 451, § 2, declares quasi-pastors equivalent to pastors in rights and obligations, without mentioning privileges." Reply of the Cardinal President of the Code Commission: "To the question, whether in virtue of canon 1125, even quasi-pastors receive *by law* the faculty to dispense mentioned in the Constitution *Populis* of Gregory XIII. *Reply*. In the affirmative." Code Commission, 3 aug. 1919; *Sylloge*, n. 72—cited Bouscaren, *Canon Law Digest*, II, 342; Winslow, *The Pauline Privilege*, p. 79, note 54; Doheny, *Informal Procedure*, p. 563.

The *vicarius cooperator*, the ordinary assistant pastor or curate, is not considered as being on a par with pastors in sharing the rights and duties of that office. An exception is made and recognized in law in the cases wherein such an assistant pastor is appointed by the bishop to assume the full discharge of the office of pastor although that office is both *de facto* and *de iure* held by another man. This unrestricted assignment must be clearly evident from the bishop's letter of appointment or from a special commission specifically given by the pastor himself.[21] Only in this latter and exceptional case could the *vicarius cooperator* be considered competent to grant a dispensation from the interpellations according to the privilege of Pope Gregory XIII.

The conditions and causes demanded as essential for the granting of a similar dispensation by a bishop are indeed necessary but also sufficient when a pastor is the dispensing power.[22]

All pastors may, therefore, validly and licitly dispense their subjects even when these are actually outside their parochial limits, as well as all others who are within these boundaries.

Again the power is ordinary, since it is attached by law to the office of pastor; it can be delegated even habitually, and in such cases with the right also of subdelegation.[23]

This general power given to pastors is in no way limited to the internal forum. Its use in the external forum, as well as in the internal non-sacramental forum, can be controlled by directives of the ordinary in the event such a control is necessary for proper order or for the avoidance of confusion

[21] Canon 476, § 6; Bernard M. Kelly, *The Functions Reserved to Pastors*, The Catholic University of America Canon Law Studies, n. 250 (Washington, D.C.: The Catholic University of America Press, 1947), p. 54; Cappello, *De Matrimonio*, n. 787, p. 777; James Joseph Donovan, *The Pastor's Obligation in Pre-Nuptial Investigation*, The Catholic University of America Canon Law Studies, n. 115 (Washington, D.C., The Catholic University of America, 1938), pp. 59-65.

[22] Chrétien, *De Matrimonio*, n. 261, p. 436; Kearney, *The Principles of Canon 1127*, p. 132.

[23] Doheny, *Informal Procedure*, p. 562.

in the administration of the diocese. Bishops may, therefore, and in fact should demand that pastors report any use of this general faculty. They may also require a written summary report of the causes upon which the dispensation was based and of what "summary and extrajudicial" means were used in the ascertainment that a sufficient cause actually existed at the time the dispensation was granted. This written report not only assures a sufficient control over the use of the privilege but also affords a valuable record for the chancery files.[24]

It is to be noted, and with emphasis, that although bishops or superiors may by reason of their authority within the diocese or religious house regulate the use of canon 1125, they cannot forbid its use, nor can the "observance of merely diocesan regulations be made a condition necessary for the valid use of the faculty granted to pastors by the Code."[25]

Any diocesan statute forbidding the use of this privilege or endorsing restrictive conditions is itself invalid, for no authority subordinate to the Holy See itself is competent to add an invalidating clause to any general law of the Church.

In this regard pastors find themselves in an exceptionally unique position, for in canon 1125 there is expressly acknowledged for them the power to dispense from the interpellations in virtue of the privilege granted by Pope Gregory XIII. Such a dispensation when operating under the unusual conditions considered by the Constitution *Populis*, can have the effect even of dissolving the bond of a legitimate marriage. To those who would object that such a faculty is too extraordinary to be conferred on mere pas-

[24] Woods, *The Constitutions of Canon 1125*, p. 98. It is suggested further that the Bishop demand submission of proofs and their approval by him before the Pastor can proceed to grant the dispensation. In ordinary procedure this will be the practice unless the policy of the Bishop and the Chancery be made known clearly to the pastors in the use of these faculties.

[25] Bouscaren, "An Inquiry into the Practical Application of Canon 1125," *Miscellanea-Vermeersch*, I, 217; Bouscaren-Ellis, *Canon Law: A Text and Commentary*, p. 559.

tors, the only answer that can be given, and it is certainly adequate, is that in this matter pastors are by law given exactly the same power that is given to bishops, for "*ubi lex non distinguit, neque nos distinguere debemus.*"[26] Identically the same effect is produced without restriction or extension, regardless of the authority granting the dispensation, provided, of course, that the dispensing authority is competent.

Shortly after the promulgation of the Code this very objection was referred to the Commission for the Authentic Interpretation of the Code for further clarification. The Commission was asked: "Utrum facultates dispensandi, quae continentur in constitutionibus relatis in canone 1125, intelligantur concessae tantum Ordinariis, an vero omnibus sacerdotibus curam animarum exercentibus." Infrascriptus Emus Commissionis Praeses respondit: "Dictae facultates dispensandi aestimandae sunt ex tenore constitutionum, de quibus in canone 1125."[27]

But the Constitution explicitly grants the privilege and the faculty to all pastors in such a way that no prudent objection can be raised against their applying of the privilege mentioned in canon 1125 and their dispensing a convert from making the interpellations as long as they have satisfied themselves upon a summary and extrajudicial investigation that the making of the interpellations would be impossible or absolutely useless, or that the infidel party has not answered the interpellations within the prescribed limit of time.[28]

[26] Bouscaren, *loc. cit.*

[27] *Sylloge*, n. 66, p. 105, as quoted by Doheny, *Informal Procedure*, p. 562, note 48; cited by Bouscaren, *Canon Law Digest*, II, 341 (26 ian. 1919).

[28] Const. *Populis*, 25 ian. 1585: "... universis et singulis dictorum locorum Ordinariis et parochis, et presbyteris Societatis Jesu ad confessiones audiendas ab eiusdem Societatibus Superioribus approbatis." —*Codex Iuris Canonici*, Documentum VIII; Gasparri, *De Matrimonio*, II, n. 1159; Ayrinhac-Lydon, *Marriage Legislation*, p. 320; Vermeersch-Creusen, *Epitome*, II, n. 435, p. 300; Woeber, *The Interpellations*, p. 126; Burton, *A Commentary on Canon 1125*, p. 173.

C. Jesuit Confessors

The faculty of dispensing from the interpellations, as incorporated in the Constitution *Populis,* is granted also to members of the Society of Jesus who are approved by their superiors for the hearing of confessions. To these confessors is conceded a faculty identical with that given to local ordinaries and pastors, and therefore the conditions for the use of the privilege are likewise the same. All that has been said in reference to the use of the privilege by pastors is to be applied also to the use of the privilege by Jesuit confessors.

There is a difference, however, in the fact that today the approbation of the superior general is necessary to allow a member of the Society to hear confessions, but this approbation is not sufficient. The general delegation of jurisdiction for the administration of the sacrament of penance can be given only by the local ordinary. This delegation of jurisdiction together with the approbation of the proper superior is necessary for all religious even exempt.[29] For that reason only those members of the Society of Jesus are to be regarded today as "approved for the hearing of confessions" who have the diocesan faculties from the ordinary of the place where the dispensation is to be granted.[30]

This delegation of faculties in no way confers upon the confessor an ecclesiastical office as defined by the Code.[31] Since, moreover, the confessor does not hold an office to which this power could be annexed, the power given to these approved confessors, even though the grant derives through the law of the Code, is not ordinary power. The faculty to dispense may, however, be subdelegated in accordance with the norm established in canon 199, § 2. This subdelegation may even be granted habitually by the terms

[29] Canon 874, § 1 .

[30] Bouscaren, "An Inquiry into the Practical Application of Canon 1125," *Miscellanea-Vermeersch,* I, 297-8; Doheny, *Informal Procedure,* p. 564.

[31] Canon 145, § 1.

of the same law.[32] And its use is not to be limited to the internal forum.[33] The restriction simply consists in this that the confessors may dispense only those whose confessions they have the faculty to hear.[34]

The Constitution *Populis* granted the faculty explicitly only to the missionary priests of the Society of Jesus who were laboring in the territories to which the Constitution was originally directed. The fact that the Constitution and its privileges are now made part of the universal law is not sufficient proof that the faculty is held today by all religious who have been approved, through the receipt of diocesan faculties, for the hearing of confessions.[35]

However, the confessors in many other religious orders do surely have the faculty, not as derived through the universal law, but as participated in through the intercommunication of this privilege. Although the Code endorses the institute of intercommunication of privileges as a lawful source of privilege,[36] it excludes for the future all such

[32] *Sylloge*, n. 66, p. 105 as quoted by Doheny, *op. cit.*, p. 562, note 48; Canon 199 § 2: Etiam potestas jurisdictionis ab Apostolica Sede delegata subdelegari potest sive ad actum, sive etiam habitualiter, nisi electa fuerit industria personae aut subdelegatio prohibita. Bouscaren, *op. cit.*, p. 297; Burton, *op. cit.*, p. 175; Woods, *op. cit.*, p. 68.

[33] Cappello, *De Matrimonio*, n. 787, p. 778: "Confessarii S.I. erga eos generatim uti poterunt, quorum confessiones audire valent, non solum in actu confessionis, sed etiam extra confessionem, pro foro quoque externo ... nulla siquidem restrictio apponitur in Const. Gregorii XIII et in canon 1125." Cf. Payen, *De Matrimonio*, II, n. 2409, pp. 745-746; Burton, *op. cit.*, p. 176; Farrugia, *De Matrimonio et Causis Matrimonialibus*, n. 324, p. 476; Winslow, *The Pauline Privilege*, n. 138, p. 79.

[34] Cappello, *loc. cit.*

[35] Vermeersch-Creusen, *Epitome*, II, n. 435, p. 301: "Quo iure ad omnes confessores extenderentur, non videmus." Cappello, *De Matrimonio*, n. 787, note 69, p. 778: "Opinio quae tenet iure communi facultatem competere omnibus confessariis caret iuridico fundamento, ut videretur, quia de iisdem silet et constitutio ipsa et canon 1125. Plures habent ex privilegio." Cf. Woods, *The Constitutions of Canon 1125*, p. 68; Payen, *De Matrimonio*, II, n. 2409, p. 746; Burton, *op. cit.*, p. 175; Vromant, *De Matrimonio*, n. 365, p. 288.

[36] Canon 63.

intercommunication among religious orders.[37] Canon 613, § 1, is not retroactive in its effect, and so all privileges intercommunicated among religious before the Code are also in the present to be considered valid. The Holy See has acknowledged this interpretation of the canon. The Pontifical Commission for the Interpretation of the Code was asked whether the words of canon 613, § 1, *"exclusa in posterum qualibet communicatione,"* are to be understood in the sense that privileges which were acquired through intercommunication and were peacefully enjoyed by religious institutes before the Code are now revoked. The Commission replied in the negative.[38]

It is certain that the confessors of many religious orders enjoyed this privilege before the Code through their participation in it by way of the intercommunication of privileges. Pope St. Pius V had declared that the Jesuits were a Mendicant Order, and therefore all the religious of other Mendicant orders shared in the habitual faculties granted in the papal constitutions of the same Pope St. Pius V, together with Paul III, and Gregory XIII. Burton states that practically all religious at that time participated in the intercommunication of privileges.[39]

All evidence indicates that the power to dispense from the interpellations as given to approved confessors in the Society of Jesus is held also by the duly approved confessors in the other Mendicant Orders, namely, the Dominicans, Friars Minor, Augustinians, Carmelites and Minims.[40] According to the present Code law all religious, even exempt,

[37] Canon 613, § 1.

[38] 30 dec. 1937—*AAS*, XXX (1938), 73; Bouscaren, *Canon Law Digest*, II, 173.

[39] *A Commentary on Canon 1125*, p. 71. Burton gives careful and ample consideration to this question, pp. 51-52; 70-71; particularly in note 29, pp. 70-71; 174-175.

[40] Doheny, *Informal Procedure*, p. 564; Vermeersch-Creusen, *Epitome*, II, n. 435, p. 301; Cappello, *De Matrimonio*, n. 787, p. 778; Woods, *The Constitutions of Canon 1125*, p. 68; Winslow, *The Pauline Privilege*, p. 79; cf. also Kearney, *The Principles of Canon 1127*, p. 132; Chrétien, *De Matrimonio*, n. 261, p. 436.

can obtain faculty for hearing the confessions of the faithful only from the Ordinary of the place. Although the permission of their superior is a prerequisite for the hearing of confessions, it is the delegation of faculties by the Ordinary and not the permission of the Superior that gives the confessor the right to dispense from the interpellations. Further, no special permission is required of the superior to use the privilege mentioned in canon 1125, since this power is given to them as approved confessors through the universal law of the Church as expressed in the Code.[41] For the very same reason the said superiors cannot deprive an approved confessor of the faculty to dispense from the interpellations, nor can they restrict it by means of invalidating conditions. The superior and the local ordinary can legitimately supervise its use; as was recommended before with pastors, so with confessors the local ordinary should demand a written report of every use of the privilege, which at least summarily lists the causes underlying the grant of the dispensation, and the means used as verification of the existence and sufficiency of these causes. These salutary regulations can aim only at assuring the reasonable and prudent use of this power; they cannot in any way affect the validity of the dispensation granted.[42]

When such a dispensation is granted by a confessor in the external forum or in the internal non-sacramental forum, it is proper that the confessor inform the pastor of the party, so that he can be made aware of the person's right to enter another marriage.[43] Woods states that the pastor has every right to demand such documentary evidence regarding the actual granting of the dispensation. This is certainly true. At the very least it is dictated by the need for good order within the parish or the diocese. Endless confusion and un-

[41] Canon 874; Woods, *op. cit.*, pp. 69, 98; Burton, *op. cit.*, p. 175.

[42] Vromant, *op. cit.*, n. 365, p. 288; Coronata, *De Matrimonio*, n. 649, p. 908.

[43] Cappello, *De Matrimonio*, n. 787, p. 778: "Si dispensatio detur pro foro externo vel foro interno non-sacramentali, necesse est ut concessa dispensatio probari possit."

necessary concern would be inevitable if the fact of the granting of the dispensation were not brought to the attention of the proper authorities, who by reason of their responsibility have a right to such knowledge. In 1935 Bouscaren wrote that his Jesuit superiors were exercising a careful and prudent control over the use of the faculty. There is every reason to believe that all religious superiors are aware of their obligation in this regard and that the same concern is being manifested today.[44]

Section 2: In Virtue of the Emergency Power Deriving from Canon 81

Although canon 1125 as part of the Church's universal law explicitly grants the faculty to dispense from the interpellations, it is not the only juridical source that warrants the granting of this kind of dispensation.

Canon 81 authorizes ordinaries to dispense from the universal laws of the Church in those cases of urgency in which recourse to Rome is difficult and any delay occasions the danger of grave harm, as long as the dispensation is one which the Holy See customarily grants.

This canon postulates only three conditions for its use: 1) that it be difficult to make recourse to the Holy See, 2) that some grave harm impend in consequence of any delayed approach to the Holy See, and 3) that it concerns a dispensation which the Holy See would regularly grant. It is necessary that all three of the conditions be verified at one and the same time.

The first condition specifies that it be difficult to reach the Holy See for the necessary dispensation. The canon refers to the ordinary means of communication by mail, and consequently any use of extraordinary means, such as telegraph, telephone, cablegram, etc., need not be used.[45]

[45] Code Commission, 12 Nov., 1922—*AAS*, XIV (1922), 663; Doheny, *Informal Procedure*, p. 536.

[44] Bouscaren, "An Inquiry into the Practical Application of Canon 1125," *Miscellanea-Vermeersch*, I, 298.

This canon is to be understood as having been restricted somewhat in its interpretation in recent years. In 1947 the Code Commission answered that the canon is not applicable whenever there is sufficient time to have recourse to the Holy See through the Apostolic Delegation in the event that the ordinary avenues of correspondence are impeded.[46]

Then there must be some grave urgency demanding the dispensation. In other words, the danger of some grave harm, physical or moral, must be occasioned through a delay in seeking and obtaining the dispensation from the Holy See. Gregory states that this urgency appears comparable to that which allows bishops to dispense from the matrimonial impediments.[47]

The Sacred Rota, in deciding the status of a marriage which for its validity depended on a dispensation granted effectively in virtue of canon 81, warned against demanding the same urgency for the application of canon 81 as is expressly required in the use of canons 1043 and 1045, for canon 81 is broader than the other two and is certainly not limited by them.[48]

Finally, the historical development of the canonical legislation on the interpellations and their necessity offers sufficient proof that the Holy See has always been eager to grant a dispensation from the interpellations in every case wherein such a dispensation would aid or favor converts

[46] Code Commission, 26 June, 1947—*AAS*, XXIX (1947), 374; Bouscaren, *Canon Law Digest Supplement through 1948*, p. 15. The Code Commission was asked: Whether the clause of canon 81, "unless recourse to the Holy See is difficult," applies when Ordinaries can easily have recourse to the Legate of the Roman Pontiff in the country, who is in communication with the Holy See. Reply: In the negative.

[47] *The Pauline Privilege*, p. 78.

[48] S. Romana Rota, *Nullitatis Matrimonii*, 10 aug. 1926, Coram R.P.D. Maximo Massini, Decano, Dec. XL,—*S. Romanae Rotae Decisiones*, XVIII (1926), 318-325; Bouscaren, *Canon Law Digest*, II, 43; Franciscus Fang, *Dispensatio Matrimonialis Urgente Morte Periculo et Instante Nuptiarum Contractu* (Romae: Officium Libri Catholici, 1946), n. 125, p. 156 (hereafter cited *Dispensatio Matrimonialis*).

to the Faith.[49] Consequently ordinaries are empowered to grant a dispensation from the interpellations when the above named conditions are present. For the use of canon 81 in the matter of dispensing from the interpellations, Woeber finds further authority in the directions of canon 20, which legislates that one is to be guided by the norms established in parallel canons and in general principles whenever the present law does not adequately cover any given situation.[50]

Before this dispensation can be granted it is necessary that the ordinary be morally certain that the infidel party will not be baptized and moreover will not live peacefully and respectfully with his convert spouse.[51] For then the interpellations do not bind *ex iure divino,* but bind merely by force of the ecclesiastical law. Even when the departure of the infidel is clearly known the formal interpellation is necessary, not indeed for validity, but only for the licit use of the Pauline privilege.[52]

The Holy Office has in the past recognized the validity of dispensing in urgent cases that did not brook any delay: "Quoties coniugem infidelem nec Christi fidem amplecti, nec sine contumelia Creatoris cum coniuge converso velle cohabitare certo constet, Episcopi tamquam Apostolicae Sedis delegati, et Vicarii Apostolici, dispensare poterunt super interpellatione, dummodo urgeat necessitas, nec tempus supetat recurrendi ad S. Sedem."[53]

This faculty as conceded to the bishops by the Holy See

[49] Vromant, *De Matrimonio,* n. 367, p. 289.

[50] *The Interpellations,* p. 129.

[51] Vromant, *op. cit.,* n. 367, p. 289: "Quando certo constat conjugem infidelem vel Christi fidem amplecti neque ullo modo aut saltem non sine contumelia Creatoris cum coniuge converso velle cohabitare, Ordinarii locorum ad normam can. 81 valent dispensare super interpellationibus ..." De Smet, *De Sponsalibus et Matrimonio,* n. 353b, p. 300; Doheny, *Informal Procedure,* p. 535; Coronata, *De Matrimonio,* n. 640, p. 895.

[52] Vromant, *loc. cit.;* Cf. Part III, Chapter I, Article III, *supra,* pp. 102-106.

[53] S.C.S. Off., 11 aug. 1859—*Fontes,* n. 954; *Coll. S.C.P.F.,* n. 1180.

has not been abrogated by the Code; rather, this faculty now is part and parcel of the powers comprised in the office of any residential bishop.[54]

In this regard Schaaf noted that the wording of the rescript did not indicate that the Holy Office was bestowing any new faculty upon the ordinaries, but simply asserted that under given urgent circumstances ordinaries could act as delegates of the Holy See. This is further evident in that the words toward the end of the declaration specify equivalently the same circumstances demanded in the last part of canon 81.[55]

This right of the ordinary to use the general faculty of canon 81 in order to dispense a convert from the obligation of making the interpellations in the cases wherein urgency does not allow sufficient time for the making of a recourse to the Holy See is recognized by commentators.[56]

Section 3: *In Virtue of Special Authorization through Canons 1043-1045*

The special concern of the Church for the welfare of souls is manifested quite obviously through the explicit delegation of faculties for dispensing from the ecclesiastical matrimonial impediments when individuals are in danger of death.[57] Such solicitude alone can explain the even more explicit and exceptional faculty of dispensing from the matrimonial impediments when they are discovered only after the preparations for the marriage have progressed to such a stage that any postponement of the marriage would cause undue inconvenience to the parties.[58]

[54] De Becker, Recensiones, "Criticism of Augustine's *Commentary*," *ETL*, II (1925), 446; De Smet, *op. cit.*, n. 353b, p. 300; Burton, *op. cit.*, p. 170.

[55] Schaaf, "Dispensation from Interpellations," *ER*, LXXXVI (1932), 535.

[56] Payen, *op. cit.*, I, n. 652, p. 485; II, n. 2413, p. 751; Gougnard, *Tractatus de Matrimonio*, p. 298; Bouscaren-Ellis, *Canon Law: A Text and Commentary*, p. 558; Ayrinhac-Lydon, *Marriage Legislation*, p. 312; Burton, *op. cit.*, p. 171, note 22; Woeber, *op. cit.*, p. 129; Doheny, *op. cit.*, p. 535; Petrovits, *The New Church Law on Matrimony*, n. 571.

[57] Canon 1043.

[58] Canon 1045.

Although the emergency faculties of both of these canons were granted explicitly with reference to the ecclesiastical impediments,[59] it is suggested further that they may be used for dispensing from the interpellations when the conditions specified in either canon are actually verified.

By far the majority of the commentators does not so much as advert to this particular possibility. Again, however, their silence cannot in any way be interpreted as sufficient reason of itself for ruling out this theory. Any argument *pro* or *con* will have to be based on the intrinsic meaning and purpose of these canons.

Vromant presents the affirmative argument by stating simply that bishops, pastors, the priests approved by canon 1098, n. 2, for assisting at marriages, and confessors may dispense from the interpellations when one of the parties is in danger of death or when the marriage cannot be further postponed. The argument is based on the interpretation of the word *impedimenta* as used in canon 1043, where this word is to be understood in its widest sense, so that it includes even such hindrances which are only improperly called impediments. In this sense an impediment is to be understood as any obstacle set up by a purely ecclesiastical law, which here and now stands in the way of the celebration or revalidation of a particular marriage.[60]

Fang defines a matrimonial impediment in the words:

> "Impedimentum communiter definitur: Circumstantia qua quis ex lege divina vel humana arcetur a nuptiis seu licite seu valide ineundis. Inde est obstaculum quoddam iuridicum et personale quod officit matrimonii liceitati vel validitati: sine quo omnes possunt contrahere matrimonium (can. 1035), cum quo tamen

[59] Fang, *Dispensatio Matrimonialis*, n. 85, p. 101.

[60] Vromant, *De Matrimonio*, n. 367, p. 290: "Vox '*impedimenta*' in can. 1043-1045 ... summenda est sensu latissimo, etiam pro impedimento improprie dicto. Immo uti nobis videtur, voce '*impedimenta*' in can. 1043-1045 intelligendum est *quodcumque obstaculum iuris mere ecclesiastici*, quod matrimonii celebrationi obstet."

persona impedita directe arcetur a contractu, consequenter a sacramento."[61]

Vermeersch-Creusen define an impediment even in the strict sense of the term: "Quidquid externum iure divino in lege ecclesiastica proposito aut iure mere ecclesiastico personas a contractu matrimoniali arcet."[62] And Gasparri noted that even in the Code the word impediment is not everywhere used in this strict sense.[63]

Vromant finds further support for his interpretation of canons 1043 and 1045 in a parallel decree of the Sacred Consistorial Congregation[64] and in a statement of the Pontifical Commission for the Interpretation of the Code,[65] both of which acknowledged the juridical existence and value of impediments other than those commonly accepted as the diriment and impedient impediments that receive mention in canons 1067-1080.

His final and perhaps most appealing argument is based upon the purpose of the law and the manifest intention of the legislator in providing for these eventualities, both of which considerations furnish valid and approved norms for the interpretation of law.[66] For canons 1043-1045 grant a faculty not contrary to, but rather concomitant with, though simultaneously outside of the regular norm in the universal law. It is evident that the faculty was granted for the spiritual good of souls insofar as it is the expressed purpose of the faculty to ease consciences and to remove the blight of illegitimacy on the one hand (can. 1043), and to forestall any undue inconvenience or possible harm on the other (canon 1045). By the same token it is the manifest intention of the legislator to extend the universal law on dis-

[61] *Dispensatio Matrimonialis,* n. 85, p. 101.

[62] *Epitome,* II, n. 296, p. 206.

[63] *De Matrimonio,* I, n. 205; cf. cans. 1971, § 1, n. 1; 1081-1102.

[64] *Proxima sacra,* 25 april 1918—*AAS,* X (1918), 190; *Periodica,* IX (1919), 116ff.

[65] 5 apr. 1929, ad V—*AAS,* XXI (1929), 171.

[66] Can. 18.

pensations as applicable to cases and circumstances not envisioned in any other faculty.[67]

This same notion is found in other authors. Vermeersch-Creusen speak of the faculty herein contained as being not only highly useful but even absolutely necessary for the good of souls.[68] Fang, with reference expressly to these canons, notes a juridical basis that rests on the fundamental principle: *Salus animarum suprema lex,* and he urges that the canons be given the widest possible application within prudent limits.[69]

Now, the interpellations are required solely by the ecclesiastical law, so that when the departure of the infidel is already known from some other source the interpellations are no longer required for the subsequent valid use of the Pauline privilege.[70] It is from this approach that Vromant deals with the interpellations. The lack of the ability to make them stand in canons 1043-1045 as an impediment to the contracting of the marriage insofar as a non-compliance with the formality of the interpellations can conceivably remain the sole obstacle to the celebration or also the convalidation of some particular matrimonial union. He accordingly, urges the use of this faculty for dispensing from the interpellations whenever, given all postulated conditions,

[67] For a thorough consideration of the relation between these canons and the faculty of canon 81 confer Wernz-Vidal, *Ius Matrimoniale,* n. 413b, note 61, pp. 536-537; resp. Comm. Codicis, 27 iul. 1942—*AAS,* XXXIV, (1942), 241; *Periodica,* XXXII (1943), 103.

[68] *Epitome,* II, n. 305, p. 214.

[69] "Vidimus . . . facultates a can. 1043-1045 datas amplissimas esse, licet vero certos intra fines circumscriptas. Principium quod Legislatorem sapientissimum ad eas concedendas induxit "salus animarum suprema lex" est: principium nobilissimum, finis altissimus! Eadem plane ratione quae suaserat ut matrimonialium impedimentorum dispensatio aeque ac constitutio R. Pontifici reservaretur, suasit ut summo in rerum discrimine atque in gravissima necessitate haec reservatio relaxaretur, pro bono animarum.

Hac quoque eadem ratione ducti, benigni potius fuimus in earum facultatum interpretatione. . ." *Dispensatio Matrimonialis,* conclusio, n. 163, p. 201.

[70] *Supra,* pp. 113-122.

the actual departure of the infidel consort is well known.[71]

The supporters of this opinion are few, but they are also the only ones who have made any reference to this consideration at all. Payen acknowledged the validity of this doctrine in his comment on the more specific faculties granted by the Sacred Congregation for the Propagation of the Faith, so that it is not altogether certain which was the actual source of power of which he spoke.[72]

Doheny, on the other hand, states unequivocally that the canons may be used to "authorize the omission of the interpellations" and notes simply that all objections that can be raised against the opinion have already been adequately answered by Vromant.[73] Woeber alludes to the same possible application of the law when he lists the causes which are recognized as sufficiently grave to justify a dispensation from the interpellations.[74] He later draws a parallel with canon 81 and the pre-Code practice of the Holy See, and allows the ordinary to dispense in virtue of canons 1043 and 1045, § 1; he concludes that, although there may be doubts as to whether this still expresses the practice of the Holy See, "one is safe in basing a course of action on this principle as long as no contrary practice is established."[75]

De Smet, in limiting the interpretation of the term *impedimentum*, represented the other viewpoint as he restricted the applicable use of canons 1043-1045 to the question simply of dispensing from impediments properly and strictly so called.[76]

[71] "*Urgente mortis periculo* necnon etiam, '*cum iam omnia sunt parata ad nuptias, nec matrimonium, sine probabili gravis damni periculo, differri possit*'; super interpellationibus, quae matrimonii christiani celebrationi obstent, dispensare possunt Ordinarius, parochus, quasi-parochus, 'sacerdos qui matrimonio, ad normam can. 1098, n. 2, assistit,' atque confessarius, omnia tamen intelligendo iuxta dispositiones can. 1043-1045—*De Matrimonio*, n. 367, p. 290.

[72] *De Matrimonio*, II, n. 2418, p. 751.

[73] *Informal Procedure*, pp. 537-538; also p. 535, note 64.

[74] *The Interpellations*, p. 113.

[75] *Op. cit.*, pp. 129-130.

[76] *De Sponsalibus et Matrimonio*, n. 763, p. 646.

At any rate, it appears that ordinarily the circumstances which open the way for a use of the faculties as mentioned in canons 1043-1045 will likewise leave room for a use of the power as granted in canon 81 as far as the dispensation from the interpellations is concerned. The allowable use of this latter canon is recognized quite generally; at present, so it seems, there is no valid reason for excluding the use of the emergency powers granted in canons 1043-1045, namely, when the peace of conscience or the good of souls is at stake, which are the very motives that prompted the legislation enacted in canons 1043 and 1045.

Article III: Competency Granted through Special Faculties

The law of the Code grants what may seem to be quite an adequate power when it authorizes ordinaries, pastors and certain confessors to dispense from the interpellations under the various but definite circumstances contemplated in several canons.[77]

Before the advent of the Code the Holy See had regularly granted directly, to individual bishops and vicars apostolic, indults that permitted the granting of a dispensation from the interpellations.[78]

But over and above these particular concessions as made in the pre-Code era, two separate but general faculties had been issued to the ordinaries, one to the mission ordinaries by the Sacred Congregation for the Propagation of the

[77] Canons 81; 1043; 1045, and especially 1125.

[78] S.C.S. Off. (ad Arch ep. Quebecen.), 8 iun. 1836—*Fontes*, n. 874; *Coll. S.C.P.F.*, n. 848; S.C.S. Off., instr. (Pro. Vic. Ap. ad Gallos), 20 iun. 1866—*Fontes*, n. 994; *Coll. S.C.P.F.*, n. 1293; S.C.S. Off. (Portland), 18 iun. 1884—*Fontes*, n. 1088; *Coll. S.C.P.F.*, n. 1620, "Quatenus vero saltem summarie et extraiudicialiter constet interpellationem vel impossibilem vel inutilem fore, utetur (Episcopus) facultate dispensandi, si ea polleat: sin minus supplicandum SSmo pro facultate pro decem casibus. SSmus approbabvit et facultatem concessit."

Faith, and the other to the remaining ordinaries by the Sacred Consistorial Congregation.[79]

With the promulgation of the Code, however, the latter of these formulas was withdrawn by a decree of the Sacred Consistorial Congregation. Upon the authority of Pope Benedict XV (1914-1922) there were withdrawn all faculties for the external forum which had been granted to ordinaries subject to the various Congregations, exclusive of the Congregation for the Propagation of the Faith and the Congregation for the Oriental Church.[80] From this revocation one cannot argue, as some could possibly wish to do, that the Holy See no longer approved the granting of a dispensation from the interpellations by ordinaries. Quite the opposite is true, for it was felt that the new Code, particularly through canon 1125, had rendered juridically superfluous these earlier faculties in all that pertained to the Pauline privilege and the wider privilege of the Faith.[81]

Actually, however, the provisions of the new Code proved inadequate in many regards to such an extent that the various Congregations felt constrained to formulate a new list of faculties, each within the field of its own competency and in line with the new Code. Pope Pius XI (1922-1939) in

[79] Vermeersch, "Facultates Prop. Fidei, Facultates Formulae III," *Periodica,* XI (1922), (33)-(144): Konings-Putzer, *Commentarium in Facultates Apostolicas* (4. ed., Cincinnati: Benziger Brothers, 1897), Formula, I, C,D,E, pp. 197 ff. Schaaf, ("Dispensation from Interpellations", *ER,* LXXXVI [1932], 534) listed a copy of the faculty formerly granted to the bishops in this country in form T, n. 13: "Dispensandi intra fines suae dioecesis coniugem fidelem super interpellatione coniugis in infidelitate relicti; dummodo adhibitis antea omnibus diligentiis etiam per publicas ephemerides, ad reperiendum locum ubi coniux infidelis habitat, iisque in irritum cessis, constet saltem summarie et extraiudicialiter, dictum coniugem infidelem moneri legitime non posse, aut monitum, intra tempus in monitione praefixum suam voluntatem non significasse." One notices the similiarity between this particular faculty and the one granted by Gregory XIII in the Constitution *Populis,* and now extended to the universal Church in canon 1125.

[80] 25 apr. 1918—*AAS,* X (1918), 190-192.

[81] Burton, *A Commentary on Canon 1125,* p. 106.

1923 decreed that all ordinaries not subject to the Sacred Congregations for the Propagation of the Faith or for the Oriental Church were to obtain all of their faculties from the Consistorial Congregation, which was authorized to collect the faculties from the various other Congregations.[82]

Shortly before this the faculties for missionary countries granted by the Congregation for the Propagation of the Faith had been reissued in new formulas. These faculties had not been abrogated by the decree of Pope Benedict XV, but were rather renewed until the first of January 1920, at which time they were replaced with new faculties formulated in the light of the provisions of the Code.[83]

These in turn were amended effective the first of January 1941, so that the three formulas of 1920 were organized into two, the formula *maior,* for those ordinaries who had episcopal consecration, and the formula *minor,* for all other local ordinaries.[84]

In these formulas three faculties explicitly grant power to dispense from the interpellations:

> *25. Dispensandi super *interpellatione* coniugum in infidelitate relictorum pro omnibus *casibus ordinariis,* quando scilicet adhibitis antea omnibus diligentiis, etiam per publicas ephemerides ad reperiendum locum ubi coniux infidelis habitat, iisque in irritum cessis, constet ex processu saltem

[82] Motu proprio, *Post datam,* 20 apr. 1923—*AAS,* XV (1923), 193-194.

[83] Letter, S.C. de Prop. Fide, 1 iul. 1919, Protoc. Num. 1522/19 referred to by Vermeersch, "Commentaria de Formulis Facultatum Quas S. Congr. de Propaganda Fide Concedere Solet," *Periodica,* XI (1922), (70) n. 29.

[84] Cf. Vermeersch-Creusen, *Epitome,* I, Appendix, n. 873, pp. 665-672, for a list of the faculties of these new formulas. Cf. also commentaries on the earlier faculties, which are also valid for these new ones insofar as these include many of the former concessions. Vromant, *Facultates Apostolicae,* p. 79; Paventi, *Brevis Commentarius,* pp. 42-44; and Winslow, *A Commentary on the Apostolic Faculties,* pp. 149-152, which covers all of the new faculties.

summario et extraiudicialiter coniugem absentem moneri legitime non posse aut monitum intra tempus in monitione praefixum suam voluntatem non significasse. Pro dispensandis infidelibus plures uxores habentibus, ut post baptismum quam ex illis maluerunt, si etiam ipsa fidelis fiat, retinere possint, nisi prima voluerit converti, cf. Canon 1125.[85]

*26. Itemque dispensandi super *interpellatione* coniugis in infidelitate relicti, siquidem certo constiterit ex processu saltem summario et extraiudicialiter, interpellationem fieri non posse sine evidenti gravis damni aut coniugi iam ad fidem converso (etsi nondum baptizato), aut christianis inferendi periculo.

*27. Permittendi ut, accedente gravi causa, *interpellatio* coniugis infidelis *ante baptismum* partis quae ad fidem convertitur fieri possit; nec non, gravi pariter de causa, ab eadem interpellatione, ante baptismum partis quae convertitur, dispensandi, dummodo hoc in casu ex processu saltem summario et extraiudiciali constet interpellationem fieri non posse, vel fore inutilem.[86]

Those who possess the faculty of dispensing from the interpellations according to the norms of the Constitution *Populis* and canon 1125 may delegate that faculty to others. This delegation may be general or given for an individual case. If the delegation is general, the one delegated may further subdelegate the faculty to dispense.[87]

In 1923 the Sacred Consistorial Congregation issued new faculties for all ordinaries not under the authority either of

[85] For the similiarity between this faculty and the one formerly granted to other ordinaries, cf. *supra*, note 79, p. 220.

[86] Winslow, *The Pauline Privilege*, pp. 34, 38, 40; Burton, *op. cit.*, p. 108; Winslow, *Commentary on the Apostolic Faculties*, pp. 152, 156 and 158.

[87] Canon 199; Winslow, *The Pauline Privilege*, p. 80.

the Congregation for the Propagation of the Faith or of the Congregation for the Oriental Church. Formula IV of these quinquennial faculties is granted to the ordinaries of North and South America and the neighboring islands, and is issued every five years according to the norms of canon 340.[88]

None of the faculties of these new formulas grant the power to dispense from the interpellations.[89] Thus the ordinaries of the United States are not by means of specially granted faculties empowered to dispense from the interpellations. If they cannot dispense in a given case in virtue of the power which the law of the Code concedes to them, they must seek the necessary dispensation or faculty from the Holy See.[90]

The Holy See has shown itself willing to grant these particular faculties to individual bishops, and does in fact urge bishops to make application for the faculty before the actual need arises, if there is reason to believe that the possession of such a faculty will prove necessary. Ordinarily the faculty is granted for a definite number of cases.[91]

The following instance of such a faculty serves as a typical example of the delegation for dispensing from the interpellations as received by certain bishops in this country.

"To dispense, for ten cases, the Catholic spouse from

[88] Cf. Vermeersch-Creusen, *Epitome*, I, Appendix III, n. 874, pp. 672-680, for a copy of the faculties; Eagleton, *The Diocesan Quinquennial Faculties, Formula IV*. These faculties are granted upon petition to those included under the term "Ordinary" in canon 198, § 1, and are granted in the years whose final number is either four (4) or nine (9), p. 34.

[89] Doheny, *Informal Procedure*, p. 534; Woeber, *The Interpellations*, p. 132.

[90] Gregory, *The Pauline Privilege*, p. 81.

[91] S.C.S. Off. (Portland), 18 iun. 1884—*Fontes*, n. 1088; *Coll. S.C.P.F.*, n. 1620; S.C.S. Off., 18 maii 1892—*Fontes*, n. 1156; *Coll. S.C.P.F.*, n. 1797; S.C. de Prop Fide (C.P. pro Sin-Sutchuen.), 3 ian 1777—*Coll. S.C.P.F.*, n. 517; Woeber, *The Interpellations*, p. 132; Doheny, *Informal Procedure*, p. 534.

interpellating the spouse who remains in infidelity, provided that, after all diligence has been used (including published notices in the papers where that is possible), it is proved with certainty, at least from a summary and extrajudicial inquiry, that the infidel spouse absolutely could not be found. The Bishop cannot delegate this faculty to anyone, but must exercise it in person. "In each case express mention must be made of the delegation from the Holy See (c. 1057).

"After these cases are exhausted, the ordinary must report to the Holy Office the circumstances in which he used the faculty each time."[92]

In other cases the dispensation is granted directly by the Holy See itself, and the ordinary becomes the executor of the rescript according to the norms of the universal law.[93]

Since the advent of the Code both the Consistorial Congregation and the Congregation for the Propagation of the Faith have issued new formulas of faculties for the various bishops and vicars under their respective jurisdictions. In the same way the general faculties for nuncios and apostolic delegates have also been revised, but none of these mention any faculty to dispense from the intrpellations.[94]

Nevertheless the Apostolic Delegate to the United States has from the Sacred Congregation of the Holy Office a special faculty by means of which he can dispense from the interpellations in individual cases and after certain specified conditions have been verified.

"Since ordinaries in this country are obliged from time

[92] Private Rescript of the Holy Office to the Bishop of Denver, November 15, 1934, Protocol Num. 2619/34—Bouscaren, *Canon Law Digest, Supplement through 1948*, p. 169; Woeber, *The Interpellations*, pp. 132-133.

[93] Cans. 51-58; Holy Office to the Archbishop of Detroit, May 22, 1947, Private, Protoc. Num. 1026/47—Bouscaren, *op. cit.*, pp. 170-171.

[94] Vermeersch-Creusen, (*Epitome*, I [7. ed., 1949), Appendix I, n. 872, pp. 658-665) list the formulas granted in 1947 for a five-year period; Cf. Vermeersch, "Facultatum quae, post Codicem, Legatis Apostolicis concedi Consueverunt Breve Commentarium," *Periodica*, XII (1923), p. (69ff.).

to time to seek dispensation from the interpellations which are required for the lawful use of the Pauline privilege, the Supreme Congregation of the Holy Office has thought it opportune to grant the faculty to dispense from the interpellations to the Apostolic Delegate.

"When, therefore, in an individual case, there is danger of delay and no time for recourse to the Holy See, Your Excellency may direct requests for this dispensation to the Apostolic Delegation. The petition, moreover, must state that the following conditions, by which the faculty is circumscribed, are verified in the case: 'Provided that after all diligence has been used (including publishing notices in the paper where that is possible), it is proved with certainty, at least from a summary and extrajudicial inquiry, that the infidel spouse absolutely could not be found, or that the interpellation could not be made without evident danger of grave harm either to the spouse who is already converted to the Faith or to Christians.' "[95]

This faculty of the Apostolic Delegate cannot possibly be understood as abrogating the general faculty granted in the law of the Code. Local ordinaries, then, may still use the emergency power which canon 81 evinces for them in dispensing from the interpellations. There is on their part no need of making recourse either to the Holy See or to the Apostolic Delegation when the postulated conditions of that canon are fulfilled.[96]

[95] Private Letter of the Apostolic Delegate to the Ordinaries of the United States, July 17, 1935, Num. 116/35; Woeber, *The Interpellations*, p. 131; Bouscaren, *The Canon Law Digest, Supplement through 1948*, pp. 169-170.

[96] The Code Commission on June 26, 1947, stated that canon 81 cannot be used when it is possible to reach the Holy See through the facilities of the Delegation, even though other avenues of approach are closed, as they were during the recent war. It does not, however, forbid the use of the canon when actually there is not sufficient time to seek the necessary dispensation from Rome. *AAS*, XXXIX (1947), 374; Bouscaren, *op. cit.*, p. 15.

When the need for a dispensation arises in a given case the ordinary should determine whether or not he is empowered to grant the dispensation by means of the faculties granted in the law of the Code before he requests a delegated faculty from the Holy See or the Apostolic Delegation. It is a valid principle of practical juridical economy never to seek an extraordinary and particular solution to a situation which is sufficiently covered through the use of ordinary or habitually possessed power. Therefore, no dispensing agent should resort to delegated power when he is competent to grant the dispensation in virtue of ordinary power. Canon 1125 grants to ordinaries, to pastors and to certain confessors the power, ordinary or at any rate habitual, of dispensing from the interpellations when a summary and extrajudicial investigation has proved that the interpellations are impossible of fulfillment, that no answer has been received with reference to them, or that they are openly and certainly useless. The far-reaching value of this canon has not been fully recognized in practice, so that there have been times when those who are expressly empowered to use it have failed to do so, and thus have made application for a delegated faculty that was wholly superfluous, and entirely unnecessary.[97]

[97] Woeber, *The Interpellations*, p. 137.

CHAPTER VIII

PRACTICAL POINTS IN THE USE OF THE DISPENSATION

Article I: Renewal of the Dispensation after the Lapse of a Year

Once the interpellations have been properly made after the baptism of the convert, and have been answered negatively by the infidel party, the marriage with the Catholic party can be postponed indefinitely by the convert without his losing the right to enter such a marriage and without incurring the obligation of repeating the interpellations at a later date before contracting a second union.[1]

The canonical requirement of interpellating the party remaining in infidelity is satisfied with a single performance.[2] Although strict juridical justice requires indeed, but at the same time is satisfied with, this single interpellation, charity may demand that it be repeated even frequently.[3]

Payen points out an exception to this rule in the case wherein the infidel was temporarily prevented from answering the interpellations when they were first made. In this and similar circumstances the interpellations are to be repeated, so that the infidel will be given the full opportunity of manifesting his intentions. It is generally agreed that a full month is certainly sufficient time to allow the infidel to make this decision. The circumstances of individual cases, however, will modulate this time requirement.[4]

[1] Payen, *De Matrimonio,* II, n. 2342, p. 666.

[2] Can. 1121; S.C.S. Off., 12 iun. 1850—*Fontes,* n. 910; Vermeersch-Creusen (*Epitome,* II, n. 431, p. 298), note that the use of the plural, 'interpellations,' in canon 1121, § 2, refers to the twofold question to be asked the infidel spouse, and not to the number of times the interpellations are to be made. Cf. Payen, *op. cit.,* II, n. 2344, n. 3, p. 668.

[3] Wernz-Vidal, *Ius Matrimoniale,* n. 632, note 74, p. 826; Cappello, *De Matrimonio,* n. 775, p. 766; Coronata, *De Matrimonio,* n. 633, p. 887.

[4] Payen, *op. cit.,* II, n. 2344, pp. 667-668; Winslow, *The Pauline Privilege,* n. 67, p. 37; Gregory, *The Pauline Privilege,* p. 93; Winslow,

At any rate, if the convert has not used his right to enter a new marriage within a reasonable time after making the interpellations, he must in some way assure himself that his former spouse has not also become a Christian in the meantime, or does not wish to resume cohabitation for else he runs the risk of entering an invalid union.[5]

If, on the other hand, a dispensation has been legitimately granted from the interpellations, it is valid only for a year. Canonical jurisprudence in the years preceding the Code recognized this time limit and required that the dispensation be renewed if the convert wished to use his right to enter a second marriage after the lapse of a year:

> Quaeritur: "Utrum dilato ex parte fidelis per notabile tempus matrimonio post interpellationem factam, vel post obtentam ab ea dispensationem, nova interpellatio, aut dispensatio nova necessaria sit? Et quantenus affirmative, quod temporis spatium intercedere debeat inter primam et secundam, aut interpellationem, aut ab ea dispensationem?"
>
> Resp: "Negative, quatenus fuerit facta interpellatio; affirmative, post annum, in casu dispensationis obtentae ab initio."[6]

It may be that the circumstances, such as the attitude of the parties and the external facts of their lives, which prevented the earlier making of the interpellations have changed during the year. In this event then, as long as it is possible, the interpellations are to be made in preference to the obtaining of a dispensation.[7]

"The Application of The Pauline Privilege," *The Jurist*, X (1950), 332; cf. also Woeber, *The Interpellations*, pp. 72, 80.

[5] Vromant, *De Matrimonio*, n. 323, p. 251; Payen, *op. cit.*, II, n. 2342, n. 4, p. 666, Stanislaus Woywod-Callistus Smith, *A Practical Commentary On the Code of Canon Law*, 10. printing (New York: Joseph F. Wagner, Inc., 1946), I, n. 1154, p. 711.

[6] S.C. de Prop. Fide (C.P. pro Sin.-Sutchuen.), 26 iun. 1820—*Coll. S.C.P.F.*, n. 743; *Fontes*, n. 4717.

[7] Coronata, *op. cit.*, n. 633, p. 887; n. 640, p. 896; Payen, *op. cit.*, II, n. 2342, p. 666.

The lapse of the year is to be computed according to the norms established in the law of the Code. The duration of the time begins to lapse from the moment the rescript comes to the bishop if the dispensation is granted *in forma gratiosa,* or from the moment the bishop himself grants the dispensation if it is given *in forma commissoria.*[8]

The Code does not contain any legislation in this regard. It seems, therefore, that the requirement of the pre-Code law has been abrogated, since the principles of the present law state that all former disciplinary laws which are neither explicitly nor implicitly contained in the Code are to be considered as revoked, except only those which are contained in approved liturgical books and those which are based on positive or natural divine law.[9]

If there were admissible an analogy between the making of the interpellations on one hand and the granted dispensation from them on the other, then it would follow that a dispensation once granted should continue in force as unaffected by any time limit, since the interpellations themselves are not in any way affected after they have once been made.[10] Yet it is commonly recognized even today that a dispensation from the interpellations must be renewed after a year's interval before the convert can enter a second and Catholic marriage.[11]

Since the former response of the Sacred Congregation for the Propagation of the Faith, which provides a safe norm in this regard, did not determine whether the renewal

[8] Cans. 31, 32; Coronata, *op. cit.,* n. 640, p. 896.

[9] Can. 6, n. 6; cf. Woeber, *The Interpellations,* p. 118; Petrovits, *The New Church Law on Matrimony,* n. 566, p. 408.

[10] Doheny, *Informal Procedure,* p. 538.

[11] Gregory, *The Pauline Privilege,* p. 80; Vermeersch, *De Casu Apostoli,* n. 75, p. 30; Wernz-Vidal, *Ius Matrimoniale,* n. 632, p. 826; Cappello, *op. cit.,* n. 781, n. 5, p. 771; Coronata, *op. cit.,* n. 633, p. 887; Winslow, *The Pauline Privilege,* p. 43; Payen, *op. cit.,* II, n. 2342 p. 666; Farrugia, *De Matrimonio et Causis Matrimonialibus,* n. 325, p. 477; De Smet, *De Sponsalibus et Matrimonio,* n. 353, p. 302; Vlaming, *Praelectiones,* n. 725; Ayrinhac-Lydon, *Marriage Legislation,* p. 312; Woeber, *op. cit.,* pp. 36, 70, 117.

of the dispensation was required for the valid or merely for the licit use of the Pauline privilege, and, moreover, since the Code has legislated nothing in this regard, it is certain that this requirement in no way affects the validity of the subsequent marriage.[12]

This is particularly true when it is known that the infidel has persisted in his evil and obstinate will, for here even the interpellations themselves are not required for the valid use of the Pauline privilege.[13] In individual cases, however, a particular rescript could demand that the dispensation be renewed after the lapse of a year under the penalty indeed of invalidity.[14]

But the procedure in these few and isolated cases cannot be understood as shaping a general principle. The marked difference occasioned through the continuity of the fulfilled interpellations on the one hand, and the lack of continuity in the dispensation granted from them on the other, can find a sufficient juridic explanation only in an equally marked difference in the ultimate effect deriving from these two factors. Even after the interpellations have been made according to the norms of the law as enacted in the Code, the Pauline privilege becomes inoperative at the moment that the second party to the infidel marriage becomes a Christian. This is true even when the convert has entered the second marriage wholly unaware of his partner's conversion. This marriage exists as an invalid union from the very beginning.

A far more extensive effect is produced by a dispensation from the interpellations, for then the second marriage as contracted in virtue of the dispensation is valid even though the unbaptized consort had been prevented from answering the interpellations or had, without any knowledge about it on the part of the convert, actually been con-

[12] Canon 11; Gregory, *op. cit.*, p. 80; Vromant, *De Matrimonio*, n. 323; p. 251; Winslow, *op. cit.*, p. 43.

[13] Cappello, *op. cit.*, n. 776, p. 766; Coronata, *op. cit.*, n. 631, p. 884.

[14] Cappello, *op. cit.*, n. 781, n. 5, p. 771; Heylen, *Tractatus de Matrimonio*, p. 347.

verted and baptized at the time the second marriage was contracted.[15]

A dispensation in the circumstances of such a case produces the unique effect of preparing the way for the dissolution of a legitimate marriage in that it authoritatively guarantees the validity of the second marriage.

In view of this extraordinary effect of a dispensation from the interpellations it is within the duty of the Church to exercise a particular control over the use of the dispensation in order to safeguard the indissolubility of valid marriages.[16]

Before such a dispensation can be renewed it is necessary that the prescribed summary and extrajudicial investigation be repeated. There must be assurance that the causes originally alleged as sufficiently grave for the dispensation are still effectively extant, otherwise every purpose in requiring such a renewal would seem futile from the beginning. This inquiry serves as an adequate check on the use of the dispensation. For the dispensation, as well as the interpellations, is of no value if the convert or the dispensing authority is aware of the conversion of the other party to the original marriage contracted in infidelity.

The renewal of the dispensation from the interpellations after the lapse of a year's time is not postulated for the validity of the subsequent marriage, but it is required by the canonical jurisprudence of the Church so that "it would be gravely illicit to use the favor after the expiration of a year from the date of its granting."[17]

Article II: Registration of the Granted Dispensation

It is of paramount importance that a careful record of every dispensation from the interpellations be made and

[15] *Supra*, pp. 193-197.

[16] Woeber (*op. cit.*, p. 118) indicates that with reason the Church does not wish in practice that the dispensation when once granted should have this effect for an indefinite and indiscriminate period of time.

[17] Woeber, *loc. cit.*

conscientiously preserved among the permanent records of the parish and the diocese. This requirement follows immediately from the very nature of the dispensation, for it can possibly produce an effect equivalent to a papal dispensation dissolving the bond of a legitimate or even ratified marriage. Such a record could be the only authentic and documentary proof of the validity of a given marriage contracted in virtue of a dispensation from the obligation of interpellating the former spouse.[18] For it is this record of the dispensation that establishes the freedom of the convert to enter a second marriage.[19] The dispensation is to be recorded both in the records of the parish of the convert as well as in the diocesan archives.[20]

An analogy in this regard is clearly found in the various instructions and decrees of the Holy See relative to matrimonial discipline and procedure. The Sacred Congregation for the Discipline of the Sacraments in its Instruction *Provida,* of 1936, explicitly required that after a second conformable decree of the nullity of a marriage both the baptismal and the matrimonial parochial records of the party are to be annotated to that effect. The Instruction imposes a two-fold obligation, the first upon the ordinary, who is to inform the pastor of the parish in which the marriage was celebrated, and the second upon the pastor, who is to make the necessary entries. If the parties were not both baptized in the parish of the marriage, it is the duty of the pastors to notify the proper parishes.[21]

[18] Woeber, *The Interpellations*, p. 135; Coronata, *De Matrimonio*, n. 649, p. 907.

[19] Vermeersch-Creusen, *Epitome*, II, n. 435, p. 301: "Ordinarius aut parochus documentum concessae dispensationis exigere poterit, quod locum tenet testimonii de statu libertatis." Cf. cans. 1019-1020.

[20] Woods, *The Constitutions of Canon 1125*, pp. 95, 98; Payen, *De Matrimonio*, II, n. 2409, p. 747; Woeber, *op. cit.*, p. 135; Coronata, *op. cit.*, n. 649, p. 907; Doheny, *Informal Procedure*, p. 564; Winslow, *A Commentary on the Apostolic Faculties*, p. 156; Burton, *A Commentary on Canon 1125*, p. 180.

[21] S.C. de Disciplina Sacramentorum, instr. (*Provida*), 15 aug. 1936, Tit. XIV, art. 225—*AAS*, XXVIII (1936), 313ff.; Bouscaren, *Canon*

In 1941 the same Sacred Congregation issued a further Instruction *Sacrosanctum* on the rules to be observed by parish priests in their making of the canonical investigations before they admit the parties to marriage. The Instruction places upon pastors a personal obligation binding *sub gravi* to carefully examine the prospective bride and groom as to their freedom to marry.[22] It explicitly requires that the parties be questioned about possible decrees of nullity or dispensations affecting the bond of previous marriages.[23]

It is evident that the pastor cannot easily satisfy his obligation to determine the freedom of the parties unless the proper notations had been carefully and accurately entered into the various records.

The III Plenary Council of Baltimore (1884) explicitly considered this recording of the dispensation from the interpellations. The Bishops assembled at the Council incorporated into the Acts and Decrees of the Council an instruction of the Sacred Congregation for the Propagation of the Faith on matrimonial causes which indicated that very often the solution of a case in which a party to the marriage contracted in infidelity had separated from his former spouse will depend entirely on whether or not the required interpellations were made or a dispensation from them obtained:

> Ad probandum vero, utrum interpellatio vel eius dispensatio intercesserit, consulendi erunt libri matrimoniorum, vel etiam regesta curiae, in quibus haec accurate erunt semper recensenda."[24]

Law Digest, II, p. 525; Joannes Torre, *Processus Matrimonialis* (Neapoli: M. D'Auria, S. Sedis Ap. Typographus, 1947), p. 154.

[22] S.C. de Disciplina Sacramentorum, instr. (*Sacrosanctum*), 29 iun. 1941, art. 4—*AAS*, XXXIII (1941), 297ff.; E. J. Mahoney. *Marriage Preliminaries* (Westminster, Maryland: The Newman Press, 1949), n. 9, p. 12.

[23] *Sacrosanctum*—Mahoney, *op. cit.*, n. 16, p. 14.

[24] Instruction *Causae Matrimoniales of the S.C. de Prop. Fide*, (1883), incorporated with the Acts and Decrees of the III Plenary Council of Baltimore. *Acta et Decreta Concilii Baltimorensis Tertii*, A.D. MDCCCLXXXIV (Baltimorae: Typis Joannis Murphy et Soci-

This warning of the Council still serves as a valuable norm to be followed in practice.

The record, particularly for the chancery, should note not only the fact of the dispensation but also the causes or reasons alleged as sufficiently warranting a dispensation. The report should also indicate what means were used for the ascertainment that the interpellations could not be made or that they would be certainly useless.[25]

Ordinaries are urged through their diocesan statutes to make specific rules which will regulate the use of canon 1125 by pastors and confessors without prejudice to the valid use of the faculty therein conceded by the Church's universal law. The statute should require that pastors and confessors who dispense from the interpellations in virtue of the power granted in this canon make the necessary report to the chancery as well as the proper notation in the parochial records.[26]

If the dispensation is granted in the internal sacramental forum, the report and notation are not to be required.[27] However, for the good order of the diocese and in view of the frequent need for documentary proof, this dispensation should be granted in the sacramental forum only in the most exceptional cases.

Article III: Canon 1127 and the Dispensation

Canon 1127 sets up the general principle that in doubtful matters the law favors the privilege of the Faith, so that in its broadest sense it is a right conceded by the ecclesiastical law in favor of converts to the Faith and is intended as a

---

orum, 1886), Appendix, *De Causis Matrimonialibus*, Pars Altera, art. IV, p. 278.

[25] Winslow, *op. cit.*, p. 156; Woeber, *op. cit.*, p. 135.

[26] Doheny, *Informal Procedure*, p. 562: "In the use of this special power, pastors should conscientiously observe the diocesan regulations as to any special norms for these cases, documents to be filed at the Chancery, and the like. Bishops have the fullest authority to designate methods for the proper recording of such cases."

[27] Coronata, *op. cit.*, n. 649, p. 907.

means to remove obstacles and thus prepare the way for further conversions.[28] Thus the law always favors the convert in all doubtful matters. The privilege of the Faith in canon 1127 is directly concerned primarily with marriage cases. This is evident from its relative position in the Code.[29]

This position of the canon further proves that the presumption in favor of Faith as established by the canon is not to be restricted to the Pauline privilege but to be extended to any and all cases wherein the bond of a legitimate marriage is dissolved in favor of the Faith, as through the use of the papal concessions mentioned in canon 1125. In this regard Kearney states: "Canon 1127, therefore, is a presumption of law in relation to all marriages which are capable of dissolution within the limits of the privilege of the Faith."[30] The Pauline privilege is but one species of the privilege of the Faith, as is also the case in which the Pope uses his supreme ministerial power to dissolve the bond of a non-sacramental union. The failure to distinguish clearly between the privilege of the Faith in general and the various specific illustrations that fall under it has occasioned much confusion and misunderstanding.[31]

The favor granted by canon 1127 quite certainly then does have application and reference to the material under consideration in this work, and commentators are explicit in applying the presumption to doubts arising in the use of the Pauline privilege and in the use of the papal constitutions which receive mention in canon 1125.[32]

[28] Ayrinhac-Lydon, *Marriage Legislation*, p. 325; Doheny, *Informal Procedure*, p. 570, Winslow, *The Pauline Privilege*, p. 83.

[29] Gasparri, *De Matrimonio*, II, n. 1168, p. 240; Winslow, *op. cit.*, p. 83; Doheny, *op. cit.*, p. 571: "The position of canon 1127 in the Code unmistakably directs, even though it does not limit, the application of the principle to marriage cases."

[30] "The Privilege of The Faith," *The Jurist*, VII (1947), 285.

[31] Vlaming, *Praelectiones*, II, n. 733, p. 329; Ayrinhac-Lydon, *op. cit.*, pp. 325-326; Vermeersch-Creusen, *Epitome*, II, n. 437, p. 303.

[32] Kearney, "The Privilege of The Faith," *The Jurist*, VII (1947), 284, "Canon 1127, then, would apply not only to the Pauline Privilege

The general principle of the privilege may be invoked to prepare the way for the dispensing from the interpellations. It is applicable in solving doubts about the sincerity of the infidel in his answers to the interpellations. In this case, if there are sufficient reasons for doubting the sincerity of the infidel, the ordinary may begin an investigation of the true attitude of the party; if, then, it is proved that the affirmative answers of the infidel were insincere, they are to be considered as negative or the interpellations are to be dispensed from.[33]

The principle is particularly applicable in solving doubts about the sufficiency of a cause in warrant of a dispensation. This is recognized in the fundamental principles of the universal law, which states that whenever there is a doubt about the sufficiency of the cause a dispensation may not only be licitly requested but also both licitly and validly granted.[34]

In most cases the causes which have been officially acknowledged and approved as sufficing for the granting of a dispensation from the interpellations will generally provide ordinaries and others who have the faculty of dispensing with a general norm for determining the sufficiency of any cause alleged in a given case. If, however, some uncertainty has remained in this regard, there is no doubt at all that canon 1127 can be invoked and the dispensation granted.[35] For the favor of the Faith demands that the

---

but also to the Constitutions of canon 1125 and to those dissolutions of the natural bond of marriage between a person baptized in heresy and one who is certainly not baptized." (*Italics this writer's*).

[33] Vermeersch-Creusen, *op. cit.*, II, n. 437, p. 304; Cappello, *De Matrimonio*, n. 788, p. 781; Coronata, *De Matrimonio*, n. 652, p. 911; Doheny, *op. cit.*, p. 575; Payen, *De Matrimonio*, II, n. 2415b, 757, Gasparri, *De Matrimonio*, II, n. 1168, p. 240.

[34] Can. 84, § 2.

[35] Vermeersch-Creusen, *loc. cit.;* Winslow, *The Pauline Privilege*, p. 84; Coronata, *loc. cit.;* Doheny, *op. cit.*, p. 576; Cappello, *loc. cit.;* Payen, *loc. cit.;* Gasparri, *op. cit.*, II, n. 1168, p. 240; Ayrinhac-Lydon, *op. cit.*, p. 327, Kearney, "The Privilege of The Faith," *The Jurist, VII* (1947), 291.

person who has the faculty of dispensing should judge in favor of the convert and grant the dispensation.[36]

Canon 1127 may be used in the application of the privileges granted by Pope Paul III in the Constitution *Altitudo.* Thus one may settle doubts regarding the person of the first wife, or relative to the validity of the first marriage in a series of polygamous unions.[37]

In each case every attempt must be made in the dispelling of doubt; ordinarily this will most effectively be accomplished by means of a summary and extrajudicial investigation similar to the one that is required in the ascertainment of the existence of a cause for the dispensation from the interpellations.[38] For the Holy See has clearly postulated this precaution for the removal of doubt.[39]

In a given case, if there is doubt whether or not there is sufficient reason for the granting of a dispensation, the doubt is always to be solved in favor of the convert. No one can question the validity of this as a practical norm; it corresponds not only to the letter, but to the spirit of the law as well. To those who may be tempted to hesitate, the writer says with Cicognani, "away with all scruple and anxiety,"[40]

[36] Kearney, *The Principles of Canon 1127,* p. 127.

[37] Woods, *The Constitutions of Canon 1125,* p. 92; Payen, *op. cit.,* II, n. 2415b, p. 757; Gasparri, *op. cit.,* II, n. 1168, p. 240; Doheny, *op. cit.,* p. 574; Kearney, "The Privilege of The Faith," *The Jurist,* VII (1947), 289.

[38] Vlaming, *op. cit.,* II, n. 733, p. 329; Winslow, *op. cit.,* p. 85; Doheny, *op. cit.,* p. 576; Ayrinhac-Lydon, *op. cit.,* p. 326; Kearney, *loc. cit.*

[39] S.C.S. Off., instr. (ad Vic. Ap. Oceaniae Central.), 18 dec. 1872—*Fontes,* n. 1024; S.C.S. Off. (Mongoliae), 20 nov. 1882—*Fontes,* n. 1075; *Coll. S.C.P.F.,* n. 1581; S.C.S. Off. (Siouxormen.), 18 maii 1892—*Fontes,* n. 1155; *Coll. S.C.P.F.,* n. 1796.

[40] Cicognani, *Canon Law,* p. 856: "In a doubt of fact, anyone may *licitly* ask for the dispensation, and the Superior may *licitly* and *validly* grant the same; nay more, in this canon [namely can. 84, § 2] the assent of the supreme legislator is expressly given for such licitness and validity. Consequently, away with all scruple and anxiety."

and with Kearney, "In view of [the] unanimity there is no reason for hesitation on the part of the local ordinary or his delegate in applying the canon under such circumstances."[41]

[41] Kearney, "The Privilege of The Faith," *The Jurist*, VII (1947), 291.

CONCLUSIONS

The maternal solicitude of the Church has from the beginning been directed in a special way to those who are converts to the Faith. Thus it was that St. Paul invoked the supreme apostolic power that was his and promulgated the privilege that bears his name.

In the sixteenth century when the spread of the Faith received a marked impetus through the discovery of new lands, the Church met the challenge presented by the conversion of those who had been parties to polygamous unions by again invoking its supreme authority in granting privileges to solve these unique and urgent matrimonial problems through the Papal Constitutions of Popes Paul III, St. Pius V, and Gregory XIII (pp. 5-15).

1) In the light of the purpose of these Constitutions, of the precise wording of their texts, and of the practice of the Holy See in the centuries before the Code, it is unmistakably clear that these papal grants were meant to be, and were in fact, given after the nature of *privileges,* and must correspondingly be interpreted as such.

2) The weight of authority today, added to the intrinsic arguments for the extensive nature of the privileges of the papal constitutions as contained in canon 1125, serves to make overwhelmingly certain the doctrine which argues for the universal application of these privileges in every case in all parts of the world without exception, whenever their use will make it easier for some convert from infidelity to accept the Faith (pp. 55-72).

3) Since the application of canon 1125 depends not upon the factors of place or time but upon the circumstances attaching to individual cases, the privileges contained therein are without any doubt applicable to the United States as they are to any other part of the Universal Church (pp. 80-87).

4) In virtue of the Constitution *Populis* of Pope Gregory XIII, all local ordinaries, pastors and Jesuit confessors in the United States are given the power of dispensing from the interpellations to prepare the way for the use of the Pauline privilege when the making of the interpellations is impossible or when the unbaptized party has not answered within the specified period of time. Although the certain uselessness or absolute futility of making the interpellations may not be commonly recognized as generally sufficient causes in themselves for granting a dispensation from the interpellations they may well warrant in virtue of this constitution a dispensation in an individual case. (pp. 171-178).

5) The faculty granted to approved Jesuit confessors is extended to approved confessors of certain other religious institutes, who have received the power through the valid agency of the intercommunication of privileges. Only those confessors can be said to be approved who have received diocesan faculties through the local ordinary (pp. 207-211).

6) The one who dispenses must satisfy himself as to the existence and sufficiency of the cause in warrant of the dispensation. According to the regulations contained in the Constitution *Populis*, these factors will obtain only upon at least a summary and extrajudicial investigation of the circumstances of the case. Every available means of modern communication must be prudently utilized in an effort to contact the infidel or to learn pertinent and necessary circumstances (pp. 178-183).

7) The faculty for dispensing from the interpellations as now granted in the Church's universal law, may be used when the preliminary investigation has patently shown that any effort to make the interpellations will be absolutely futile or useless. Thus the privilege is applicable when the infidel party is permanently insane or even when he has civilly divorced the convert and subsequently has entered a second civil union, for in the latter case any continued cohabitation with the second consort belies any vocal or written manifestation of sincerity on the part of the infidel (pp. 175-178).

8) The faculty of dispensing from the interpellations, as it is now granted through the Constitution *Populis*, derives from the Church's universal law, and, therefore, no authority other than the Holy See can effectively forbid its use. Ordinaries, however, through their diocesan statutes should regulate the practical application of the faculty, and should require the necessary registration of the dispensation in the parochial records and the chancery files. Any diocesan statute to which there would be added an invalidating clause in regulation of the use of this faculty for dispensing from the interpellations would remain totally without juridical effect (pp. 231-234).

In conclusion, it is to be emphasized that these privileges, and therefore also the faculty of dispensing from the interpellations, were originally granted, and subsequently extended universally throughout the Church, for the benefit of converts to the Faith. It is not unthinkable that some prospective converts in this country have been deprived of their rightful privilege because of a scrupulous and unfounded hesitation on the part of those who have the right and the duty to grant the dispensation whenever sufficient cause is alleged and then established as approved upon the required investigation. The academic objection that the use of this faculty will eventually lead surely to laxity in its application betrays on the part of those who object a suspicion that was unknown to the early missionaries and to the Supreme Authority of the Church. As always, prudence is the guiding norm. The prescribed investigation together with the required registration of the dispensation in the parochial records and in the report sent to the chancery serves as an adequate safeguard for the prudent use of the faculty.

The use of the privileges must ever be accompanied with discretion, for otherwise their very purpose, namely the spread of the Faith and the salvation of souls, would be frustrated through the scandal given those outside the Church. In an individual case the fear of possible scandal will of itself not prove a sufficient reason for denying the dispensation to a deserving convert, for in many cases the scandal is indeed prompted by insincerity and pharisaical duplicity. Christ did not hesitate to use His supreme power in the face of frequent and violent objection on the part of His opponents.

When the recounted necessary conditions are verified the privileges should be used freely and apart from all undue fear, for it may well be that the known usage of the granting of a dispensation from the interpellations will remain the only means of preparing the way for the conversion of many who otherwise would not accept the Faith. That was the reason for the original grant of the privileges; it was the reason for their being extended through the universal law of the Church. And that is precisely why the faculty ought to be unhesitatingly used in every single case today when the few but necessary conditions are verified. The salvation of a soul may be at stake!

APPENDIX

A

Ex Constitutione Pauli PP. III *Altitudo* 1 iunii 1537

Venerabilibus Fratribus Universis Episcopis Occidentalis et Meridionalis Indiae Salutem et Apostolicam Benedictionem.

Altitudo divini consilii, quod humana nequit ratio comprehendere, ex suae immensae bonitatis essentia, aliquid semper ad salutem humani generis pullulans, tempore congruo et solo suo secreto ministerio, quod Ipse Deus novit, opportune producit et manifestat: ut cognoscant mortales, ex suis meritis, tamquam ab ipsis, nihil proficere posse; sed eorum salutem et omne donum gratiae ab Ipso Summo Deo, et Patre luminum provenire. Sane cum sicut, non sine grandi et spirituali mentis nostrae laetitia, accepimus, quam plures incolae occidentalis et meridionalis Indiae, licet divinae sint legis expertes, S. Spiritu tamen cooperante, illustrati, errores, quos hactenus observarunt, penitus ab eorum mentibus et cordibus abiecerint, ac fidei catholicae veritatem et S. Ecclesiae unitatem amplecti, et secundum ritum eiusdem Romanae Ecclesiae vivere desiderent et proponant . . . Super eorum vero matrimoniis hoc observandum decernimus, ut qui ante conversionem plures iuxta eorum mores habebant uxores, et non recordantur quam primo acceperint, conversi ad fidem unam ex illis accipiant, quam voluerint, ut cum ea matrimonium contrahant per verba de praesenti, ut moris est; quivero recordantur quam primo acceperint, aliis dimissis, eam retineant. Ac eis concedimus, ut coniuncti etiam in tertio gradu tam consanquinitatis, quam affinitatis, non excludantur a matrimoniis contrahendis donec huic S. Sedi super hoc aliud visum fuerit statuendum.[1]

[1] *Coll. S.C.P.F.*, n. 114; *Codex Iuris Canonici*, Documentum VI.

B

Constitutio S. Pii PP. V *Romani Pontificis* 2 augusti 1571

Romani Pontificis aequa et circumspecta providentia, ne ea quae pro salubri Indorum noviter ad fidem conversorum directione sanciri debent et terminari, alicuius haesitationis scrupulo subiaceant, declarationibus et aliis opportunis consuevit providere remediis. Cum itaque, sicut accepimus, Indis in sua infidelitate manentibus plures permittantur uxores, quas ipsi etiam levissimis de causis repudiant, hinc factum est quod recipientibus baptismum permissum sit permanere cum ea uxore, quae simul cum marito baptizata existit; et quia saepenumero contingit illam non esse primam coniugem, unde tam ministri quam Episcopi gravissimis scrupulis torquentur, existimantes illud non esse verum matrimonium; sed quia durissimum esset separare eos ab uxoribus, cum quibus ipsi Indi baptismum susceperunt, maxime quia difficilimum foret primam coniugem reperire; ideo Nos, statui dictorum Indorum paterno affectu benigne consulere, atque ipsos Episcopos et ministros ab huiusmodi scruplis eximere volentes, motu proprio et ex certa scientia Nostra, ac apostolicae potestatis plenitudine, ut Indi, sic ut praemittitur baptizati, et in futurum baptizandi, cum uxore, quae cum ipsis fuerit baptizata et baptizabitur, remanere valeant, tamquam cum uxore legitima, aliis dimissis, apostolica auctoritate, tenore praesentium, declaramus, matrimoniumque huiusmodi inter eos legitime consistere, etc.[2]

C

Constitutio Gregorii PP. XIII *Populis* 25 ianuarii 1585

Populis ac nationibus nuper ex gentilitatis errore ad fidem catholicam conversis expedit indulgere circa libertatem contrahendi matrimonia, ne homines, continentiae servandae

[2] *Codex Iuris Canonici*, Documentum VII.

minime assueti, propterea minus libenter in fide persistant, et alios illorum exemplo ab eius perceptione deterreant. Quoniam igitur saepe contingit multos utriusque sed praecipue virilis sexus infideles, post contracta gentili ritu matrimonia, ex Angola, Aethiopia, Brasilia, et aliis Indicis regionibus, ab hostibus captos, a patriis finibus et propriis coniugibus in remotissimas regiones exterminari, adeo ut tam ipsi, captivique qui in patria remanent, si postea ad fidem convertantur, coniuges infideles tam longo locorum intervallo disiunctos, an sine contumelia Creatoris secum cohabitare velint, ut pars est, monere nequeant, vel quia interdum ad hostiles et barbaras provincias ne nuntiis quidem accessus pateat, vel quia ignorent prorsus in quas regiones fuerint transvecti, vel quia itineris longitudo magnam afferat difficultatem: idcirco Nos, attendentes huiusmodi connubia inter infideles contracta, vera quidem, non tamen adeo rata censeri, ut necessitate suadente dissolvi non possint, talium gentium infirmitatem paterna pietate miserati, universis et singulis dictorum locorum Ordinariis et parochis, et presbyteris Societatis Iesu ad confessiones audiendas ab eiusdem Societatis Superioribus approbatis et ad dictas regiones pro tempore missis vel in illis admissis, plenam auctoritate Apostolica, tenore praesentium, concedimus facultatem dispensandi cum quibuscumque utriusque sexus Christifidelibus incolis dictarum regionum et serius ad fidem conversis qui ante baptisma susceptum matrimonium contraxerunt, ut eorum quilibet, superstite coniuge infideli, et eius consensu minime requisito, aut responso non expectato, matrimonia cum quovis fideli alterius etiam ritus contrahere et in facie Ecclesiae solemnizare, et in eis postea carnali copula consummatis quoad vixerint remanere licite valeant: dummodo constet etiam summarie et extraiudicialiter, coniugem, ut praefertur, absentem moneri legitime non posse, aut monitum intra tempus in eadem monitione praefixum suam voluntatem non significasse; quae quidem matrimonia, etiamsi postea innotuerit coniuges priores infideles suam voluntatem iuste impeditos declarare non potuisse, et ad fidem etiam tempore transacti secundi matrimonii conversos fuisse, nihilominus rescindi numquam debere, sed valida et firma, prolemque inde suscipiendam legitimam fore decernimus. Non obstantibus *etc.*[8]

[8] *Codex Iuris Canonici,* Documentum VIII.

BIBLIOGRAPHY

SOURCES

Acta Apostolicae Sedis, Commentarium Officiale, Romae, 1909—

Acta et Decreta Concilii Plenarii Baltimorensis Tertii, A.D. MDCCCLXXXIV, Baltimorae: Typis Joannis Murphy et Sociorum, 1886.

Acta et Decreta Sacrorum Conciliorum Recentiorum, Collectio Lacensis, 7 vols., Friburgi Brisgoviae, 1870-1892.

Acta et Decreta et Normae—Vota—Primum Concilium Sinense, Tou-se-we, Zi-ka-wei, Shanghai: Typographia Missionis Catholici, 1929.

Acta Pii Pp. XII: Motu Proprio, De Disciplina Sacramenti Matrimonii pro Ecclesia Orientali, AAS, XLI (1949), 89-119.

Acta Sancta Sedis, 41 vols., Romae, 1865-1908.

Appendix ad Bullarium Pontificium Sacrae Congregationis de Propaganda Fide, 2 vols., Romae: Typis Collegii Urbani, 1839.

Bouscaren, T. Lincoln, *The Canon Law Digest*, 2 vols., and *Supplement through 1948*, Milwaukee: The Bruce Publishing Company, 1934, 1943, 1949.

Bullarium Sanctissimi Domini Nostri Benedicti Papae XIV, 4 vols., in 10, Venetiis, 1777-1784.

Bullarium Pontificium Sacrae Congregationis de Propaganda Fide, 8 vols., Romae: Typis Collegii Urbani, 1839-1858.

Canones et Decreta Concilii Tridentini ex Editione Romana 1834, Neapoli, 1859.

Codex Iuris Canonici Pii X Pontificis Maximi Iussu Digestus, Benedicti Papae XV Auctoritate Promulgatus, Romae: Typis Polyglottis Vaticanis, 1917, reimpressio, Westminster, Maryland: The Newman Bookshop, 1942.

Codicis Iuris Canonici Fontes, cura Emi Petri Card. Gasparri, editi, 9 vols., Romae: Typis Polyglottis Vaticanis, 1923-1939, Vols. VII-IX, cura Emi Iustiniani Card. Serédi.

Codicis Iuris Canonici Schema (sub secreto pontificio publicata) cum notis Petri Card. Gasparri, Romae: Typis Polyglottis, 1913.

Collectanea S. Congregationis de Propaganda Fide, 2 vols., Romae: Ex Typographia Polyglotta Sacrae Congr. de Prop. Fide, 1907.

Concilium Tridentinum Diaria, Tomus I, Herculis Severoli Commentarius, Angeli Massarelli Diaria I—IV, collegit, eddidit, illustravit Sebastianus Merkle, Friburgi Brisgoviae, St. Ludovici, Americae: Sumptibus Herder, 1901.

Corpus Iuris Civilis, Codex Iustinianus, ed. sterotypa 10, recognovit et retractavit Paulus Krueger; Berolini: apud Weidmannos, 1929;

Digesta Iustiniani Augusti, ed. sterotypa 15, recognovit Theodorus Mommsen, retractavit Paulus Krueger, Berolini: apud Weidmannos, 1928; *Codices Gregorianus Hermogenianus, Theodosianus*, ed. Gustavus Haenel, Lipsiae: Prostat Bonnae apud Adolphum Marcum, 1837.

Corpus Iuris Secundus, A Complete Testament of the Entire American Law, Donald Kiser, Editor, Brooklyn, New York: The American Book Company, 1944.

Mansi, I. D., *Sacrorum Conciliorum Nova et Amplissima Collectio*, 53 vols. in 60, Parisiis-Arnhemii-Lipsiae, 1901-1927.

The New Testament, Confraternity of Christian Doctrine Edition, Patterson, New Jersey: St. Anthony Guild Press, 1941.

North-Eastern Reporter, 2. ed., Sept., Dec. 1937, St. Paul, Minn.: West Publishing Company, 1938.

Pallottini, S., *Collectio omnium conclusionum et resolutionum quae in causis propositis apud Sacram Congregationem Cardinalium S. Concilii Tridentini Interpretum Prodierunt ab eius institutione anno MDLXIV ad MDCCCLX, distinctis titulis alphabetico ordine per materias digesta, cura et studio Salvatoris Pallottini*, 17 vols., Romae, 1868-1893.

Regesta Pontificum Romanorum inde ab anno post Christum natum 1198 ad annum 1304, ed. Augustus Potthast, 2 vols., Berolini, 1874-1875.

S. Romanae Rotae Decisiones seu Sententiae ab anno 1909—, Romae: Typis Polyglottis Vaticanis, 1912—.

Schroeder, H. J., *Canons and Decrees of the Council of Trent*, St. Louis: B. Herder Book Company, 1941.

Thesaurus Resolutionum Sacrae Congregationis Concilii, 167 vols., Romae, 1718-1908.

AUTHORS

Augustine, Charles, *A Commentary on the New Code of Canon Law*, 8 vols., Vol. V, 2. ed., St. Louis: B. Herder Book Company, 1920.

Augustine, Charles, *The Rights and Duties of Ordinaries According to the Code and Apostolic Faculties*, St. Louis: B. Herder Book Company, 1924.

Ayrinhac, H. A.,-Lydon, P. J., *Marriage Legislation in the New Code of Canon Law*, New Revised Edition, New York: Benziger Company, 1946.

Badii, Cesare, *Institutiones Iuris Canonici*, 3. ed., 2 vols., Florentiae: Libreria Editrice Fiorentina, 1922.

Benedictus XIV, *De Synodo Dioecesana*, 3 vols., Romae: Ex Typographia Ioannis Baptistae Connetti, 1783.

Biederlack, Josephus, *Institutiones Iuris Ecclesiastici de Fundamentali Ecclesiae Constitutione*, Romae, 1907.

Billot, Ludovicus, *De Ecclesiae Sacramentis Commentarius in Tertiam Partem S. Thomae,* 6. ed., 2 vols., Romae, 1895.

Blat, Albertus, *Commentarium Textus Codicis Inuris Canonici,* 5 vols. in 6, Romae: Ex Typographia Pontificia in Instituto Pii IX, 1919-1927.

Boggiano-Pico, Antonio, *Il Matrimonio nel Diritto Canonico,* Torino: Unione Tipografico-Editrice Torinese, 1936.

Bouscaren, T. Lincoln,-Ellis, Adam C., *Canon Law: A Text and Commentary,* Milwaukee: The Bruce Publishing Company, 1946.

Burton, Francis James, *A Commentary on Canon 1125,* The Catholic University of America Canon Law Studies, n. 121, Washington, D.C.: The Catholic University of America Press, 1940.

Caponi, Iulius, *Institutiones Canonicae,* Coloniae Allobrogum, Sumptibus Marci Michaelis Bousquet, 1734.

Cappello, Felix M., *Tractatus Canonico-Moralis de Sacramentis,* Vol. V, *De Matrimonio,* 5. ed., Romae: Domus Editorialis Marietti, 1947.

Cappello, Felix, *Summa Iuris Canonici,* 3 vols., Vol. II, 4. ed., Romae: Apud Aedes Universitatis Gregorianae, 1945.

Cerato, P., *Matrimonium a Codice I. C. integre Desumptum,* 4 ed., Patavii: Libreria Gregorianiae Edidit Typis Seminarii, 1929.

Chelodi, Ioannes, *Ius Matrimoniale,* 3 ed., Tridenti: Libr. Edit. Tridentum, 1921.

Chelodi, Ioannes-Ciprotti, Pius, *Ius Canonicum, De Matrimonio,* Vicenza: Società Anonima Typografica Editrice, 1947.

Chrétien, P., *De Matrimonio,* 2. ed., Metis: Typis Imprimerie du Journal "Le Lorrain," 1937.

Cicognani, Amleto G., *Canon Law,* revised ed., authorized English version, translated by J. M. O'Hara and F. Brennan, Philadelphia: Dolphin Press, 1935.

Claeys Bouuaert, F.,-Simenon, G., *Manuale Iuris Canonici ad Usum Seminariorum,* 3 vols., Vol. II, Gandae et Leodii, 1931.

Coronata, Matthaeus, Conte a., *Institutiones Iuris Canonici: De Sacramentis, Tractatus Canonicus,* Vol. III, *De Matrimonio,* Taurini: Domus Editorialis Marietti, 1946; Vol. V, Taurini: Domus Editorialis Marietti, 1936.

D'Annibale, Josephus, *Summula Theologiae Moralis,* 5. ed., 3 vols., Romae, 1908.

De Becker, Julius, *De Matrimonio,* ed. nova, Louvain: Establis, Fr. Ceuterick, 1931.

De Smet, Alois, *Betrothment and Marriage,* 2. ed., trans. from 3rd Latin ed. of 1920 by W. Dobell and A. Owens, Brugis: Beyaert, 1923-1925.

De Smet, Aloisius, *De Sponsalibus et Matrimonio,* 4. ed., Brugis: Carolus Beyaert, 1927.

Doheny, William J., *Canonical Procedure in Matrimonial Cases*, Volume II, *Informal Procedure*, Milwaukee: The Bruce Publishing Company, 1948.

Donovan, James Joseph, *The Pastor's Obligation in Pre-Nuptial Investigation*, The Catholic University of America Canon Law Studies, n. 115, Washington, D.C.: The Catholic University of America, 1938.

Eagleton, George, *The Diocesan Quinquennial Faculties, Formula IV*, The Catholic University of America Canon Law Studies, n. 248, Washington, D.C.: The Catholic University of America Press, 1948.

Eloy, A. L., *Variae Institutiones Practicae ad Matrimonium et ad Causas Matrimoniales Spectantes*, Hongkong, 1915.

Fahrner, Ignaz, *Geschichte der Ehescheidung im kanonischen Recht, und Geschichte des Unauflöslichkeitsprinzips, und der vollkommenen Scheidung der Ehe im kanonischen Recht*, Freiburg im Breisgau, 1903.

Fang, Franciscus, *Dispensatio Matrimonialis Urgente Mortis Periculo et Instante Nuptiarum Contractu*, Romae: Officium Libri Catholici, 1946.

Farrugia, Nicolaus, *De Matrimonio et Causis Matrimonialibus*, Taurini, Romae: Marietti, 1924.

Feije, Henricus, *De Impedimentis et Dispensationibus Matrimonialibus*, 3. ed., Lovanii, 1885.

Gandolphus Bononiensis, *Sententiae Libri Quattuor*, ed. Joannes Walter, Vindobonae et Vratislaviae: Aemilius Haim et Soc., Bibliopolae Academici, 1924.

Gasparri, Petrus, *Tractatus Canonicus de Matrimonio*, ed. nova, 2 vols., Romae: Typis Polyglottis Vaticanis, 1932.

Genicot, E.,-Salsmans, I., *Institutiones Theologiae Moralis*, 11. ed., 2 vols., Bruxellis: Alb. Dewit, 1927.

Gonzales-Tellez, Emmanuel, *Commentaria Perpetua in Singulas Textus Librorum Decretalium*, Lugduni: Sumptibus Laurentii Arnavdi et Petri Barde, 1673.

Gougnard, Armandus, *Tractatus de Matrimonio*, 7. ed., Mechliniae: H. Dessain, 1931.

Gregory, Donald, *The Pauline Privilege*, The Catholic University of America Canon Law Studies, n. 68, Washington, D.C.: The Catholic University of America, 1931.

Heiss, M., *De Matrimonio Tractatus, Usui Venerabilis Cleri Americani Accommodatus*, Monachi: Ex Typographia E. Stahl, 1861.

Henriquez, Henricus, *Summa Theologiae Moralis*, Venetiis, 1660.

Heylen, V., *Tractatus de Matrimonio*, Mechliniae: H. Dessain, 1945.

Joyce, George Hayward, *Christian Marriage: An Historical and Doc-*

trinal Study, 2. ed., London and New York: Sheed and Ward, 1948.

Kearney, Francis Patrick, *The Principles of Canon 1127*, The Catholic University of America Canon Law Studies, n. 163, Washington, D.C.: The Catholic University of America Press, 1942.

Kelly, Bernard M., *The Functions Reserved to Pastors*, The Catholic University of America Canon Law Studies, n. 250, Washington, D.C.: The Catholic University of America Press, 1947.

Knecht, August, *Handbuch des katholischen Eherechts*, Freiburg im Breisgau: B. Herder and Company, 1928.

Konings, Antonius-Putzer, Joseph, *Commentarium in Facultates Apostolicas*, 3. ed., Ilchester College, Maryland: Typis Congr. Sanctissimi Redemptoris, 1893.

Konings, Antonius-Putzer, Joseph, *Commentarium in Facultates Apostolicas*, 4. ed., Cincinnati: Benziger Brothers, 1897.

Laymann, Paulus, *Theologia Moralis in Quinque Libros Distributa*, ed. nova, ab auctore recognita, Venetiis: Typis Georgii Valentini, 1630.

Léry, Louis Chaussegros de, *Le Privilège de la Foi*, Montréal: Ex Typis Collegii Maximi Immaculatae Conceptionis, 1938.

Lehmkuhl, Augustinus, *Theologia Moralis*, 10. ed., 2 vols., Friburgi, Brisgoviae, 1902.

Leurenius, Petrus, *Forum Ecclesiasticum in quo Ius Canonicum Universum Librorum ac Titulorum Ordine Exploratur*, Venetiis: Apud Ioannem Baptistam Recurti, sub signo Religionis, 1729.

Liguori, Alphonsus, *Theologia Moralis*, 4 vols., ed. L. Gaudé, Romae, 1905-1912.

Mahoney, E. J., *Marriage Preliminaries*, Westminster, Md., The Newman Press, 1949.

Marc, Cl.-Gestermann, F. X.-Raus, J. B., *Institutiones Morales Alphonsianae*, 18. ed., 2 vols., Lugduni: Typis Emmanuelis Vitte, 1927-1928.

Matulenas, Raymond A., *Communication, A Source of Privileges*, The Catholic University of America Canon Law Studies, n. 183, Washington, D.C.: The Catholic University of America Press, 1943.

Merkelbach, Benedictus, *Summa Theologiae Moralis*, 3 vols., Parisiis: Typis Desclée de Brouwer et Soc., 1931-1933.

Michel, P., *Ce qu'il y a de plus pratique pour le prêtre dans le Nouveau Code canonique*, 2. ed., Alger, 1919.

Motry, Hubert Louis, *Diocesan Faculties According to the Code of Canon Law*, The Catholic University of America Canon Law Studies, n. 16, Washington, D.C.: The Catholic University of America, 1922.

Nau, Louis J., *Marriage Laws of the Code of Canon Law*, New York: Frederick Pustet Company, Inc., 1933.

Navarrus, *Consilia et Responsa*, Lugduni, 1594.

Neufeld, E., *Ancient Hebrew Marriage Laws*, New York: Longmans Green and Co., 1944.

Palmieri, Dominicus, *Tractatus de Matrimonio Christiano*, Romae, 1880.

Paventi, Xaverius, *Brevis Commentarius in Facultates S. Congregationis de Propaganda Fide*, Romae: Officium Libri Catholici, 1944.

Payen, G., *De Matrimonio in Missionibus ac Potissimum in Sinis: Tractatus Practicus et Casus*, altera editio, 3 vols., Zi-ka-wei: in Typographia T'ou-se-we, 1935-1936.

Perrone, Ioannes, *De Christiano Matrimonio Libri Tres*, 3 vols., Romae: Typis S. Congregationis de Prop, Fide, 1858.

Petrovits, Joseph, *The New Church Law on Matrimony*, The Catholic University of America Canon Law Studies, n. 6, Washington, D.C.: The Catholic University of America, 1919.

Pirhing, Ernricus, *Ius Canonicum*, ed. novissima, Dilingae, 1722.

Piscetta, A-Gennaro, A., *Elementa Theologiae Moralis*, 7 vols., Vol. VI, Torino: Società Editrice Internazionale, 1929.

Pontius, Basilius, *De Sacramento Matrimonii Tractatus cum Appendice de Matrimonio Catholici cum Haeretico*, 2. ed., Bruxellis, 1627.

Pruemmer, Dominicus, *Manuale Theologiae Moralis*, 2. ed., 3 vols., Friburgi Brisgoviae: Herder, 1922.

Ramstein, Matthew, *The Pastor and Marriage Cases*, 3 ed., New York: Benziger Brothers, 1945.

Ramstein, Matthew, *The Pastor and Marriage Cases*, 3. ed., New York: Terminal Printing and Publishing Company, 1947.

Raus, J. B., *Institutiones Canonicae*, 2. ed., Lugduni, Parisiis, 1931.

Rebellus, Fernandus, *Opus de Obligationibus Iustitiae, Religionis, Charitatis*, Lugduni, Sumptibus Horatii Cardon, 1608.

Romani, Sylvius, *Institutiones Iuris Canonici*, Vol. II, Pars II, *De Matrimonio*, Romae: Editrice 'Iustitia', 1945.

Sanchez, Thomas, *De Sancto Matrimonii Sacramento Disputationum Libri Tres*, 3 vols., Venetiis, 1614.

Scherer, Rudolph Ritter von, *Handbuch des Kirchensrechts*, 2 vols., Graz, 1886-1898.

Schmidt, John Rogg, *The Principles of Authentic Interpretation in Canon 17 of the Code of Canon Law*, The Catholic University of America Canon Law Studies, n. 141, Washington, D.C.: The Catholic University of America Press, 1941.

Sipos, Stephanus, *Enchiridion Iuris Canonici*, 2. ed., Pécs: Ex Typographia "Haladás R. T.," 1931.

Torre, Ioannes, *Processus Matrimonialis*, Neapoli: M. D'Auria, S. Sedis Ap. Typographus, 1947.

Ubach, Josephus, *Compendium Theologiae Moralis*, 2 vols., Friburgi Brisgoviae, 1927.

Vaughan, William E., *Constitutions for Diocesan Courts*, The Catholic University of America Canon Law Studies, n. 210, Washington, D.C.: The Catholic University of America Press, 1944.

Vazquez, Gabriel, *Commentaria ac Disputationes in Primam Secundae D. Thomae*, 2 vols., Lugduni, 1630.

Vermeersch, Arturus, *De Matrimonii Casu Quem Apostoli Vocant seu de Fidei Privilegio*, Brugis: Typis Houdmont Fratrum, 1911.

Vermeersch, Arturus, *Theologia Moralis*, 4 vols., Vol. III, 3. ed., Roma: Pontificia Università Gregoriana, 1933.

Vermeersch, A.-Creusen, J., *Epitome Iuris Canonici cum Commentariis*, Vol. I, 7. ed., Vols. II and III, 6. ed., Mechliniae, Romae: H. Dessain, I, 1949, II and III, 1940 and 1946.

Verricelli, Angelus Maria, *Questiones Morales et Legales in Octo Tractatus Distributae*, Venetiis: apud Franciscum Beda, 1635.

Vlaming, Theodorus M., *Praelectiones Iuris Matrimonii*, 3. ed., Bussum in Hollandia: Sumptibus Societatis Editricis Anonymae, olim Paulus Brand, 1919-1921.

Vromant, G., *Facultates Apostolicae quas Sacra Congregatio de Propaganda Fide Delegare Solet Ordinariis Missionum*, Louvain: Editions du Museum Lessianum, 1926; ed. 3, Paris: Desclée de Brouwer, 1947.

———, *Ius Missionariorum*, Tom. V, *De Matrimonio*, Louvain: Museum Lessianum, 1931.

Wernz, Franciscus, *Ius Decretalium*, 6 vols., Vol. IV, *Ius Matrimoniale*, Romae: ex Typographia Polyglotta, 1904.

Wernz, Franciscus,-Vidal, Petrus, *Ius Canonicum ad Codicis Normam Exactum*, 7 vols. in 8, Vol. V, *Ius Matrimoniale*, 3. ed., a P. Aguirro, Romae: apud Aedes Universitatis Gregorianae in Piazza della Pilotta, 1946.

Winslow, Francis J., *A Commentary on the Apostolic Faculties*, New York: The Field Afar Press, 1946.

———, *The Pauline Privilege and the Constitutions of Canon 1125*, New York: The Field Afar Press, 1948.

Woeber, Edward M., *The Interpellations*, The Catholic University of America Canon Law Studies, n. 172, Washington, D.C.: The Catholic University of America Press, 1942.

Woods, Francis, *The Constitutions of Canon 1125*, Milwaukee: The Bruce Publishing Company, 1935.

Wouters, Ludovicus, *Manuale Theologiae Moralis*, 2 vols., Brugis, 1933.

Woywod, Stanislaus,-Smith, Callistus, *A Practical Commentary on the Code of Canon Law*, 10 printing, New York: Joseph Wagner Co., Inc., 1946.

ARTICLES

Arendt, G., "De Clausula Restrictiva Can. 1123", *ETL*, III (1926), 328-337.

Aryinhac, H. A., "Indissolubleness of Non-Catholic Marriages," *ER*, LXXII (1925), 405-409.

Bouscaren, T. Lincoln, "An Inquiry into the Practical Application of Canon 1125 outside of Mission Territories," *Miscellanea-Vermeersch*, I, 279-302.

De Becker, Julius, Recensiones, "Criticism of Augustine's *Commentary*," *ETL*, II (1925), 444-447.

———, Recensiones, Criticism of Charles Augustine's *Rights and Duties of Ordinaries According to the Code and Apostolic Faculties*," *ETL*, II, (1925), 444-447.

———, "Criticism of Wernz-Vidal's *Ius Matrimoniale*," *ETL*, II (1925), 271-275.

Kearney, Francis P., "The Privilege of the Faith," *The Jurist*, VII (1947), 281-293.

Kieda, Francis J., "Direct Dissolution of a Legitimate Marriage," *The Jurist*, II (1942), 134-144.

Rayanna, Puthota, "De Constitutione S. Pii Papae V, *Romani Pontificis*," *Periodica*, XXVII (1938), 295-331; XXVIII (1939), 24-52; 112-134; 190-209.

Roelker, Edward, "The Meaning of the Term 'Rationabilis' in the Code of Canon Law," *The Jurist*, IX (1949), 163-166.

Schaaf, Valentine, "Dispensation from the Interpellations," *ER*, LXXXVI (1932), 533-537.

Vermeersch, Arturus, "Commentaria de Formulis Facultatum Quas S. Congr. de Propaganda Fide Concedere Solet," *Periodica*, XI (1922), (33)-(144).

———, "De Canone 1125 eiusque vi extensiva," *Periodica*, XX (1931), 1*-5*.

———, "Facultatum quae, post Codicem, Legatis Apostolicis Concedi Consueverunt Breve Commentarium," *Periodica*, XII (1923), (69)-(98); (125)-(159).

Vromant, G., "De Dispensatione ab Interpellationibus in Ordine ad Privilegium Fidei—Applicationes Practicae Canonis 1125," *Periodica*, XX (1931), 108*-117*.

Winslow, Francis J., "The Application of the Pauline Privilege," *The Jurist*, X (1950), 304-333.

"Die neuen Missionsfakultäten von 1915," *AKKR*, XCVII (1917), 423-434.

PERIODICALS

The American Ecclesiastical Review (*AER*), Vols. I-XXXII, Philadelphia, 1889-1905; from 1905: *The Ecclesiastical Review* (*ER*), Vols. XXXIII-CIX, Philadelphia, 1905-1943; from 1944: *The American Ecclesiastical Review* (*AER*), Vol. CX—, Washington, D.C., 1944—.

Archiv für katholisches Kirchenrecht, **Innsbruck, 1857-1861, Mainz, 1862—.**

Ephemerides Theologicae Lovanienses, **Lovanii-Brugis, 1924—.**

The Jurist, **The Catholic University of America, Washington, D.C., 1941—.**

Periodica de Re Canonica et Morali utili praesertim Religiosis et Missionariis, **Brugis, 1905—.**

Miscellanea-Vermeersch, **2 vols., Romae: Pontificia Universita Gregoriana, 1935.**

ABBREVIATIONS

AAS—Acta Apostolicae Sedis

AER—The American Ecclesiastical Review

AKKR—Archiv für katholisches Kirchenrecht

ASS—Acta Sanctae Sedis

Bullarium—Bullarium Pontificium Sacrae Congregationis de Propaganda Fide

Coll. S.C.P.F., Collectanea Sacrae Congregationis de Propaganda Fide

Coll. Hong.—Collectanea Constitutionum, Indultorum ac Instructionum ad usum Societatis Missionum ad exteros, 2. ed.

Coll. Lac.—Acta et Decreta Sacrorum Conciliorum Recentiorum, Collectio Lacensis.

Collectio Resolutionum, S.C.C.—Collectio omnium conclusionum et resolutionum quae in causis propositis apud Sacram Congregationem Cardinalium S. Concilii Tridentini prodierunt ab eius institutione anno MDLXIV ad MDCCCLX

ER—The Ecclesiastical Review

ETL—Ephemerides Theologicae Lovanienses

Mansi—*Sacrorum Conciliorum Nova et Amplissima Collectio*

Periodica—Periodica de Re Canonica et Morali utili praesertim Religiosis et Missionariis.

BIOGRAPHICAL NOTE

Arthur Anthony Sego was born August 7, 1921, at Kentland, Indiana. After completing the eight years of his primary education at St. Joseph's School, Kentland, he entered St. Meinrad's Seminary, St. Meinrad, Indiana. There he pursued his entire Seminary course in the Minor and Major Seminaries, and received the degree of Bachelor of Arts on the completion of his philosophical course. He was ordained to the priesthood at Lafayette, Indiana, on June 15, 1946, and served for a year as assistant pastor at St. Lawrence Parish, Muncie, Indiana. Then, after a brief term as administrator of Holy Family Parish, Gas City, Indiana, he entered the School of Canon Law at the Catholic University of America in October of 1947. He received the degree of the Baccalaureate in Canon Law on June 9, 1948, and the degree of the Licentiate in Canon Law on June 8, 1949.

Alphabetical Index

CANON LAW STUDIES*

306. WATERS, REV. JOSEPH L., S.S.J., J.C.L., The Probation in Societies of Quasi-Religious.
307. REGAN, REV. MICHAEL J., J.C.L., Canon 16.
308. BYRNE, REV. HARRY J., J.C.L. Investment of Church Funds.
309. GALLAGHER, REV. THOMAS V., J.C.L., The Rejection of Judicial Witnesses and Testimony.
310. CHATHAM, REV. JOSIAH G., PH.D., S.T.L., J.C.L., Force and Fear as Invalidating Marriage: The Element of Injustice
311. BROWN, REV. JAMES VICTOR, O.R.S.A., J.C.L., The Invalidating Effects of Force, Fear, and Fraud upon the Canonical Novitiate.
312. DUERR, REV. CHARLES J., B.A., J.C.L., The Judicial Notary.
313. GONZALEZ, REV. FRANCISCO J., O.S.A., J.C.L., De Parocho Religioso Eiusque Superiore Locali.
314. HANNON, REV. JAMES J., J.C.L., Holy Viaticum.
315. SADLOWSKI, REV. EDWIN L., J.C.L., The Sacred Furnishings of Churches.
316. SEGO, REV. ARTHUR A., J.C.L., Dispensation from the Interpellations.
317. WATERHOUSE, REV. JOHN M., J.C.L., The Power of the Local Ordinary to Impose a Matrimonial Ban.
318. FREIN, REV. EUGENE B., J.C.L., The Discretionary Power of the Defender of the Matrimonial Bond.
319. CARTON, REV. GEORGE A., J.C.L., The Time Factor in the Gaining of Indulgences.
320. WALSH, REV. JOHN J., C.S.Sp., J.C.L. The Jurisdiction of the Interritual Confessor in the United States and Canada.
321. UNTERKOEFLER, REV. ERNEST L.. S.T.L., J.C.L., The Presiding Judge in Matrimonial Causes of First Instance.

* A complete list of the available numbers in the series will be found in earlier studies. Send orders to: The Catholic University of America Press, 620 Michigan Ave., N.E., Washington 17, D.C.

www.ingramcontent.com/pod-product-compliance
Lightning Source LLC
LaVergne TN
LVHW050255080826
844660LV00012B/640

* 9 7 8 0 8 1 3 2 2 4 9 1 6 *